ENDING DISABILITY DISCRIMINATION

Strategies for Social Workers

Edited by

GARY E. MAY
University of Southern Indiana

MARTHA B. RASKE
University of Southern Indiana

PEARSON

Boston ■ New York ■ San Francisco
Mexico City ■ Montreal ■ Toronto ■ London ■ Madrid ■ Munich ■ Paris
Hong Kong ■ Singapore ■ Tokyo ■ Cape Town ■ Sydney

This work is dedicated with love to the memory of David Pfeiffer,
a colleague, an advocate, an activist, an enthusiast,
a friend, and a mentor.

Series editor: Patricia Quinlin
Editorial assistant: Annemarie Kennedy
Marketing manager: Kris Ellis-Levy
Manufacturing buyer: Andrew Turso
Cover design: Joel Gendron
Production coordinator: Pat Torelli Publishing Services
Editorial-production service: Stratford Publishing Services, Inc.
Electronic composition: Stratford Publishing Services, Inc.

For related titles and support materials, visit our online catalog at www.ablongman.com.

Chapter 1 "Academic Debates and Political Advocacy" by Harlan Hahn, first published in *Disability Studies Today*. Edited Colin Barnes et al. © Polity Press 2002.

Library of Congress Cataloging-in-Publication Data

Ending disability discrimination : strategies for social workers / edited by Gary E. May, Martha B. Raske.
    p.   cm.
  Includes bibliographical references.
  ISBN 0-205-37942-7
  1. Social work with people with disabilities—United States.   2. Discrimination against people with disabilities—United States.   3. People with disabilities—Civil rights—United States.   4. People with disabilities—United States—Social conditions.   I. May, Gary E. II. Raske, Martha B.

HV1553.D547 2005
362.4′0453—dc22   2004047743

Printed in the United States of America

10 9 8 7 6 5 4 3 2 1   08 07 06 05 04

CONTENTS

PREFACE

This work is intended to give social workers a new framework for conceptualizing disability in contemporary U.S. society and strategies for implementing this new framework. The book builds upon the growing interest in reconsidering old truths about disability and is consistent with the profession's commitment to empowerment, self-determination, and commitment to populations at risk. As the movement toward community-based services and supports for people with disabilities gains momentum, social workers will increasingly be on the front lines of this movement. Therefore, they will need a useful model for understanding disability as a social construct and for intervening effectively at multiple levels and with diverse populations.

Although the editors and most of the contributors are social workers, the text is based on the groundbreaking efforts of scholars from the field of disability studies. Since the 1980s, a growing number of disability studies programs/departments have been organized at universities to lead the search for new insights about disability policies. Scholars, such as Harlan Hahn and David Pfeiffer, whose contributions are included in this book, speak out against prevailing theories and practices that stigmatize and marginalize persons with disabilities. Their contributions set the broad parameters for the Disability Discrimination Model set forth in this book. The social work authors (Reiko Hayashi, Vanmala Hiranandani, Martha Raske, and Gary May) write from an "insiders" perspective as social work educators and practitioners. We are hopeful that you will find these perspectives both informative and engaging and that this book will contribute to this new understanding. Stereotypes and myths about disability need to be challenged and debunked. This approach is consistent with social work's historic commitment to social justice.

The Disability Discrimination Model integrates social work theories, such as empowerment and the strengths perspective, with new insights from disability studies to reshape social work practice and policy regarding disabilities. The model introduces social workers to a set of concepts that structure a new way to think about the complex issues of disability policy, practice, and research, and initiates the process of theory construction. The Disability Discrimination Model is not yet a complete social work theory because it is not yet accepted as a standard for professional practice and it lacks empirical evidence. We hope this text will spark the discussion and research needed to bring a theory of disability-related impairment into the mainstream of social work practice.

The book is divided into two parts. Part I, Chapters 1–4, provides an overview and historical perspective on the development of thinking about disability and related issues. The contributors include outspoken policy critics and advocates for social change from disability studies (Hahn & Pfeiffer) and social work

(Hayashi & Hiranandani). Their diverse points of view are presented as background for the Disability Discrimination Model.

Hahn, in Chapter 1, provides a comprehensive history of the movement toward a socially oriented, dynamic understanding of disability. He describes events and activities within the disability-rights movement, including acts of civil disobedience that sparked policy changes in the latter part of the twentieth century. In addition to reporting the policy shift brought about by the passage of Section 504 of the Rehabilitation Act of 1973, Hahn introduces the concept of "disabling environment" and the increasing awareness among disability rights advocates of the role of prejudice and discrimination. The chapter includes a critique of the concept "quality of life," and describes the serious concerns persons with disabilities have about the popularity of this concept.

Pfeiffer, in Chapter 2, makes the distinction between and among various paradigms for understanding disability. He summarizes and critiques the major frameworks (social constructionist, social model, impairment model, oppressed minority, independent living, postmodern, continuum model, human variation approach) that purport to explain disability, and then lays the foundation for creating a discipline known as Disabilities Studies, a discipline that would be comparable to psychology, history, or political science. In his search for a common theme that draws all the frameworks together, Pfeiffer offers the discrimination model, proposing that persons are disabled by the attitudes and actions of others, and the remedy is civil rights.

Hayashi, in Chapter 3, describes the discriminatory and oppressive nature of residential/nursing home services for many persons with disabilities. A social worker and advocate for persons with disabilities, Hayashi argues that social work lacks the leadership needed to transform institutional care and create effective community-based alternative forms of housing. She uses Thompson's (2000) distinction between formal and informal practice theories to describe how typical agency practices interfere with the introduction of newer practice ideas, such as empowerment theory and the strengths perspective. A critic of the medically oriented model of disability, Hayashi incorporates first-person narratives of persons facing both new opportunities and foreclosed options.

Finally, in Chapter 4, Hiranandani draws from broad theoretical frameworks (humanities, social sciences, and disability studies) to support a departure from the entrenched social work paradigms for defining, treating, and training about disability for our profession. She describes how the dominant discourse on disability has been based on the medical model that defines disability as individual deficit. Hiranandani proposes that social workers examine their mainstream ideas about disability by joining with other disciplines, such as disability studies. She argues that such a partnership will challenge the prevailing socially constructed view that disability is a personal tragedy linked to inadequacy and deficiency.

Part II, (Chapters 5–8) defines the Disability Discrimination Model and gives a detailed description of the model's application to social work practice, policy, and research. Whereas Part I includes the somewhat divergent views that brought the model to life, Part II describes one overarching framework (the Disability Discrimination Model). Part II explicitly links the model to social work and describes how the model fits with other accepted perspectives (empowerment theory and the strengths perspective) and applies to various components of practice. Case examples are included to aid reader understanding.

In Chapter 5, May begins with a description of the Disability Discrimination Model. The model is that of an interactive, socially constructed definition of disability-related impairment. The model asserts that, contrary to conventional wisdom and pervasive professional judgment, disability and pride can coexist. Discrimination, not disability, results in impairment. Therefore social work interventions must focus on multiple levels and engage several target systems. This is a challenge to many popular practice theories as well as the research upon which current practice models are based. A case example is provided to illustrate the application of this model in a real situation.

In Chapter 6, Raske describes the application of the Disability Discrimination Model to clinical social work practice. She integrates accepted theoretical perspectives (the medical model, empowerment theory, the strengths perspective, and the resiliency model), but uses the Disability Discrimination Model as the monitor or lens through which all social work practice must take place. The chapter includes specific strategies that challenge the reader to reconsider social work practice truths about working with people with disabilities.

In recognition of the important role that policy practice plays in social work, Chapter 7 describes the application of the Disability Discrimination Model in policy practice. Because the model defines disability-related impairment as a consequence of the environment, policy practice is an essential component for all social work practitioners, including those who view themselves as clinical social workers. Case examples are offered to illustrate the application of this model in policy practice.

In Chapter 8, Hahn and Raske address research-related issues and application of the Disability Discrimination Model. The authors present contrasting viewpoints of the challenges facing a new paradigm for disability research. First, the chapter describes emerging trends in disability research and lays out a conceptual and theoretical framework as the foundation for the discipline of disability studies. Then, the authors critique current methodological research practices and describes a model for transformational studies of issues related to disabilities.

Finally, the Epilogue serves as a clarion call to the profession to take a more active and enlightened role in advocating for a more useful and humane understanding and treatment of persons with disabilities and a renewed recognition of the profession's obligation to promote personal empowerment and true choices.

We wish to acknowledge the thousands of students from whom we have learned so much. The support for this endeavor from colleagues and contributors has also been significant, encouraging, and humbling. We are particularly grateful to Cynthia Christy Baker, a valued colleague at our university, who provided important direction and guidance especially in the early phases of this project. Obviously, a project of this magnitude relies on the contributions of many people. We thank those who took the time to review manuscript drafts, to offer helpful criticisms and suggestions, and to prompt us to do our best work, especially our colleagues, Drs. Michelle Blake and Thomas Bordelon. Notable among these reviewers are Tami Grismore and Megan McGinn. The editors thank all who helped bring this project to life. While acknowledging and appreciating the contributions of the many, we, the editors, accept full responsibility for this work. Any errors of commission or omission exist in spite of our best effort to eliminate such oversights.

Gary E. May
Martha B. Raske

ABOUT THE CONTRIBUTORS

Harlan Hahn holds joint appointments as professor of political science and professor of psychiatry and the behavioral sciences in the medical school of a large university in Los Angeles. He holds a Ph.D. in political science from Harvard University, and advanced degrees in rehabilitation as well as public health from other universities in the Los Angeles area. He has written or edited eight books and more than 100 articles in professional journals.

Reiko Hayashi, Ph.D. MSW, is an assistant professor at University of Utah's College of Social Work. She is a member of the Commission on Disability and Persons with Disabilities under the Council on Social Work Education. Her research interests include environmental obstacles faced by people with disabilities, policies that facilitate the integration of people with disabilities into the community, and roles of social workers in the lives of people with disabilities.

Vanmala Hiranandani is assistant professor in the department of social work at the University of Northern Iowa. She worked for several years in urban and rural India as a medical social worker in a hospital and on research projects concerning community health, women's rights, displacement of minority groups from their traditional sources of livelihood, producing educational documentaries related to health and social justice, and training local communities and government officials in effective community organizing and disaster relief. She has conducted participatory action research with women with disabilities in Canada as well as qualitative research to study the consequences of Medicaid managed care for adults with physical disabilities in Pennsylvania, USA. Her current research and scholarship focuses on the health consequences of corporate-driven globalization, especially for marginalized populations.

Gary E. May, MSSW is an associate professor of social work at the University of Southern Indiana. He has been a disability advocate and serves on the Indiana Governor's Council for People with Disabilities. He has presented workshops, consulted and written on disability issues since the mid-1980s.

David Pfeiffer was resident scholar in the Center on Disability Studies and visiting scholar in the department of political science at the University of Hawaii at Manoa. He was formerly department chair and professor of public management in the Frank Sawyer School of Management at Suffolk University in Boston. Pfeiffer, who held a doctorate in political science from the University of Rochester, taught in universities for more than three decades, serving as mentor to numerous young disability studies scholars. Throughout his life, he was also active in numerous disability rights initiatives on both the state and federal level. Dr. Pfeiffer died at his home in Honolulu on December 17, 2003.

Martha Raske, associate professor of social work at the University of Southern Indiana, earned the MSW and Ph.D. from the University of Illinois at Chicago and teaches undergraduate and graduate policy, practice, and research. She is a licensed clinical social worker who worked many years as a rehabilitation counselor and social worker.

ACADEMIC DEBATES AND POLITICAL ADVOCACY: THE U.S. DISABILITY MOVEMENT*

HARLAN HAHN

INTRODUCTION

The issue of disability in the USA and elsewhere has reflected widely divergent orientations as well as radical shifts in public policy during the twentieth century. Contrary to popular belief, efforts to improve the status of disabled citizens have been marked by significant changes. Much of the variation can be explained by the fact that so-called "experts" and professionals have never been able to reach agreement on policies concerning the struggles of disabled people. Four issues in these developments seem especially important. First, most political changes have been preceded by an intense conflict among researchers and professionals about the most appropriate framework for studying disability. Second, despite the seemingly abstract—or even esoteric—nature of these debates, the outcome of the arguments has been shaped, at the end of the day, by social and political considerations rather than by the alleged success or failure of plans based on any of these studies. Third, even the limited or begrudging acceptance of a new approach ordinarily did not occur because an earlier paradigm was vanquished. Instead, prior theoretical constructs ordinarily have survived alongside the latest plans. Finally, at least until recently, disabled people themselves seldom have been invited to participate in such discussions.

Obviously these tendencies have had many different effects. One consequence has become particularly evident when the remedies implied by established paradigms have not been successful in achieving the results they initially appeared to promise. In such circumstances, researchers and policymakers have frequently been provoked to begin a renewed search for innovative ideas and creative solu-

*This study was supported in part by a Mary Switzer Distinguished Rehabilitation Research Fellowship from the National Institute on Disability and Rehabilitation Research (NIDRR).

tions. Unfortunately, many of the individuals who formulated earlier measures have already invested so much intellectual energy and resources in existing plans that they are reluctant to advance new proposals. The capacity of politicians or professors to change their minds or to relinquish reputations based on previous work in order to pursue alternative solutions is rare.

The purpose of this analysis is to examine several different concepts that have previously been adopted as a basis for improving the status of disabled people and to explore new thoughts and proposals that might achieve this objective in coming years. Although an effort is made to include comparative data, this investigation focuses primarily on a case study of changes in U.S. disability laws and programmes. The first section contains a brief history of disability policy, including the problems created by judicial resistance to antidiscrimination statutes such as the Americans with Disabilities Act. An attempt will be made to assess the strengths and weaknesses of proposals that stem from the emerging social model for research and advocacy on behalf of disabled people. The second portion assesses the threat to the lives of disabled citizens posed by plans such as rationing health care, assisted suicide, and other medical interventions founded, in part, on quasi-utilitarian constructs and on cost–value analysis. The final part investigates several possible innovations implied by the principle of empowerment. In particular, emphasis is devoted here to the possibility of enhancing the strength of disabled citizens through permanent, systemic, and institutional change in the policymaking process.

A BRIEF HISTORY OF DISABILITY POLICY

One dominant issue in early controversies surrounding disabled people and society has revolved about competing claims concerning the association between disability and work. Prior to the transition from feudalism to capitalism, many disabled individuals working in families supported by peasant farms and small shops made important contributions to household economies. Yet, policies dating from the early English Poor Laws, which defined disabled people as almost the only group worthy of receiving so-called outdoor relief that did not require them to live in dreaded almshouses or workhouses, also seemed to be founded on the supposition that disability signified an inability to work. The first major disability policy adopted in the United States, for example, was designed to aid officers of the revolutionary army who "became so disabled as to prevent their . . . getting their livelihood, and may stand in need of relief" (quoted in Liachowitz, 1988, p. 22). Such programmes were also designed exclusively for military officers rather than enlisted personnel; money for the first such benefits was not appropriated by Congress until long after most eligible recipients had died. In the nineteenth century, the so-called Arrears Act of 1879 was enacted seemingly on the premiss that veterans who had survived for more than twenty years after the Civil War had become eligible through disability or other means to receive benefits that a Republican Congress wanted to dispense to former members of the Union Army

(Skocpol, 1992). Nonetheless, the keystone of U.S. welfare policy, the Social Security Act, enacted during the administration of a powerful disabled president, was designed to provide government benefits only on the basis of age not disability. During World War II, extensive provisions were made for the medical rehabilitation of veterans with disabilities. However, direct payments to unemployed disabled persons were not provided in the USA until a post-war compromise defining disability as an inability to engage in "substantial gainful activity" was finally adopted by Congress (Erlanger & Roth, 1985).

As Western nations emerged from the transition from feudalism to capitalism, as well as the separation of home and work, the economic value of disabled workers became a growing concern. Despite the prior resistance of the Supreme Court to almost any form of government regulation of the U.S. economy, state workers' compensation laws were passed in the early twentieth century to protect labourers from serious injury or disability due to accidents in operating crude machinery (Erlanger & Roth, 1985). Perhaps the principal public response to the growing problem of joblessness and begging among disabled citizens, however, was the introduction of vocational rehabilitation programs. These plans were first adopted for disabled veterans of World War I, and they were broadened in 1920 to include unemployed disabled civilians (Obermann, 1965). As predicted by Marx's concept of an "industrial reserve army," when the demand for labour in defense industries increased during World War II, due to the absence of young, nondisabled, heterosexual, and predominantly white males serving in the military abroad, disabled workers, along with other oppressed groups such as ageing individuals, gays and lesbians, African-Americans, Latinos, and housewives, were temporarily admitted to the work force. Disabled adults, who compiled favourable work records during these years, were granted the opportunity to hold jobs primarily through the waiver of requirements that all employees pass a medical examination. But, with the return of nondisabled veterans after the war, these requirements were frequently reinstated; and unemployment among disabled workers continued to soar. The ubiquitous questions about disability on job applications and admission forms became a device primarily to sort out an excessive number of candidates during a period of high demand for employment and, thereby, to simplify the complex decisions that must be made in the hiring process. Despite the boasts of rehabilitation counsellors, who claimed extraordinary success in job placements to impress gullible politicians, the incredible unemployment rate that plagued disabled persons in the USA and other industrialized countries remained at the level of approximately two-thirds (Bowe, 1978; Hahn, 1984). The major theme of rehabilitation research in the post-war years was an emphasis on so-called "psychological adjustment" (Abberly, 1993), which in the USA could mean either a relentless struggle to "overcome" an impairment or a passive acceptance of supposed limitations during extended periods of unemployment.

By the final quarter of the twentieth century, there was a growing search for new programmatic approaches to the social and economic problems that confronted disabled people everywhere in the world. In both developing and industrialized nations, disabled citizens have been compelled to encounter extraordinary levels of poverty; massive unemployment, formidable barriers to housing, transportation, and freedom of movement; as well as exclusion or segregation in education and public accommodations. At least part of the source of these developments can be traced to extraordinarily high rates of unemployment, vocational programmes primarily for the most cooperative, middle class, and least impaired clients; as well as the lack of effective services for significantly impaired individuals. Hence, the initial objectives of the U.S. Rehabilitation Act of 1973, which was finally passed by Congress over President Nixon's veto, included plans to conduct a study of environmental barriers, to reverse the priority in rehabilitation programmes that had previously favoured their least impaired clients, and to establish plans to aid disabled individuals for whom employment did not appear to be a "feasible" economic goal. Perhaps the most crucial component to this measure, however, was an antidiscrimination clause known as Section 504, copied almost verbatim from the Civil Rights Act of 1964, that applied to institutions receiving "substantial Federal financial assistance." This clause was inserted into the rehabilitation bill by Congressional staff members almost as an afterthought (Scotch, 1984). In accordance with conventional procedures, the Department of Health, Education, and Welfare (HEW) was designated as the lead agency to draft administrative rules to implement this portion of the legislation. Despite attempts by disabled citizens to persuade government officials to sign the regulations, no action had been taken during three presidential administrations.

The first national law to protect disabled Americans from the effects of pernicious discrimination, therefore, was not enacted after an intense legislative controversy, a relentless struggle to gain broad political support, or massive public protests and demonstrations. Moreover, most of the members of Congress who voted for the final version of the Rehabilitation Act had little understanding of the content or meaning of Section 504. When HEW lawyers began to comprehend the sweeping implications—and the potential costs—of this legal requirement, top administrators responded by attempting—in a word that would eventually become an infamous part of the Washington lexicon—to "stonewall" the issue simply by not taking any action on it. Despite the repeated efforts to persuade government officials to sign regulations drafted by attorneys, nothing had been done about the matter when President Jimmy Carter entered office in 1977. The unenviable task of choosing between the claims of disabled people and political worries about budgetary concerns as well as broad legal precedents, therefore, fell to Carter's new Secretary of Health, Education, and Welfare, Joseph A. Califano, Jr. For a while, Califano continued to stall, but the imperative to sign the regulations became almost inescapable when a group of disabled people organized sit-ins and protests at HEW offices and elsewhere. These demonstrations have been described as exemplary models of political protest (Johnson, 1999; Shaw, 1996). Another event that may have contributed to Califano's decision to sign the regulations on April 28, 1977, happened twenty-five days earlier. While disabled protestors were picketing his home, Califano suddenly realized that his dog was not in the house. Califano (1981, p. 260) allowed his imagined fears to influence his judgment. Later he said," I saw the television pictures and the newspaper headlines: CALI-

FANO DOG ATTACKS CRIPPLED WOMAN . . . CALIFANO DOG BITES BLIND MAN."

The perception of rigid cultural norms that moulded his behaviour certainly seemed to permit less discretion than the attitudes that shaped Sheriff Bull Connor's decision to use police dogs and fire hoses against a group of demonstrators led by Rev. Martin Luther King, Jr., almost fifteen years earlier in Birmingham, Alabama. Califano's action may reveal the faint residue of paternalistic sentiments that had moulded nondisabled beliefs about disabled people for centuries, but the signing of the regulations signalled a victory that would open up opportunities for many new developments in the interpretation of disability rights.

Suddenly aware that the signing of the Section 504 regulations had actually been caused by these protests, the disabled segment of U.S. society, which had been almost politically dormant even when a prominent disabled leader was elected President, began to stir slightly. Several new developments began to indicate that many disabled people were prepared to claim a direct role in decisions affecting their fate. At the University of Illinois and the University of California, Berkeley, for example, disabled college students demanded to leave hospitals and nursing homes in order to live on their own. This defiance of professional authority led to the emergence of the concept of independent living which was, at first, so closely intertwined with the struggle for equal rights that they were frequently described as the "independent living/disability rights movement." Other goals were sought in the courts by disabled individuals who initiated litigation (Olson, 1984) before the formation of groups such as the Disability Rights Education and Defense Fund (DREDF). The trend marked by protests, demonstrations, and acts of civil disobedience, of course, was also pursued in local incidents such as the one-day stoppage of bus traffic in Denver, Colorado, by the 'gang of nineteen' and the Rev. Wade Blank, one of the founders of a group known initially as Americans Disabled for Accessible Public Transportation (ADAPT).

Some of the changes that occurred in the disability rights movement are illustrated by transitions within ADAPT in the final quarter of the twentieth century. For several years, ADAPT focused on attempts to persuade the American Public Transit Association (APTA) to pass a resolution calling upon its membership, which consists primarily of municipal transportation bureaus, to provide full access to disabled passengers on public vehicles. Blocking the sightseeing buses of APTA delegates after their business meetings, wheelchair users frequently revived another theme from the civil rights movement by demanding "access to the bus, even if it is the back of the bus." APTA often called the police to arrest the demonstrators, and ADAPT leaders later held news conferences to disseminate information about the inaccessibility of local jails.

While government policy on the accessibility of public buildings and transportation evolved at a glacial pace (Katzmann, 1986), the conflict between ADAPT and APTA was constantly reenacted throughout the 1980s. In the last decade of the century, however, several factors, including the death of the Rev. Blank, caused ADAPT to concentrate on efforts to get disabled men and women out of nursing homes and enable them to gain the support needed to live in their own homes. ADAPT wanted to allocate a fraction of the funds dedicated for nursing homes and grant them directly to disabled individuals so that they could hire their own personal assistants and defray other costs of living independently. By replacing the American Public Transit Association with the nursing home industry, ADAPT challenged a formidable adversary. The issue, however, embodied numerous themes—including deinstitutionalization, attendant or assistive services, and personal autonomy—that had been a significant part of the disability movement for years. Moreover, these acts of civil disobedience may have contributed to the growth of a new sense of personal and political identity among disabled citizens. A survey of ADAPT demonstrators, for example, found that more than half would not take a "magic pill" to become cured, and these feelings were most closely related to a positive rather than a negative orientation toward their experience as disabled people (Hahn & Beaulaurier, in press).

Meanwhile, the instability stirred by the growing influence of disabled Americans was also reflected by a mounting debate among academicians engaged in the study of disability. While some members of the nondisabled public seemed willing to accept at least some of the objectives implied by the concept of independent living, researchers as well as ordinary citizens appeared to resist the goal of equal rights. During the last quarter-century, a group of university professors, many of whom were disabled themselves, began to dismantle the conventional paradigm that had long dominated investigations of disability. Oliver (1990) performed a crucial task by dissecting "the sense of personal tragedy" that permeated perceptions of disability in Western culture. In addition, increasing controversy began to revolve around the definition of disability (Liachowitz, 1988; Higgins, 1992; Bickenbach, 1993; Swain, Finkelstein, French, & Oliver, 1993). Much of this debate also focused on a sociopolitical concept, which defined disability as the product of interactions between individuals and the surrounding environment (Hahn, 1982, 1985a, 1985b, 1986b, 1987a, 1993a, 1993b). From this perspective, of course, disability can be perceived as the product of a disabling environment instead of organic impairments, defects, or deficiencies. This understanding provided an agenda for the examination of topics such as personal identity, architectural or communications barriers, accessible transportation and public accommodations, and unfair practices in employment, education, and government programmes. In addition, it formed the foundation for legal and political arguments about the principle of equality. Most disabled people simply wanted "to level the playing field." They did not seek special favours. They wished to gain the same rights and privileges that had been granted to nondisabled citizens. They sought only to be treated equally.

Many disabled Americans identified discrimination as the principal problem that they confronted in everyday life. This perception was founded on several sources of information. First, a large proportion recalled specific encounters in their lives when nondisabled persons had displayed unsophisticated and blatantly prejudicial attitudes. Because they had been told that they lived in a world where such opinions were virtually nonexistent, these incidents were especially salient and hurtful. The assumptions that shaped their behaviour had been suddenly destroyed. They frequently felt vulnerable and defenseless. Similarly, some disabled people analysed factors such as circumstances, nonverbal behaviour, and so on, to form an interpretation in which their disabilities represented the only possible explanation for rejection or animosity. The expectation of a few activists that the prohibition of discrimination would yield equal or impartial treatment for disabled people, however, was soon shattered. Finally, there is definitive empirical evidence of unfavourable attitudes towards disabled people in the research literature of the social sciences. While the dominance of a medical model of disability—as well as the absence of survey questions about visible or labelled traits that might elicit prejudicial reactions—precluded further analyses of this issue, the early psychological experiments by Kleck (1966) and the sociological studies concluded by Richardson (1970) and by Richardson and his colleagues (1968) provided strong and incisive data about attitudes toward disabled people that could be cited to build a persuasive case against bias and discrimination (Hahn 1996).

The quest for equality aroused intense covert resistance from the nondisabled majority. Some opponents simply felt that disabled people were biologically inferior. According to this belief, since disabled citizens did not possess the same abilities as their nondisabled counterparts, critics were not prepared to recognize that the alleged inequality of disabled persons was spawned primarily by a disabling environment instead of bodily impairments. While few so-called "experts" seemed willing to claim publicly that disabled people were biologically inferior, the lack of a definitive refutation of this allegation fuelled lingering suspicions.

Part of the hidden opposition to the goals of disabled people also reflected a dawning realization that, if major features of the architectural and communications environment were no longer regarded as fixed or unalterable, the granting of equal status to disabled citizens would entail major expenditures. Unlike changes that had been achieved by other minority groups, the agenda of the disability rights movement carried a high price tag. In order to fulfil the promise of equal rights for all persons, the inclusion of disabled citizens in many facets of society required a sizeable allocation of economic resources. Both social institutions and physical structures would need to be changed permanently. Many entrenched interests recognized that spending increased funds to gain equal rights for disabled citizens necessarily meant that less money would be available for other purposes.

Most of the organizations that were secretly opposed to the objectives of disabled people, however, did not proclaim their resistance either in legislative chambers or in corridors haunted by lobbyists. They were probably influenced by the phenomenon of paternalism, which prevented nondisabled professionals and others from calling attention to the advantages they enjoyed as the alleged protectors of disabled people (Hahn, 1983). Because of historical traditions that had defined disabled people as the "deserving poor," the disability movement was enmeshed in a legacy of charity. Most nondisabled observers claimed that they were sympathetic to disabled people, even if they did not actively support their objectives. Paternalism implies that benefits for disabled people are motivated by private philanthropy instead of government decision making. Prevailing assumptions about charitable sentiments placed people with disabilities in an unequal and subordinate position, where they could expect support only from personal benefactors not from the government or from themselves. Paternalism also prevented the emergence of opportunities for compromise or a healthy debate concerning disability policies. Since everyone appeared to favour increased rights for disabled people, the relative absence of conflicting opinions about solutions to the problem stemming from disability reduced the prominence of these issues. Politicians were reluctant to admit to their constituents that they had voted against rights for disabled people. Most of the bills endorsed by the disability rights movement were passed without major opposition and by overwhelming legislative majorities. Instead, as evidenced by the failure to sign the regulation for Section 504, most of the hidden disagreements about disability rights were revealed by official inaction concerning the implementation and enforcement of these laws. Decades after the acceptance both of the legislative provisions and of administrative rules that later accompanied them, observable evidence reveals pervasive noncompliance in many U.S. communities with legal mandates to provide accessible facilities and programmes for persons with sensory and mobility impairments.

The prevalence of paternalistic sentiments, however, produced a situation in which many members of Congress were prepared to extend and expand legal rights. Disabled people were finally granted protection against discrimination in the private sector as well as within entities receiving "Substantial Federal Financial Assistance" that were covered by Section 504. Under the leadership of Senator Tom Harkin from Iowa, the Americans with Disabilities Act (ADA) was passed and signed by the President in 1990. The approval of this statute, which was the only measure to be endorsed by a conservative presidential administration, seemed remarkable in many respects. The legislative history of the bill suggested that Congressional representatives who voted for the law also appeared to understand the social model of disability and the need to combat the discrimination imposed by a disabling environment. Most legal and other commentators anticipated that the principal controversy regarding the ADA would revolve around the clause requiring "reasonable accommodations" in employment, public accommodations, and other areas of everyday life (Hahn, 1993a). This was the first legal provision to impose an affirmative obligation upon members of the dominant majority in order to bestow equal rights on a disadvantaged group.

Despite the potential threat that such mandates could be subverted either by inaction or by escalating opposition, many activists in the disability movement felt that they had achieved another unqualified victory. The path to securing equal rights for disabled Americans was amply buttressed by available literature in disability studies. Extending the arguments implied by the sociopolitical definition and the concept of a disabling environment, for example, Hahn (1987a, 1993a, 1994, 1996, and 1997a) proposed a "minority group model" for the study of disability. From this perspective, the problems faced by disabled citizens are essentially similar to the difficulties encountered by other minorities. The basic issues are prejudice and discrimination evoked by visible or labelled human differences (Hahn, 1988). Like other physical traits indicating age, race or ethnicity, and gender, the principal features differentiating disabled and nondisabled persons frequently are obvious and perceptible to others. In addition, visible characteristics signifying a disability usually are devalued. On other occasions, evidence of a so-called "hidden disability" may be found only in dossiers, files, and other sources containing information from medical records, employment applications, insurance forms, and similar sources. Nondisabled people, of course, often react to both visible and labelled attributes of disabled individuals. These phenomena have prevented an explicit test of the "minority-group model." Nevertheless, there are strong reasons to believe that adverse reactions by nondisabled persons comprise the basic source of the problems of disabled people. As a result, like other minorities, disabled citizens have been plagued by social inequalities such as extraordinarily high rates of unemployment, poverty, and welfare dependency; school segregation; inadequate housing and transportation; and exclusion from many public facilities that appear to be reserved exclusively for the nondisabled majority (Bowe, 1978). Moreover, laws prohibiting discrimination on the basis of disability appeared to be the primary remedy for these obstacles.

One of the last remaining obstacles to the quest by disabled people for equal rights entailed the interpretation of antidiscrimination laws by the judicial branch of government. The first Supreme Court controversy involving Section 504 of the Rehabilitation Act of 1973 appeared to be a harbinger of future events. In 1979, by refusing to reverse the decision of a community college to deny admission to a nursing student because of her hearing impairment, the judges concluded that accommodations for disabled people could not "fundamentally alter" the nature of a public programme (*Southeastern Community College v. Davis*, 442 U.S. 397). In *Cleburne v. Cleburne Living Center* (473 U.S. 432), a 5–4 decision by the justices held that discrimination against disabled Americans would not be struck down unless the acts violated the minimal constitutional standard of "reasonableness." Although this 1985 case invalidated a municipal ordinance banning "group homes" for persons with developmental disabilities in residential neighbourhoods on the grounds that it was "unreasonable," the finding seemed to imply that only the most blatant acts of bigotry and irrationality would be invalidated by the courts. Under the leadership of Chief Justice William Rehnquist, the Supreme Court also nullified a Bill of Rights for developmentally disabled people in 1981 (*Pennhurst v. Halderman* 451 U.S. 1) and equal educational opportunities for disabled students in 1982 (*Rowley v. Hudson Central Board of Education* 458 U.S. 176).

Perhaps more importantly, most appellate courts continue to subscribe to a "functional limitations" rather than a "minority group" model of disability. The crucial parts of Section 504 and the ADA which prohibit discrimination against "otherwise qualified" disabled individuals were interpreted in a highly restrictive manner by U.S. courts. The judges appeared to think that if plaintiffs alleging discrimination were disabled, they could not be "otherwise qualified." Conversely, of course, if they were "otherwise qualified," they could not be disabled. By the end of the twentieth century, the misunderstanding of disability in American law was so grievous that some disabled researchers began to urge the movement to abandon a strategy based solely on lawsuits and to explore other means of seeking political objectives (Hahn, in press). After nearly forty years of litigation, the courts seemed reluctant to heed the plea of Jacobus tenBroek (1966) to grant disabled people "the right to live in the world."

THE PURSUIT OF POLITICAL AND CONCEPTUAL ALTERNATIVES

Increasing disillusionment with the legal process prompted many disabled researchers and activists in the USA to pursue alternative means of fulfilling their aspirations. In addition to litigation, another major objective of the disability movement has revolved about strategies to enhance the political influence of disabled citizens. Eventually, a significant proportion of disabled people began to consider the struggle to improve their status in society as a more significant aspiration than their own personal rehabilitation. The first national survey of disabled Americans disclosed in 1986 that the largest percentage felt that disabled persons are "a minority group in the same sense as are Blacks and Hispanics" (Harris, 1986, p. 114). The fundamental goals of the disability movement are nearly identical to the aim of other minorities. They are striving to improve their status in society. They want to achieve genuine equality, or parity between the privileges afforded disabled and nondisabled citizens. In addition, the tactics adopted by disadvantaged groups, which range from community organizing to nonviolent civil disobedience, are essentially similar. Perhaps the primary differences between the experience of disabled people and other minorities are reflected by the residual effects of medical concepts that have been inherited from earlier studies of disability.

QUALITY OF LIFE

In many respects, the search outside the courtroom for methods of improving the status of disabled people seemed to converge with a growing interest in the consequences of health care. Increasingly, doctors became discontented with a continual—and almost exclusive—emphasis on refining their procedures and forms of treatment. In a period of growing medical costs and fiscal stringency, the emphasis on the effects of professional intervention promoted intensified attempts to measure health-care outcomes. This trend coincided with a mounting demand to scrutinize the conduct of professionals (Haug & Sussman, 1969). In addition, legal restrictions prompted by the exposure of grave violations of ethical principles compelled health professionals to secure the consent of the client before embarking on most interventions (Rothman, 1991). The first attempts to assess the satisfaction or dissatisfaction of patients or clients were, of course, denounced as too subjective by medical researchers. Thus, scientists began to search for other methods of analyzing the consequences of their practices.

The barriers to the study of health-care outcomes for disabled people seem to be especially formidable. By definition, of course, impairments are usually permanent. The purpose of medical rehabilitation is not to eradicate a functional problem. Despite the desire of many physicians to "fix" what they view as unacceptable bodily anomalies, often the most that can be expected from a lengthy process of rehabilitation is the arrest of a steady deterioration of physical or mental attributes. "Cure," or even the amelioration of chronic conditions, is usually not a viable prospect. Researchers cannot easily measure improvements in such characteristics. Although some studies have attempted to appraise personal improvements, a great deal of research on outcomes has consisted of investigations within separate diagnostic categories. From the perspective of disability studies, however, diagnostic classifications may be of limited value. While they may help to identify useful information about the aetiology or cause of impairments for planning prevention strategies, they provide little data either about the functional status of a disabled individual or about the presence of traits that may spawn prejudice and discrimination. Finally, the standards posed by "quality of life" often have been invoked to the detriment of disabled people. One of the first versions of the notion of "quality of life," for example, appeared in the "bioethical" formula: $QL = NE \times (H + S)$, where NE is natural endowment, H is home, and S is society (Shaw, 1977). However, within the same society, S drops out of the equation, so the formula becomes $QL = NE \times H$. In other words, where people in society are treated similarly, "quality of life" is determined by "natural endowments" times the influence of the "home." And the "home" variable generally reflects the inheritance from parents and opportunities shaped by socioeconomic status. To put it simply—and some might claim crudely—nondisabled rich people enjoy a higher "quality of life" than persons who are poor and disabled. The "formula," therefore, merely becomes a tautology. Nourishment and water sometimes have been withheld from disabled infants and adults who are "allowed" to die because the prospects for their lives do not meet the expectations of medical practitioners.

In addition, relatively few studies have focused on the social participation of disabled people after they leave hospitals or rehabilitation facilities. In fact, an investigation employing the Craig Handicap Assessment and Reporting Technique (CHART) discovered no relation between the community reintegration subscale and other predictors of rehabilitation effectiveness. The Harris survey (1986, pp. 37–41) found that disabled people were much less likely than their nondisabled counterparts to engage in everyday activities such as shopping at supermarkets, eating at restaurants, attending concerts or seeing films, and visiting neighbours or friends. In fact, much of the isolation and exclusion of disabled people can be attributed to the prevalence of architectural and communications barriers, even where they are prohibited by law, that frequently prevented them from leaving their own dwellings or "back bedrooms."

The increased realization that disabled people might sometimes need to move beyond their homes and enter the outside world gradually encouraged the development of measurements that departed from strictly clinical assessments by encompassing the external environment. One of the first significant steps in this direction was taken when the *International Classification of Impairments, Disabilities, and Handicaps (ICIDH)* was published by the World Health Organization (1980). This classification scheme included a separate category, called "Handicap," for "a disadvantage . . . resulting from an impairment or a disability, that limits or prevents the fulfillment of a role that is normal (depending on age, sex, and social and culture factors) for that individual" (p.183). While some disabled leaders viewed this category as an opportunity to collect important data about environmental accessibility, others felt that the *ICIDH* signified the first wave of a renewed eugenics movement (Pfeiffer, 1998). One valuable by-product of the *ICIDH*, however, was a model that incorporated environmental dimensions in plans for research on disability (Fougeyrollas et al., 1998). Finally, environmental components of research on disability were featured prominently in an important Institute of Medicine report on rehabilitation science and engineering (1977). Despite these indications of gradual progress toward the acceptance of measures that would incorporate environmental as well as intrapersonal variables in assessing health-care outcomes, most medical rehabilitation professionals preferred to engage in arduous and often futile attempts to operationalize a concept, such as "quality of life," that allegedly could be related in a more direct manner to clinical evaluations of individual functioning. A review of articles containing "quality-of-life" instruments disclosed troubling inconsistencies. Within a relatively short period of time, however, research and publications on measures of Health-Related Quality of Life (HRQOL) expanded profusely. Many of these conceptualizations were promoted by international scientists in organizations such as the WHOQOL Group, the Euro-Qol Group, REAVES (the International Network on Health Expectancy and the Disability Process), and similar informal and formal organizations. Reiser (1993) noted that interest in the perceptions of the so-called "patient" and the appraisal of "quality of life" eventually converged.

Another major impetus for the increasing popularity of so-called quality of life measures emerged, ironically, from trends in the social sciences. Prominent researchers in the 1960s who witnessed dramatic outbreaks of ghetto violence prompted by long-standing grievances began to dream about the possibility of conducting periodic surveys to gather data on "social indicators" similar to the economic indicators that had been used so successfully as a basis for fiscal policy. Drawing upon Cantril's (1965) studies of "self-anchoring scales," in which respondents were asked to indicate their position on a ten-rung ladder representing the best (top) and worst (bottom) life they could lead, social scientists sought to fashion instruments that could be used longitudinally in frequent surveys (Campbell, Converse, & Rodgers, 1976). Along with employment and family life, health was consistently rated throughout the world as one of three principal human concerns. Perhaps the major drawbacks to the "social indicators" movement, however, entailed both the difficulty of applying them in a deterministic manner to complex phenomena such as urban uprisings and the inability to find a funding source willing to invest as much in social problems as it spends on economic forecasts.

The proliferation of the so-called health-related quality of life measures, however, seemed destined to continue unabated. Biomedical scientists appeared to stumble over themselves in a frantic rush to discover a composite indicator of health outcomes both to satisfy the demands of administrators who sought to end escalating costs and to attract a consensus among professional colleagues that could yield personal rewards for the inventor of such an instrument. The inappropriateness of the use of such scales in the study of disability is indicated by evidence revealing that disabled people tend to rate the quality of their lives higher than most nondisabled individuals (Albrecht & Devliger, 1999). A significantly disabled psychotherapist reported that many of her clients who were almost comatose derived pleasure from "the sensuous touch of the sheets on the skin." Most HRQOL assessments, however, were based on clinical definitions that restrict the measure of observable differences in outcomes to organic conditions within the human body. Implicit within these measures is the incorrect and unspoken assumption that "quality of life" is a direct, unmediated reflection of physiological traits and that impaired people must, therefore, experience a lower quality of life than individuals without bodily impairments. Despite the supposed familiarity of health professionals with the controversy about the so-called handicap dimension of *International Classification of Impairments, Disabilities, and Handicaps,* these scientists were reluctant either to extend their research beyond the physiological boundaries of the body or to admit researchers from other disciplinary traditions into the exclusive province of medical investigations. As a result, social or environmental measures were neither accepted as a supplement nor appended to the clinical or biomedical model.

Continual reliance on the clinical approach in nearly all branches of the health sciences imposes additional restraints on the progress of such investigations. The well-established standards of "universal design" or an accessible environment for disabled people were never added to the "medical model." For many disabled persons who actually know that their organic conditions cannot be ameliorated and for health practitioners who realize that they cannot "fix" or repair such impairments, changes that make the surrounding environment more accessible may represent the only feasible means of improving major facets of life, including their mobility, navigational skills, community participation, and opportunities for social interactions with families, neighbours, and friends. Without an accessible environment and public or private transportation, many disabled people are condemned to live indefinitely either in institutions or in their own domiciles and "back bedrooms" where they remain virtually incarcerated without any real chance to interact with other human beings. Disabled people are seldom confined to wheelchairs, but often they are confined to nursing homes, residential institutions, houses, or apartments. They are frequently barred from obtaining needed health care or social services simply because architectural or communication barriers prevent them from "getting from here to there." The persistent adherence to a clinical perspective that has excluded the accessibility of the environment from analysts of "health related quality of life" has prevented researchers from exploring many significant issues. Obviously, the most important advances in human mortality have resulted from environmental rather than clinical changes through improved sanitation and related policies adopted in nineteenth-century cities. As organized medicine acquired increasing power in the twentieth century, however, the dominant emphasis in health affairs shifted from the analysis of public policies that affect large numbers of people to the refinement of clinical techniques performed on individuals. As a result, the major unit of analysis in health-related research reflected a corresponding tendency to move from aggregate entities such as governmental jurisdiction to the free-standing individual.

This trend has had the unfortunate consequence of inhibiting the development of adequate measurements for rigorous examination of the impact of government policy on public health. Analyses of such policies and programmes have not been fully or effectively integrated into the study of health services. At least this research literature has not provided political leaders with clear guidance about the best means of improving public health. These lacunae have had a detrimental impact on disabled people. In particular, the absence of such investigations has impeded the ability of researchers to answer many crucial questions. Do disabled residents of communities that strictly enforce laws requiring accessible public accommodations, for example, enjoy increased social interaction and participation in comparison with counterparts who live in localities that have not fully implemented such statutes? Such an investigation would clearly seem consistent with the "assessment" function of public health. Does the reduced social isolation and confinement that may presumably result from such legislation have a positive effect on personal health or longevity?

The use of traditional methods to examine "health-related quality of life," however, also has confronted two other obstacles. What is "health"? What is "quality"? The first issue, of course, revived debate about the World Health Organization's definition of health as a "state of complete physical, mental, and social well-being rather than simply the absence of disease." This formulation frequently has been attacked as too idealistic. For many years, few, if any, prominent scholars devoted their work exclusively to the search for a more practical meaning. Most theoreticians and practitioners seemed content to allow health to be defined by an individual need which represented a deficiency from a condition that was often approximated by a bell-shaped curve or some notion of "normality." Such a conceptualization appeared to work reasonably well in a period dominated by acute problems, in which the subjective appraisal of signs or symptoms represented need and a cure was the desired outcome. In this paradigm, of course, disabled people usually were perceived as individuals with deficiencies from a customary norm, or as "outliers" on a bell-shaped curve, who could not be helped by conventional techniques. Gradually, as predominant health concerns shifted from acute to chronic difficulties, however, "cure" no longer represented a feasible outcome. In fact, disabled participants in civil disobedience who tended to express favourable attitudes about many of their experiences with disability also stated that they would reject a "cure," even if it were offered to them (Hahn & Beaulaurier, in press). The change from predominantly "acute" to "chronic" health problems meant that researchers had to redefine both "need" and outcomes as practicable objectives.

People with chronic conditions frequently seek health care for secondary conditions, but they may seldom "need" medical treatment because of permanent impairments. Often the most that physicians can do for disabled individuals is to treat ordinary health problems or to monitor increases or decreases in functional capabilities. Full cognizance of the implications of these circumstances may require a significant redefinition of common medical objectives. For many years, such goals have revolved around the implications of morbidity *and* mortality. In the modern era, however, chronic limitations cannot be eliminated. Even though people with chronic health problems can survive, the full restoration of "normal" functioning is usually not a viable prospect. A crucial question that appears to emerge from these trends, therefore, might be stated as follows: If "cure" is not an appropriate goal of medical intervention in chronic health problems, what can disabled people reasonably expect from health professionals? What should health professionals expect of themselves? How can their efforts be measured? What are the criteria of success or failure?

Possible answers to such questions have not yet reached the level of extensive public discussion. Some disabled people have urged that rigid evaluations need to be applied to professional conduct in order to prevent further damage, and a few have even proposed that the goal of "fixing" impairments be abandoned so that physicians and scientists can concentrate exclusively on the aim of extending life. Most nondisabled people still appear to believe that they must consult medical experts when a disabling incident occurs or, at least, that few other service providers can effectively perform these activities. And the demand for norms or criteria regarding the performance of these duties seems almost inevitable.

Even more fundamentally, there seems to be a pressing need to revamp the theoretical framework in which the standard of "quality of life" initially emerged. The basic precepts of the principles of utilitarianism are, of course, guided by the familiar maxim about "the greatest good for the greatest number." Almost by definition, since disabled people probably are destined to remain a minority for several decades, they are not likely to benefit from the application of judgments based on such logic. Utilitarianism appears to fit most comfortably in a legal context of individualistic choice based on the concept of liberty rather than the standard of equality. In addition, choice often implies a trade-off between people or goods of greater or lesser value. Thus, health care practices that yield the most benefit for the largest number of people ordinarily can be expected to provide rewards primarily for the nondisabled segment of the population that fits in the area under the "normal" curve within a fraction of a standard deviation from the mean.

Perhaps even more fundamentally, utilitarian concepts have been adopted as a foundation for "cost-benefit" or "cost-value" calculations, yielding an outcome that justifies neglect of the needs and interests of disabled citizens. The clearest example is the concept of DALYs, literally Disability Adjusted Life Years. This formulation, which emerged from a project sponsored by the World Bank, seemed to combine indices of mortality, or death, and morbidity, or "a diseased state" of some kind, into a single measure of "health." Disability is defined exclusively both as a negative factor that subtracts from a healthy life and as a form of ill health that imposes a substantial "burden" on society as well as the individual. Part of the fallacy of this concept appears to reflect confusion about the concepts of disability, sickness or illness, disease, and impairment. Disability is neither a disease, a term that often stands for diagnostic classifications, nor a sickness, a word that usually implies an acute health problem from which a person can be expected to recover fully. Nor does it result exclusively from bodily impairments; in fact, disability is produced primarily by the effects of a disabling environment. Disability may be, in part, a chronic or persistent condition, but, because environmental configurations seldom are unalterable, it can be mitigated or ameliorated especially through improvements in the architectural and communications milieux. It is entirely possible to have a significant disability and to be perfectly "healthy," in the conventional meaning of the term, simultaneously. DALYs signify not only an outdated notion, but this measure also seems oddly incongruent with an era in which growing numbers of disabled people are beginning to consider disability as a positive source of personal and political identity as well as an experience from which many valuable perspectives can be derived (Groce, Chamie, & Me, 1998; Hahn, 1997a).

Perhaps most importantly, DALYs pose a substantial danger to the lives and well-being of disabled people. As Nord (1999, p. 123) concluded, this threat "is a heritage from utilitarian thinking in the QUALY [quality adjusted life years] approach, in which . . . the equal valuation of life for disabled people was not recognized as a salient societal concern." The widespread use of DALYs and the increasing costs of medical treatment could promote numerous life-threatening plans, including a revival of the eugenics movement, the rationing of health care, and the legalization of euthanasia. For many disabled people, breathing in an atmosphere fostered by ideas that characterize "a healthy life" as "living without a disability" has been permeated by the stale, sweet taste of death. Many disabled people have privately expressed the fear that the paternalistic attitudes displayed by the nondisabled may actually conceal unacceptable feelings of hostility and repugnance that, if they were ever to become exposed, might be related to a repressed desire even to kill disabled people. Obviously, women would feel justifiably threatened by the prevalence of measures that weight life as a female as only a fraction of the value of the life of males. Yet, for reasons which have not been fully uncovered and which comprise a pressing mandate for future scholars in disability studies, the general public does not display similar reactions when this formula is applied to disabled people. Although the World Bank has claimed that the DALYs score of a particular country will not be used as a basis for decisions about the extension or foreclosure of loans, there is nothing to prevent other agencies from using the statistic in this manner. Many nations might curtail social services to disabled people in the belief that fewer services might mean fewer disabled citizens, which would reduce costs and contribute to a higher DALYs measure to convey the impression of a healthy and productive workforce. One example of the application of these concepts to contemporary American policy was provided by efforts of the state of Oregon to obtain a waiver from Federal Medicaid standards by rationing health care on the basis of discriminatory priorities from a public-opinion survey that were deemed inconsistent with the ADA (U.S. Department of Health and Human Services, 1992). Eventually, other political leaders may find it difficult, if not impossible, to resist the temptation to invoke such medical excuses which were used during in the Holocaust to exterminate millions of disabled people.

Obviously there is a pressing need for an alternative method of measuring advances toward the goals of the disability movement. Experience in the United States has demonstrated that the principles of civil rights embodied in laws such as Section 504 and the ADA have been subverted by the reliance of the courts upon an antiquated functional understanding of disability that has prevented disabled people from fulfilling the aspirations implied by this legislation. Moreover, the utilitarian suppositions embedded in "quality of life" measures have rebounded to the disadvantage—and even to the life-threatening detriment—of disabled people. Consequently, a high priority must be assigned in coming years to the search for objectives and strategies to replace concepts that have been exposed as antithetical to the interests of the disability rights movement. In fact, without a new agenda and priorities, there is a danger that the movement could flounder and lose its sense of purpose.

EMPOWERMENT: AN ALTERNATIVE REMEDY

Perhaps one of the most popular recent strategies for social change has revolved around the concept of empowerment. Unlike quasi-utilitarian notions that emphasize principles of liberty and free choice almost to the exclusion of other values, empowerment seems to imply at least an opportunity to consider the standard of equality. A fundamental goal of empowerment is to increase the influence of relatively powerless sectors of society. Since disabled people comprise a group that has been significantly disadvantaged by the environment surrounding them, empowerment would mean that they could eventually be elevated to a level commensurate with the benefits traditionally enjoyed by their nondisabled counterparts. The first stage of the agenda, therefore, might be achieved merely by "leveling the playing field." Part of this task would require that criteria take into account the so-called taken-for-granted environment that confers major privileges upon nondisabled persons and corresponding disadvantages upon disabled people (Hahn, 2000). The disability movement cannot become a full participant in decisions about the distribution of resources until this initial goal is accomplished.

There is, however, still considerable debate about whether or not the struggle by disabled people for equal rights is a zero-sum game. From one vantage point, resources may appear to be so plentiful that the interests of a minority such as disabled Americans can be accommodated without disturbing the rewards that have previously been allocated to other segments of the population. By contrast, some analysts may contend that granting the demands of disabled citizens would entail redistribution of resources that could require political leaders to take privileges away from groups that traditionally have enjoyed them. The latter prospect obviously entails more political difficulties than the former scenario. Even when dominant interests display a supposedly sympathetic or paternalistic attitude toward disabled people, there is still a strong likelihood that powerful groups will not voluntarily surrender their traditional advantages for altruistic reasons.

Since disabled people seem destined to remain a minority at least until longevity extends beyond existing parameters, it is also unlikely that they can fulfil all their aspirations within the confines of a political system based on the rule of the majority. Certainly, there are some strategies that disabled people can pursue to enhance their influence. Perhaps one of the most important of these is the effort to redefine disability as a positive source of identity instead of a trait enveloped by feelings of shame or inferiority. This way of expanding the constituency of disabled people admittedly rests upon the shaky premise that votes count in free elections, that the verdict of the electorate exerts some influence on the selection of government representatives, and that political institutions are capable of shaping the behavior of financial elites. Many Americans believe that all of these myths were shattered by the presidential elections of 2000. But, in a supposedly democratic country, politics appears to remain the only possible means by which ordinary people can seek to shape the policies that affect their lives. The mobilization of alienated citizens has not *yet* seemed to emerge as a viable option. In addition, leaders of the disability rights movement must always be mindful of the possibility of improving the status of disabled people through sweeping changes in the economic system. Capitalism is undoubtedly a root cause of the oppression of disabled people, and any act that diminishes the stranglehold of this form of control on human behaviour must be counted as an achievement for the movement.

Perhaps one of the most effective means of securing empowerment for disabled people, however, involves permanent systematic alterations in the decision-making process. Some local governments in the USA have attempted to augment the legislative strength of racial or ethnic minorities through devices such as proportional representation, which permits the weighting of votes and sometimes the recounting of ballots based on second or third choices after winners with a specified number of first choices have been selected. Other localities have experimented with cumulative voting, which allows the electorate to distribute votes for candidates in various combinations in order to maximize the strength of their preferences (Guinier, 1994). Yet these measures were frequently repealed after their consequences were revealed, and they seldom have achieved the desired results. Unless the strivings of disabled people have a continuing effect on the political and economic institutions of a nation or the globe, they may never exert an impact that extends beyond a temporary and constantly shifting scorecard of wins and losses. Animus toward disabled people seems to be an endemic and deep-seated characteristic of most cultures of the world. Thus, the battles of the disability movement cannot be waged solely within the confines of the existing political process; they must also seek to impose an imprint on the structure of society. In addition, and perhaps most importantly, the empowerment of disabled people must be permanent. In a legacy within social work that has been perpetuated by early works about community organizing, empowerment is frequently equated with a temporary intervention into a neighbourhood or locality that is intended to have lasting and sustained effects. Ironically, political science, as a discipline that is supposed to be concerned with the issues of power, minority rights, and majority rule, has devoted relatively little attention to the concept of empowerment. Studies by Browing, Marshall, and Tabb (1984) have suggested that local ethnic groups often are able to satisfy their political goals through governing coalitions; but another investigation indicated that the empowerment of disadvantaged groups may be relatively short-lived after the election of a minority candidate to high public office (Gillam, 1998).

Perhaps the principal countries in which disabled people have been granted the greatest opportunity to participate in government decision making, however, are the countries of Uganda and South Africa. Although Western lawmakers ordinarily may be unwilling to accept recommendations born in developing nations, increased attention might be devoted to justifications for the creation of seats on local councils that are reserved for the representation of disadvantaged groups, including disabled people. Democratic government must be concerned not only about majoritarian rule, but it must also discover mechanisms by which groups such as mentally and physically disabled people, ex-convicts, and others who have been almost permanently excluded from the political process might be able to secure official recognition of their needs and interests. Details of this proposal, such as decisions about the citizens who would participate in the selection of representatives, as well as the qualifications of officeholders who would occupy these seats, could be negotiated after governments endorse the principles of the plan. By seeking a voice on local councils, disabled people would not be asking for pity or charity. Instead, they would be seeking to become full participants in political decision making on an equal basis with the nondisabled portion of society. As a result, establishing seats to represent disadvantaged and marginalized groups may also be regarded, at least in the USA, as an effort to fulfil a frequently neglected commitment to diversity and inclusion.

CONCLUSION

Disabled people, like other minorities, have followed a long and somewhat torturous path toward full inclusion in social, economic, and political structures. They have been told that they must complete long and seemingly senseless rehabilitation programmes in order to work, and later they were granted public benefits for *not* working. Many disability policies in the nineteenth and early twentieth centuries were designed to support groups such as Republican Congressmen, who sought to reinforce the loyalties of Civil War veterans with specious assumptions about the link between aging and disability almost twenty years after the war. Similarly, there were conflicts between labourers and business interests that were willing to support workers' compensation laws to protect themselves from the dangers of crude machinery and the potential liability that could result from a shift in prevailing legal doctrines about employer responsibilities. Rehabilitation measures, of course, were introduced after World War I in part to avoid the embarrassment of unemployed disabled veterans begging on city streets. Subsequently, however, employers were permitted to continue the discriminatory practice of using questions on employment applications or visible evidence from interviews to sort out—and to reject—disabled workers seeking jobs; and the unemployment rate for disabled workers has held consistently at approximately two-thirds. Only during World War II, when most young nondisabled males were in military service, were disabled people admitted to the labour force, ordinarily through the waiver of medical requirements. After this war, disabled veterans were offered medical rehabilitation to "fix" their impairments; and disabled civilians in vocational rehabilitation were told by psychiatrists and administrators that their inability to find jobs could be ascribed to a lack of psychological "adjustment." In addition, Congress finally enacted social welfare policies to provide SSI [Supplemental Security Income] and SSDI [Social Security Death Index] payments to disabled people who were declared to be "unable to engage in substantial gainful activity."

The relatively abrupt shift to civil rights remedies began with the adoption, almost as an afterthought, of Section 504 of the Rehabilitation Act of 1973. Perhaps even more importantly, the failure of several administrations to sign regulations to implement the law prompted a series of sit-ins and protests that contributed significantly to the birth of the disability movement in the USA. Early indications of unremitting judicial attempts to undercut such laws were revealed by an initial Supreme Court case in which a hearing-impaired nurse was denied acceptance by a community college programme on the grounds that her admission would result in a "fundamental alteration" of the curriculum. Despite such forewarnings, Congress continued to pass even more stringent bans against disability discrimination, including the Individuals with Disabilities Education Act (IDEA), the Civil Rights Restoration Act, and the Americans with Disabilities Act (ADA). In subsequent litigation, however, the Supreme Court decided that disabled people were not entitled to a strong defence against discrimination under the "equal protection" clause of the Fourteenth Amendment to the U.S. Constitution; that a deaf student who was merely passed by her teachers was receiving an "appropriate" education, even though she may not have been able to learn what was being said in the classroom; that disabled people in institutions may not claim "habilitation" or other minimal forms of training; and that a Bill of Rights for developmentally disabled people was not really a "bill of rights" after all. Plaintiffs were frequently caught in a dilemma by judicial interpretations of statutes prohibiting discrimination against "otherwise qualified" disabled individuals and, if they were "otherwise qualified," they could not be disabled. Similarly, numerous appellate courts have refused to apply the

ADA against employers who fired personnel suspected of having AIDS merely because they did not have the symptoms of the disease. Many of these results could be attributed to judicial understandings of the functional thrust of the definition of disability in ADA. Although this clause also prohibited discrimination against persons who are "regarded as" having a disability or who have a "history" of disability, courts have viewed medical evidence of a functional impairment as an essential precondition for legal findings about disability. Perhaps at least part of the explanation of this interpretation can be ascribed to the absence of data based on the visible or labelled characteristics of a disability. Visibility and labelling can be operationalized, and information about these attributes would not be difficult to collect, but neither the government nor private foundations have exhibited much interest in funding the surveys. Once again, public policies can be traced to the availability of research findings and to the theoretical or conceptual orientations that guide such investigations.

The strong popular interest in quasi-utilitarian concepts of "quality of life" that emerged during the latter part of the twentieth century, along with a mounting concern about measuring the costs and outcomes of health care, prompted a relatively detailed analysis of the effects of this approach on disabled people. Thinly concealed within this perspective, for example, are majoritarian assumptions that tend to treat disabled people as the "outliers" or deviants from the norms prescribed by the bell-shaped curve. Perhaps even more significantly, utilitarianism seems to be an inappropriate source of measurements related to disability or chronic health conditions. Emerging from an era in which the signs or symptoms of acute sickness indicated a need for medical treatment, the difficulty of measuring outcomes has been exacerbated by the prevalence of chronic problems which denote the absence of such a "cure" and the persistence of the condition. Perhaps the most dangerous of "quality of life" issues involves their use in "cost–benefit" or "cost–value" calculations, in which the worth of disabled people is purposely diminished in relation to nondisabled persons. Another manifestation of the inordinate stress on "quality of life" is revealed by the invention of so-called DALYs, which purport to measure "health" by subtracting the number of years lived with a disability from the longevity of individuals. Such concepts have provoked a major fear among disabled people about a possible resurgence of eugenics, euthanasia, and the rationing of health.

The defects of existing conceptualizations have sparked a new search for a replacement to prior methods of assessing the status of disabled people. In this analysis, the principle of "empowerment" is proposed as an excellent potential replacement for earlier measures. Unlike utilitarian notions that emphasize choice almost to the exclusion of other values, empowerment also encompasses an opportunity to examine the issue of equality. In fact, empowerment often is characterized by an increase in the social, economic, and political influence of disadvantaged groups in relation to privileged segments of society. In fields such as social work, empowerment has tended to revolve around temporary interventions that are supposed to produce enduring effects. Experiments with proportional representation, cumulative voting, and "gerrymandering" have seldom produced the results desired by their originators. But the prospects for disabled people will be able to satisfy their aspirations without systemic and permanent modifications of the decision-making process are slight. The high levels of political participation displayed by disabled people in Uganda and South Africa may provide a foundation for a debate about new arrangements, such as the representation of disabled and other disadvantaged people through a reserved seats in local councils. Both the dissatisfaction aroused by prior approaches and the promise indicated by untried plans demonstrate the need for a lively debate about the future of disabled people framed by innovative approaches to the controversy.

REFERENCES

Abberley, P. (1993). "Disabled people and 'normality'." In J. Swain, V. Finkelstein, S. French, & M. Oliver (Eds.), *Disabling Barriers, Enabling Environments* (pp. 107–115). London: Sage.

Albrecht, G. L., & Devliger, P. (1999). "The disability paradox: High quality of life against all odds." *Social Science and Medicine, 48*, 977–988.

Bickenbach, J. E. (1993). *Physical Disability and Social Policy.* Toronto: University of Toronto Press.

Bickenbach, J. E., Chattedi, S., Badley, E., & Ustun, T. B. (1999). "Models of disablement, universalism, and the international classification of impairments, disabilities, and handicaps." *Social Science and Medicine, 48*, 1173–1187.

Bowe, F. (1978). *Handicapping America: Barriers to disabled people.* New York: Harper and Row.

Browning R. P., Marshall, D. R., & Tabb, D. H. (1984). *Protest is not enough: The struggle of Blacks and Hispanics for equality in urban politics.* Berkeley, CA: University of California Press.

Califano, J. (1981). *Governing America: An insider's report from the White House and the Cabinet.* New York: Simon and Schuster.

Campbell, A., Converse. P., & Rodgers, W. L. (1976). *The quality of America life: Perceptions, evaluations, and satisfactions.* New York: Russell Sage Foundation.

Cantril, H. (1965). *The Pattern of Human Concerns.* New Brunswick, NJ: Rutgers University Press.

Dijkers, M. P. J. M., Whiteneck, G., & El-Jaroudi, R. (2000). "Measures of social outcomes in disability research." *Archives of Physical Medicine and Rehabilitation, 81*, supp. 2, S63–S80.

Erlanger, H. S. & Roth, W. (1985). "Disability policy: The parts and the whole." *American Behavioral Scientist, 28* (3), 319–345.

Fougeyrollas, P., Noreau, L., Bergeron, H., Cloutier, R., Dion, S. A., & St. Michel, G. (1998). "Social consequences of long-term impairments and disabilities: Conceptual approach and assessment of handicap." *International Journal of Rehabilitation Research, 21*(1), 127–141.

Gillam, K. L. (1998). "Is there an empowerment life cycle?" *Urban Affairs Review, 33*, 741–766.

Groce, N., Chamie, M., & Me, A. (1998). "Measuring the quality of life: Rethinking the World Bank's disability adjusted life years." *International Rehabilitation Research Review, 4*, 12–16.

Guinier, L. (1994). *The tyranny of the majority: Fundamental fairness in representative democracy.* New York: Free Press.

Hahn, H. (1982). "Disability and rehabilitation policy: Is paternalistic neglect really benign?" *Public Administration Review, 43*, 385–389.

Hahn, H. (1983). "Paternalism and public policy." *Society, 20*, 36–46.

Hahn, H. (1984). *The issue of equality: European perceptions of employment policy for disabled persons.* New York: World Rehabilitation Fund.

Hahn, H. (1985a). "Changing perceptions of disability and the future of rehabilitation." In L. G. Perlman, & G. F. Austin (Eds.), *Societal influences on rehabilitation planning: A blueprint for the twenty-first century* (pp. 53–64). Alexandria, VA: National Rehabilitation Association.

Hahn, H. (1985b). "Disability and the problem of discrimination." *American Behavioral Scientist,* 28(3), 293–318.

Hahn, H. (1986b). "Public support for rehabilitation: The analysis of U.S. disability policy." *Disability, Handicap, and Society,* 1 (2), 121–137.

Hahn, H. (1987a). "Adapting the environment to people with disabilities: Constitutional issues in Canada." *International Journal of Rehabilitation Research,* 10 (4), 363–372.

Hahn, H. (1988). "The politics of physical differences." *Journal of Social Issues,* 44, 39–43.

Hahn, H. (1993a). "Equality and the environment: The interpretation of 'reasonable accommodations' in the Americans with Disabilities Act." *Journal of Rehabilitation Administration,* 17, 101–106.

Hahn, H. (1993b). "The political implications of disability definitions and data." *Journal of Disability Policy Studies,* 4 (2), 41–52.

Hahn, H. (1994). "The minority group model of disability: Implications for medical sociology." In R. Wetz, & J. J. Kronenfeld (Eds.), *Research in the Sociology of Health Care* (pp. 3–24), 11. Greenwich, CT: JAI Press.

Hahn, H. (1996). "Antidiscrimination laws and social research on disability: The minority group perspective." *Behavioral Sciences and the Law,* 14, 1–19.

Hahn, H. (1997a). "An agenda for citizens with disabilities: Pursuing identity and empowerment." *Journal of Vocational Rehabilitation,* 9 (1), 31–37.

Hahn, H. (2000). "Accommodations and the ADA: Biased reasoning or unreasonable bias?" *Berkeley Journal of Employment and Labor Law,* 21(1), 166–192.

Hahn, H. (in press). "Adjudication or empowerment: Contrasting experiences with the social model of disability." In L. Barton (Ed.), *Society and Disability.*

Hahn, H., & Beaulaurier, R. (in press). "ADAPT or perish: A research on interviews with participants in nonviolent protests." *Journal of Disability Policy Studies.*

Harris, L. (1986). *The ICD survey of disabled Americans: Bringing disabled Americans into the mainstream.* New York: Louis Harris.

Haug, S., & Sussman, M. (1969). "Revolt of the Clients." *Social Problems,* 13, 108–114.

Higgins, P. C. (1992). *Making disability: Exploring the social transformation of human variation.* Springfield, IL: Charles C. Thomas.

Johnson, R. A. (1999). "Mobilizing the disabled." In J. Freeman, & V. Johnson (Eds.), *Waves of protest: Social movements since the sixties.* Landon, MD: Rowman and Littlefield.

Katzmann, R. (1986). *Institutional disability: The saga of transportation policy for the disabled.* Washington, DC: Brookings Institution.

Kleck, R. (1966). "Emotional arousal in interactions with stigmatized persons. *Psychological Reports,* 19 (3), 1226.

Liachowitz, C. H. (1988). *Disability as a social construct: Legislative roots.* Philadelphia: University of Pennsylvania Press.

Nord, E. (1999). *Cost–value analysis in health care: Making sense out of QUALYs.* New York: Cambridge University Press.

Obermann, T. E. (1965). *A history of vocational rehabilitation.* Minneapolis, MN: T. S. Denison.

Oliver, M. (1990). *The Politics of Disablement.* Basingstoke: Macmillan.

Olson, S. M. (1984). *Clients and lawyers: Securing the rights of disabled persons.* Westport, CT: Greenwood Press.

Pfeiffer, D. (1998). "The ICIDH and its need for revision." *Disability and Society,* 13 (4), 503–523.

Richardson, S. A. (1970). "Age and sex differences in values toward physical handicaps." *Journal of Health and Social Behavior,* 11(3), 207–214.

Richardson, S. A., & Royce, J. (1968). "Race and handicap in children's preferences for other children." *Child Development,* 39, 457–480.

Rothman, D. (1991). *Strangers at the bedside: A history of how law and bioethics transformed medical making.* New York: Basic Books.

Scotch, R. K. (1984). *From good will to civil rights: Transforming federal disability policy.* Philadelphia: Temple University Press.

Shaw, A. (1977). "A short formula for quality of life." *Hastings Center Report,* 5 (1), 37–43.

Shaw, R. (1996). *The Activist's Handbook.* Berkeley, CA: University of California Press.

Skocpol, T. 1992: *Protecting soldiers and mothers: The political origin of social policy in the United States.* Cambridge, MA: Harvard University Press.

Swain, J., Finkelstein, V., French, S., & Oliver, M. (Eds.). (1993). *Disabling Barriers, Enabling Environments.* London: Sage Publications.

tenBroek, J. (1966). "The right to live in the work: The disabled in the law of torts." *California Law Review*, 54, 84, 1–864.

U.S. Department of Health and Human Services (3 August, 1992). Press release.

World Health Organization (1980). *International classification of impairments, disabilities, and handicaps*. Geneva: World Health Organization.

CHAPTER 2

THE CONCEPTUALIZATION
OF DISABILITY*

DAVID PFEIFFER

INTRODUCTION

Disability studies is the field which examines the experience of being disabled and the lives of people with disabilities. As the Society for Disability Studies describes itself:

> [The Society] is a nonprofit academic, professional, and educational organization committed to developing theoretical and practical knowledge about disability and to promoting the full and equal participation of persons with disabilities in society. (Society for Disability Studies, 2000)

Although the Society for Disability Studies hesitates to call disability studies a discipline, it fits the definition offered by Kuhn (1970) in that it has common problems and common methodologies, much like the disciplines of political science, psychology, sociology, history, and others. Disability studies has a wide variety of problems to be studied and methodologies to be used. It is today an academic discipline with, as Kuhn would say, its own paradigm which sets forth the variables in the field and their relationships.

The disability paradigm did not arise out of nothing. It is the product of the disability movement, which has its U.S. roots in the activities of parents of children with disabilities and adults with disabilities during the first half of the twentieth century (Pfeiffer, 1993). In 1977, the White House Conference on Handicapped Individuals became a watershed in the history of the disability movement, both in terms of policy recommendations and in creating a national network of the leaders of the disability movement. As a result of their accom-

*Published in *Exploring theories and expanding methodologies: Where we are and where we need to go*, edited by Sharon N. Barnartt and Barbara Mandell Altman in the series Research in Social Science and Disability, New York: Elsevier Science, volume 2 (2001), pp. 29–52.

plishments, independent-living centers were founded, political activity increased, and new policy was created.

Out of the 1997 White House Conference recommendations came the National Institute on Disability and Rehabilitation Research (NIDRR) which is part of the U.S. Department of Education. In the 1980s, NIDRR took the leadership in research that introduced a new paradigm of disability.

> This disability paradigm . . . maintains that disability is a product of an interaction between characteristics of an individual (e.g., conditions and impairments, functional status, or personal and socioeconomic qualities) and characteristics of the natural, built, cultural, and social environments. The new paradigm . . . [focuses] on the whole person functioning in his or her environment. (U.S. Department of Education, 2000, pp. 2–3)

The old paradigm, the medical model, studied disability in terms of deficits which kept a person from carrying on certain functions and activities.

THE OLD DISABILITY PARADIGM

The key to understanding the medical model and why it is inadequate for the study of disability is its depiction of the "sick role" (Parsons, 1957, pp. 146–150; Parsons, 1975; Bickenbach, 1993, pp. 61–92). In the medical model the individual has a condition (a deficit) which is unwanted or which in the past caused something unwanted in the individual. As a result, the individual is viewed as being in the "sick role," as being sick.

In the sick role, the individual is excused from social obligations (Parsons, 1951, p. 285) and has a reason for not going to work or to class. If someone is sick and goes to work or to class, he or she has an excuse to be less than cordial and even have other people carry out responsibilities. Moreover the person who is sick must follow the orders of the professional—the doctor's orders—to become "well." The professional is the one who makes the decisions to be followed so the sick one can recover.

If the person in the sick role rejects the doctor's orders, then he or she is described as "noncompliant" and suffers. The person may be labeled as maladjusted or not accepting of reality. The consequence is often the denial of services or, with some persons who have "mental disabilities," forceful medication.

Not everyone in the medical, health, and rehabilitation fields accepts the medical model (Scullion, 1999; Longino & Murphy, 1999). As Engel (1977) pointed out some years ago, over time the medical model was continually accepted and not challenged. It became ". . . a cultural imperative, its limitations easily overlooked. . . . [It] acquired the status of dogma" (Engel, 1977, p. 130). There are major problems using this model to study and understand disability, as Marks (1999b, pp. 51–76) points out.

One of the fundamental problems with the medical model is that it blames the "victim." If a person has a permanent impairment that necessitates using a wheelchair to move around, that person will never get "well." To get "well" the person must no longer need the wheelchair; but that person will need the wheelchair and thus will remain in the "sick role" forever and will always be viewed as dependent. Experiences with a permanent impairment are depicted as aberrant and as targets for intervention.

In the medical model people are judged as "sick" or "unemployable" on the basis of their ability to function as a "normal" person does. As Amundson (2000a) writes, the idea of "normal" is a fiction. People categorize themselves in a number of ways. Some of them—like the distinction between women and men—appear to reflect biological reality in a way that the distinction between Methodists and Presbyterians does not.

The medical model, relying heavily on the concept of "normal function," accepts functional determinism. Amundson (2000a, 2000b) asks if these concepts are objective and their use scientific, or are they simply the catchwords of the dominant class of society which they use to preserve their power and position. He writes:

> [T]he doctrine of biological normality is itself one aspect of a social prejudice against certain functional modes or styles. The disadvantages experienced by people who are assessed as "abnormal" derive not from biology, but from implicit social judgments about the acceptability of certain kinds of biological variation. (Amundson, 2000a, p. 33)

This argument is one of the criticisms, presented by Pfeiffer (1998), of the International Classification of Impairments, Disabilities, and Handicaps (ICIDH), which is based on the medical model. An extensive discussion of the concepts of normal and normality as used by biomedical ethicists can also be found in Silvers (1988) and in Crossley (2000).

Kirchner (1995) gives an excellent critique of conclusions about people who are blind or have severe visual limitations based on the medical model. Conrad (1992), Barbour (1997), and Crossley (2000) also provide excellent discussions of the problems of the medical model.

THE NEW DISABILITY PARADIGM

The alternative today to the medical model is the disability paradigm. It has at least nine interpretations or versions: (1) the social constructionist version as found in the United States; (2) the social model version as found in the United Kingdom; (3) the impairment version; (4) the oppressed minority (political) version; (5) the independent living version; (6) the postmodern (poststructuralist, humanist, experiential, existential) version; (7) the continuum version; (8) the human variation version; and (9) the discrimination version. All of them have some characteristics in common, which will be used to present a composite disability paradigm.

Each of these versions will be summarized in turn with references for further reading. The more developed the version the longer will be the summary. They will also be critiqued. As with all summaries and most critiques, some things will be left out and some things may appear over emphasized. The reader should review the references provided for the overall view of each version of the disability paradigm.

The Social Constructionist Version in the United States

Disability as a social construct can be traced back a number of years in the United States. See Chapter 4 for a more comprehensive discussion of the Social Constructionist Version. The classic statement was made by Goffman (1963) regarding the interaction of stigmatized and "normal" people in social situations: People with disabilities (and others) have an unexpected differentness which causes "normal" people to stigmatize them and to socially construct their identities based on that differentness.

Other early writings that use the social constructionist approach are Meyerson (1948); Barker (1948), which is cited by some authors as the first treatment of disabled persons as a minority group; Becker (1963); Scott (1969); Schur (1971 & 1979); Albrecht (1976); Blaxter (1976); Wikler (1979); Gove (1980); Altman (1984); and Bogdan, Taylor, and Stevan (1982). Birenbaum (1975 & 1979) gives the earliest clear statement of the social construction of disability, but he failed to elaborate in a theoretical way.

The concept of disability as being socially constructed was widely discussed during the 1970s and 1980s. In *Missing Pieces*, Zola (1982a) presents a chronicle of living with a physical disability which begins to explain the disability experience as a social construction. He sets forth much of the intellectual framework needed to understand people with disabilities and their experiences from the social constructionist viewpoint. These ideas are further elaborated in Zola (1982b). Wright (1983) and Osberg, Corcoran, DeJong, & Ostroff (1983) carry the analysis further by emphasizing that environmental factors play an important role in constructing the disability identity. By the mid 1980s, the social constructionist version of the disability paradigm was well developed in the United States. Albrecht (1992, pp. 17–18) has a good summary discussion.

There are three objections to the U.S. social constructionist version of the disability paradigm. First, by accepting the roles as found in society this version makes disability appear to be "real" (inevitable) and not changeable. Second, the roles are based on "normal" activities that actually embody white, male, Western values, which seriously limits its usefulness. Third, by defining disability in terms of social roles, it blames the person with a disability for not conforming and falls into the (medical model) trap of wanting to change the person and not society. It is helpful for explaining how people with disabilities come to be called disabled (because they are not "normal"), but it is not very useful for research and for advocacy purposes.

The Social Model Version in the United Kingdom

The social model paradigm found in the United Kingdom is a Marxist or class perspective of disability wherein the disabled are viewed as "oppressed," a view which is not often found in the United States (Pfeiffer, 1996). Scholars and advocates who use this model identify themselves as working class and stress their working-class origins. The model was formalized in a 1976 statement by the Union of the Physically Impaired Against Segregation (UPIAS, 1976) as to why people with disabilities are oppressed. It was further elaborated by Finkelstein (1980) and Oliver (1983 & 1990) and it is vigorously and often contentiously debated and discussed by its supporters (Oliver, 1990 & 1996; Barton, 1996; Germon, 1998 & 1999; Branfield, 1999; Marks, 1999a).

According to the social model of disability the problem is "society's failure to provide appropriate services and adequately ensure [that] the needs of disabled people are fully taken into account in its social organization" (Oliver, 1995, p. 32). A major problem, according to Oliver, is that physicians inappropriately make decisions about social issues that are unrelated to medicine. In addition, the agencies in the UK which are responsible for various social concerns important to people with disabilities have the power to decide what people with disabilities need, whereas they are not responsible for helping them meet these needs. Disability, according to the social model, is generally seen by other people as an individual tragedy and pathology.

According to this version of the disability paradigm, it is the structures of society, especially the means of industrial production, which places people with disabilities at a disadvantage in society, politics, and the economy. There must be a radical restructuring of society to resolve the problems facing people with disabilities. Only when one recognizes that truth can the experience and reality of disability be understood. Only then can it be viewed clearly enough to be studied.

However, many disability studies scholars in the UK (including Oliver, 1983, 1990, 1995, 1996) say that no model, including the social model, can totally explain disability, because as they say, it is not a social theory, but only a model that says why people with disabilities are disadvantaged.

There are problems with the UK social model, including distrust. Humphrey (2000) says that the UK social model can be interpreted in a way which excludes some disabilities, and the persons with them feel alienated from other people with disabilities. In addition, she writes, the model suffers from the distrust of academics and especially nondisabled researchers. For example, people who are survivors of brain injury say that discussions of the social model often involve, implicitly, the medical model's negative assumptions about impairment, when their brains are described as "defective." Persons who have facial disfigurements or have dyslexia also say that the social model keeps them from feeling accepted in the disability community because it says that they are not disabled enough. Survivors of the mental health system also express these criticisms of the social model and of most every model or paradigm of disability (Beresford, 2000).

Shakespeare and Watson (1997) write that the UK social model of disability is ignored by the social and behavioral sciences, such as psychology and most areas of sociology. This "ignorance" might be understandable in medical science because it challenges the medical model for disability, but not in psychology and medical sociology. Further discussion of the social model as used in the UK can be found in Barton (1996), Oliver (1996), Barnes (1996), and Marks (1999b).

The Impairment Version

Some critics of the social model argue that impairment and personal experience are overlooked, but they must be included (Morris, 1991; French, 1993; Crow, 1996; Paterson & Hughes, 1999). After all, they say, it is impairment that distinguishes people with disabilities. Impairment means some mental or physical aspect of the person is diminished or damaged from normal capacities. Take away the impairment and all people are equal.

The impairment version is rejected by defenders of the social model. Some proponents of the social model say that everyone has an impairment of some type and so such a version is not distinct enough to be of use. Other writers say that the impairment version focuses blame on the individual with the impairment and not on the social structures that produce the disadvantage. And others say this approach reintroduces the tragic version of disability, in other words, the impairment is seen as a tragedy that can only be fought against (Branfield, 1999; Barnes, 1999; Marks, 1999b; Paterson & Hughes, 1999).

In any event the impairment version of the disability paradigm is useful in some contexts. It is not yet fully developed and may become more useful in the future.

The Oppressed Minority (Political) Version

A good overview of the oppressed minority (political) version can be found in Bickenbach (1993), Branfield (1999), and Moore & Feist-Price (1999). A succinct description of the oppressed minority version and its impact on the shaping of ADA can be found in Scotch (2000, pp. 213–218). This version is often wrongly thought to be the underlying paradigm for many disability studies scholars who are presenting research findings, but who are then characterized as partisan advocates (Ustun, Bickenbach, Badley, & Chatterji, 1998).

The oppressed minority (political) version says that people with disabilities face discrimination because they are confronted with architectural barriers as well as sensory, attitudinal, cognitive, and economic barriers. They are treated as second-class citizens. Although children with disabilities are no longer (in most cases) excluded from public school, today they are routinely segregated into special education classes. In spite of the Individuals with Disabilities Education Act in the United States, which requires placement in the least restricted classroom setting, children with disabilities spend their time in separate rooms doing little of educational value according to critics. As a result of this discrimination, many persons with disabilities perceive a similarity between their personal experiences and those of an oppressed minority group.

Using a standard definition of a minority group (Vander Zanden, 1972), a minority group has five attributes: (1) As a group and individually the members face prejudice, discrimination, segregation, or persecution, or a combination of them; (2) it has a trait which is viewed negatively by the dominant group; (3) it has a collective awareness of itself and its problems; (4) it has an involuntary membership, usually from birth; and (5) it practices endogamy or intragroup marriage (marriage within a specific group as required by custom or law).

A number of groups exhibit these five traits: African Americans, Hispanics, Jews, Asian Americans, Native Americans, and women. All of them experience discrimination and segregation. All of them have a common trait held in low esteem: color, religion, culture, language, and gender roles. All of them have a collective awareness, although it varies in intensity. In most cases people are born into the group. And all but women experience endogamy. Are people with disabilities a minority group under this definition?

People with disabilities face prejudice and discrimination daily: They are denied jobs; they must often live in segregated "handicapped units"; they face inaccessible public transportation; their "special education" is simply segregated education. In all these ways they are excluded from society.

People with disabilities have a trait—a disability—which is viewed in a very negative way. People with disabilities are beginning to have a common awareness. People with disabilities are either born with a disability or become disabled involuntarily. They experience endogamy, but less today than in previous years. Clearly, people with disabilities are a minority.

As a minority, people with disabilities are denied rights and share of society's resources. As other minorities have concluded, the only way to break out of this constraining and deadly condition is to rebel, either through political action or by violent acts. The rebellion of people with disabilities is usually very quiet, except for members of ADAPT, activists who use techniques such as occupation of premises and demonstrations to make their point. Other persons with disabilities use the more traditional political means and court actions to overcome their oppression.

Corker (1999) discusses some of the problems with the oppressed minority (political) version of the disability paradigm. According to her, the major problem is that this version has an inadequate theoretical basis. It emphasizes structure (such as power and recourse inequity) too much and excludes the importance of discourse. It needs to move away from the idea that all experience can be explained in terms of a dichotomy (e.g., disabled/non-disabled, rich/poor) because that is limiting of what people with disabilities can do and understand.

Another basic problem with the oppressed minority (political) version is that there are a number of people with disabilities who live in the mainstream of society who are *not* oppressed and in fact are sometimes the oppressors of other people with disabilities. They are not about to lead a revolution to secure their share of the resources of society because they already have them. Furthermore, this version, it is said, is unrealistic and turns off nondisabled people with its militancy.

On the good side, however, the oppressed minority (political) version does produce insights into cultural group dynamics that can be incorporated into research. It is also the most useful of all the versions in organizing and advocacy. For purposes of understanding the behavior of many people with disabilities this version is very useful.

The Independent Living Version

The independent living version of the disability paradigm (well expressed in DeJong, 1983) sees the person with a disability as a responsible decision maker. The disability does not mean that the person is sick, nor is she or he unhealthy because of the disability. Professionals may or may not be asked for expert knowledge and others may or may not be asked for assistance. Unlike the medical model, in the independent living version a refusal to follow a professional's advice is not grounds for limiting social rights in society. The person with a disability has the fundamental right to choose.

The problems for people with disabilities are seen as controlling attitudes on the part of professionals and others, inadequate support services, and attitudinal, architectural, sensory, cognitive, and economic barriers. But the solution to the problems under this paradigm consist of self-advocacy, system advocacy, elimination of barriers, and outcomes chosen by the person with a disability. As Morris (1991) states, "Nothing about me without me."

Ratzka (1999) writes that independent living is both a philosophy and a movement that works for equal rights, equal opportunities, self-respect, and self-determination. It does not mean that people with disabilities want to live in isolation. Instead, it means that people with disabilities want the same opportunities and choices in life as other people. Most importantly, people with disabilities must be in charge of their own lives and to speak for themselves. Another excellent presentation of the philosophy of independent living and how it can be applied in society through independent living centers is to be found in Brown (1994).

The DeJong (1983) interpretation was not only influential in the disability movement in the United States, but it had a high impact on research in the field of disability studies. However, Williams (1983) writes that the DeJong version is too narrow, that his terminology is very ambiguous and his methodology unnecessarily complex, to the point of self-contradiction; but, most importantly, DeJong's stress on individualism and the free market arise from a misunderstanding of the social, political, and economic mechanisms at work. So Williams suggests: "If we remain entrapped by images of individual consumers and clients, divorced from any sense of power and social structure, we will only replicate the current weaknesses of research in rehabilitation" (Williams, 1983, p. 1009).

Further problems are suggested, which are parallel to the problems presented by Williams (1983). The independent living version only looks for supports and not rights. Without the rights the supports either will not be obtained or else will be short-lived. In a similar vein, it can be argued that the independent living version plays into the hands of the professionals, who pretend to support it, but do so only because through it they become providers, which helps maintain their dominance.

The Postmodern (Post-Structuralism, Humanist, Experiential, Existential) Version

Cultural studies is the source for this version of the disability paradigm. It is based on the idea that culture is a social and political construct (Gramsci, 1971; Foucault, 1980). The ideas underlying a culture are presented in texts or material things. To understand the world these things must be decoded (Marks, 1999b). This same approach is used with the experience of disability.

Sometimes called interdisciplinary, cultural studies is more nondisciplinary or even antidisciplinary because it does not stake out an area of knowledge in which to use a common methodology to produce a body of knowledge. Instead it uses whatever field of knowledge necessary and it is very politicized in a good way. This version of a disabilities paradigm attacks the Enlightenment idea of a rational, progressive human actor in society. It aggressively deconstructs existing knowledge to discover the fundamental orientations and unstated assumptions about disability and people with disabilities. The focus is on the subjective experience of disability and both the explicit and implicit assumptions that shape that experience.

Historians, literary critics, and some philosophers are natural participants in this endeavor because they closely examine texts and cultural artifacts searching for the underlying meanings. For further discussion see Eagleton (1983), Huyssen (1986), Butler (1990), Arnold (1993), and John (1996).

Some writers have reservations about this approach, asking if it is, indeed, possible to reconstruct a theory of modern society and culture and thereby understand disability. Further, they contend, the nonacademic cannot understand this approach, and the academic community soundly rejects it. (Whether this last statement is correct will not be discussed here, but there are many academics who do reject this version of the disability paradigm.) In addition, this version is so divorced from reality that it is not at all useful as an organizing and advocacy strategy, and it is of no help to the person with a disability facing barriers and discrimination and badly in need of services.

The Continuum Version

Running through, under, and over all of the versions so far is an idea, not always explicit, that there are many different representations of disability and that they are related. As Zola (1989, 1993a, 1993b, 1994) noted, the fit between the environment and the impairments of people produces the issues confronting persons with disabilities. There are changes that can be made in housing, transportation, and employment policies that would increase the quality of the daily life of disabled persons and of everyone in society. Everyone will eventually have a chronic illness and activity limitations so that universal adaptations are needed to avoid the segregation of persons with disabilities which exist today.

The continuum version is more of a nuance than a developed version. It should be kept in mind when researching disability, but it may not qualify as a complete version in and of itself. Although, it is not as fully developed as the other versions, it may, at some future date, emerge as a true rival to the others and not just a means of seeing commonalities. It is useful for explaining why "nondisabled" people should be concerned with the needs and experiences of persons with disabilities.

The Human Variation Version

Schriner and Scotch (1998) and Scotch and Schriner (1997) present the human variation version of the disability paradigm, based in part on Higgins (1992), which presents additional implementation strategies to achieve policy goals.

In their presentation they say that while similarities between people with disabilities, racial minorities, ethnic group members, and women exist and were recognized over thirty years ago (tenBroek, 1966; tenBroek & Matson, 1966; Safilios-Rothschild, 1970), people with disabilities suffered discrimination not because of shared group characteristics, but because of the way in which people viewed and reacted to them (Gliedman & Roth, 1980). Scotch and Schriner (1997) perceive the minority (political) version as the dominant version of the disability paradigm and conclude that the minority group version not only is inadequate for understanding disability, but it also fails in helping to resolve the numerous problems facing people with disabilities. They present a number of arguments and facts to support their contention.

They write that the multidimensions of disability must be the foundation of any useful paradigm of disability. However, there is a huge problem in coming to an agreement on a definition of disability. Any definition must deal with diverse impairments, various cultural implications, and varying social settings in which a barrier to one person with a disability is of little consequence to another (Zola, 1993a).

Schriner and Scotch (1998) and Scotch and Schriner (1997) also write that this human variation version is based on the fact that social institutions were not constructed to deal with as wide a variation in people as is found in the population of people with disabilities. In other words, institutional efficiency based on standardization does not work with people with disabilities.

Scotch & Schriner (1997) point out that in the twenty-first century, inflexible, narrowly standardized social institutions, especially economic ones, will not work. Systems that are quite flexible and adaptable are needed. In a flexible social system which fully accommodates a person with a disability, the disability disappears. Universal design (environments and facilities that are usable by everyone), as it sometimes is called, will be able to accomplish such a disappearance.

Disability does introduce complexity (such as interaction with the healthcare system and making accommodations) into lives and families and the social system that surrounds them. An approach based on this understanding will increase the understanding of disability. It will help as social services examine the issues of resource allocation and institutional adaptation. Discrimination does exist, but there is also the incapacity of social systems to respond to the kind of human variations that are found in people with disabilities. Even if all discrimination and stereotyping disappeared, there would still be problems facing people with disabilities.

To deal with these kinds of problems Scotch & Schriner (1997) say that today's inflexible organizations and institutions, when confronted with obligations to include people with disabilities, will achieve "satisfactory" outcomes in a process described as "satisficing" by March and Simon (1958). However, they write, satisficing excludes "exceptional cases," which describes many persons with disabilities as well as others, such as single mothers and people caring for elderly parents. In the case of employers, for example, it is better to accommodate through maximizing a person's productivity than to rely on legal entitlements such as ADA. Such flexibility is necessary in the global economy (and society) of the twenty-first century.

However, the problem with the human variation version of the disability paradigm is twofold. First, it relies on the concept of "normal." This concept is culturally bound, and in most discussions of disability, what is normal is what Western, white, male, middle-class people do and what they value. In addition, the concept of normal is ambiguous. The normal way of carrying out functions is neither agreed upon generally nor is it clearly defined, as discussed above.

The second problem with the human variation version is that it is partly based upon a misconception of ADA, which is a civil rights statute, and not an entitlement of any type. ADA says that people with disabilities in our system, like all other people, have a right to due process and equal protection. People, especially people with disabilities, have the right to be treated fairly and the same as others are treated. The U.S. legal system is based on these rights, which will be discussed below.

Disability As Discrimination

This version of the disability paradigm comes from the fact that many people with disabilities live their daily lives not acting as if they are disabled. It is only when they encounter acts of discrimination based upon an artificial barrier (their disability) that they feel disabled. It could be discrimination based on a lack of architectural access or on sensory, attitudinal, cognitive, and economic barriers. They are not being treated fairly because they are not being treated as other, nondisabled people.

It is true that disability is socially constructed, is based upon social mechanisms, is related to an impairment, is the basis for oppression, is the need for services to live independently, is the product of the wrong ontology, is based on an ignorance of the continuum of human experience, and is related to the idea of "normal." In all of these perspectives, however, discrimination is the thread which makes sense of what is happening. It is discrimination which draws all of the versions together.

Because of the prominent role which discrimination plays in understanding disability, disability is a policy issue, not a health nor a medical issue. By prescribing behavior and activities, policy (including laws) disable people (Liachowitz, 1988). Laws and policies very effectively produce the expectation of certain behavior in the minds of nondisabled people, which is conveyed to people with disabilities. Because of these expectations on the part of people with and without disabilities, laws and policies "lead to an ostensible 'self-inflicted' disability" (Liachowitz, 1988, p. 19). The same thing happens with race, gender, religion, and national origin. People with disabilities, non-Caucasians, women, and people of certain religions and national origins all begin to behave as expected by the dominant class of people. Such behavior is learned and makes it easier to survive in a world of discrimination.

There is an important point to be made when disability is seen as a policy issue: Disability rights are civil rights. The right of a person with a disability to be treated as other persons are treated and in a fair way (equal protection and due process) is a civil right. And civil rights are *not* dependent on available funding or even the appropriation of funds. Waddington (1996), Gewirth (1996), and Percy (1989) discuss this point.

However, Percy (1989) writes that there are three ways to view disability rights as civil rights in terms of implementation: equal treatment, equal access, or equal outcome. By viewing these three ways as separate, Percy and many others find themselves in conflicting positions. The three ways are actually all part of one. A person with a disability cannot receive equal treatment unless society is as equally accessible as it is for a nondisabled person. To a person with a disability, receiving equal treatment and equal access has no meaning unless there are equal outcomes possible. A person with a disability must be treated in the same way as a person without a disability (Illingworth & Parmet, 2000). No distinction based on the existence of a disability can be tolerated because such an approach is the essence of discrimination. Advocates who do not understand this position and judges who are ignorant of this approach fall back on some type of special privilege required by people with disabilities which results in both inadequate remedies and partial discrimination.

In an alternative approach, Burgdorf (1997), citing tenBroek (1966) and tenBroek and Matson (1966), argues that the integration of people with disabilities into society is both the more equitable and the more practical alternative to segregation and dependence. In addition he argues that artificial barriers contribute to segregation, limit integration, and are discriminatory. Full participation in society (not special privilege) is the objective of antidiscrimination laws such as Section 504 and ADA (Pfeiffer, 2000).

Burgdorf (1997) continues by pointing out how treating people with disabilities as different because of a characteristic (a disability) produces pity, patronizing behavior, and negative stereotypes in other people. It is no different than prejudice on the basis of race, gender, or religion. Some people need certain services and other people need different services. As he writes: "Nondiscrimination is a guarantee of equality. It is not a special service reserved for a select few" (Burgdorf, 1997, p. 568).

This point is well exemplified by gender discrimination. The discriminatory practices toward women do not put them on a pedestal, but in a cage. The idea that people with disabilities are different and in need of special services such as protection and professional direction is, in the same way, plain discrimination. People with disabilities must not be perceived as being in a protected class because that practice destroys all vestiges of equality. Such an approach under ADA requires that people with disabilities prove how badly disabled they are and then prove how well they can carry out a job, use a service, or access a public accommodation. People with disabilities are different from each other and from nondisabled people, but all people are different (Johnson, 1981). All people need their differences acknowledged and have them accommodated.

A beginning discussion of the discrimination version of the disability paradigm can be found in Bickenbach (1993). However, he trips over a call for entitlements in the same way as Percy (1989). Bickenbach writes that people with disabilities are entitled to certain rights because they are disabled. In his discussion of how these rights are to be justified, he develops the key idea of equality—they are entitled to these rights to make them equal. However, it is here contended, that if all people are treated in the same manner and are treated fairly (equal protection and due process), then there is no reason to justify the way a person with or without a disability is treated. Illingworth and Parmet (2000) agree that ADA clearly supports the need for due process and equal protection.

Equal protection means receiving similar treatment in similar circumstances and no discriminatory treatment from the government, employers, and operators/owners of public accommodations. It means being treated like others and in a fair way. Personal liberties can only be violated after due process or in an extreme emergency. Due process means a fair procedure in a legal sense to ensure a person receives equal protection, such as a jury trial before being sent to prison. It usually includes: adequate/reasonable written notice of reason(s) for a hearing before the hearing is held, an open hearing if the individual wants one, a full opportunity to express the person's position, unbiased hearing personnel who understand any technical information necessary, a transcript of the hearing in a written and print-accessible form, access to counsel, questioning of any witnesses used, examination of any physical evidence presented, receiving the decision in a written and print-accessible form in a reasonable time after the hearing is over, and the right to appeal the decision to unbiased other(s) who can overturn the decision, order a new hearing, or affirm the decision. In other words, be treated like other people and be treated in a fair manner. Admittedly it does not always work out that way as Gerstmann (1999) and Burgdorf (1997) show.

It is often argued that people with disabilities require unusual and expensive accommodations. Curb cuts, ramps, Braille printing, accessible buses, special equipment, reserved parking spaces, and expensive medical care are all cited to support this contention. However, other people receive subsidies and services such as snow plowing; fire and police protection; ambulance service; tax-supported sports arenas; mass transit; enterprise zones; and tax breaks. Some "special services" are useful to a large number of people. Curb cuts are helpful to anyone on wheels (people pushing baby carriages, furniture movers, bicyclers, skaters, wheelchair users). Many persons who do not need ramps find them useful.

One might argue that snow plowing is important to keep the streets open, but mass transit with accessible buses is also important for taking people to work. And one might argue that fire, police, and ambulance services are necessary to make society work for the people who need them, but so are reserved parking spaces necessary to make society work for people who need them. One might argue that tax-supported sports arenas are nice for people who want to go to games, but Braille is nice for people who need it to read public documents. One might argue that enterprise zones with their special breaks to businesses provide special services, but so does special equipment enable the user to move about in society. One might argue that tax breaks to developers are necessary to have new housing, but expensive medical care is often necessary for plain survival.

The argument could go on for a very long time. There is no doubt that certain people receive privileges in society and others have to fight for equal treatment. Wildman (1996) shows how some persons get big benefits while other people—such as people with disabilities—are told that it costs too much. It is a matter of privilege based on race (being white), class (being rich), gender (being male), sexuality (being heterosexual), and two things which Wildman does not cover: age (being young) and, for lack of a better term, not being disabled (being able bodied).

WHAT DISABILITY DOES NOT MEAN

It is important to discuss what disability does not mean because it is expressed in several propositions which form a foundation for the disability paradigm: (1) Disability is not a tragedy; (2) disability does not mean dependency; (3) disability does not mean a loss of potential, productivity, social contribution, value, capability, ability, and the like; (4) disability is a natural part of life, everyone's life; and (5) there is as much variation between people with disabilities as between people in general.

In other words, disability does not mean grief, guilt, and bitterness. People with disabilities are not courageous, noble, and brave any more than any one else. People with disabilities can be very sexual and sensual. People with disabilities can be very good parents. People with disabilities are not poor unless they are unemployed. People with disabilities are not ignorant unless they were segregated from mainstream education and even then many are quite brilliant in spite of so-called special education. People with disabilities do not have to be with "their own kind," whatever that means.

People with disabilities (like all people) are human, fallible, make mistakes, and are capable of taking risks, hopefully learning from failures. People with disabilities are not necessarily confrontational (maybe some are) and most of the research done on people with disabilities in public health, medicine, and rehabilitation is of little value

Perhaps part of the problem is that other minority groups—such as women and African Americans—self identify. People with disabilities are diagnosed. With no true input from them, people with disabilities are labeled, forever.

A STATEMENT OF THE DISABILITY PARADIGM

What is to be made of these different versions of the disability paradigm? Can they be combined to produce a statement of the disability paradigm? Yes, but there will be many protests and (hopefully) much discussion about the result.

The disability paradigm states that the study of the experience of people with disabilities focuses on the following variables which impinge on the phenomenon of disability and interact with each other and other human characteristics:

1. The process in which the performance of social roles and tasks produces discrimination.
2. The discriminatory treatment of people with disabilities produced by the organization of society.
3. The recognition that an impairment does not imply tragedy and a low quality of life.
4. The stark reality that people with disabilities are an oppressed minority which experiences discrimination.
5. The need of all people, including people with disabilities, for various services in order to live independently.
6. The realization that all people have agendas so that the unstated assumptions of disability policy must be revealed.
7. The knowledge that people over time move on a continuum from non-disabled to disabled so that eventually everyone experiences disability.
8. The rejection that there is "normal" human behavior on which social policy can be based.
9. The all pervasiveness of discrimination against persons with disabilities.

There are methodological problems in this statement of the disability paradigm. The whole question of identifying and measuring disability is open. The interpretation of the results of advocacy and research is varied. In some research, different variables will be studied more than others. In some advocacy activities different variables will be more prominent than others. There are other problems in obtaining adequate data. Similar variables are explicit or implied in the earlier quote from NIDRR's Long-Range Plan 1999–2003, Executive Summary, which bears repeating here:

> This disability paradigm . . . maintains that disability is a product of an interaction between characteristics of an individual (e.g., conditions and impairments, functional status, or personal and socioeconomic qualities) and characteristics of the natural, built, cultural, and social environments. The new paradigm . . . [focuses] on the whole person functioning in his or her environment (U.S., Department of Education, 2000, pp. 2–3).

There is still much refinement to be carried out, but the basic statement of the disability paradigm exists.

CONCLUSION: IMPLICATIONS OF THE DISABILITY PARADIGM

Some implications of the disability paradigm need to be pointed out. First, professionals are not the decision makers in the field of disability. The person with a disability is the one who makes the decision on his or her own behalf. Second, social change must occur and people with disabilities are not the ones who should be forced to change. And third, research based on the disability paradigm must include people with disabilities as active partners because they are the decision makers. These three implications need further elaboration.

Stone and Priestley (1996) and Kitchen (2000) point out that many persons with disabilities view disability research as occurring within an oppressive theoretical paradigm supported by social oppression. They set forth an emancipatory research model to be applied to all disability research. This research model not only states that the outcomes must be relevant to the lives of people with disabilities, but that active participation in the research by people with disabilities must occur.

A considerable amount of disability related research is plainly oppressive. The World Bank uses Disability Adjusted Life Years (DALYs), which view disability and people with disabilities as burdens (Murray & Lopez, 1996a, 1996b; World Bank, 1995). The irony of the DALYs is that they cannot stand up to methodological criticism (Groce, Chamie, & Me, 1999.) The concept is essentially meaningless.

The World Health Organization and many researchers use the International Classification of Impairments, Disabilities, and Handicaps (ICIDH) which is handicapist in its language, furthers eugenics for people with disabilities, and has considerable problems in its logic (Pfeiffer, 1992, 1994, 1998).

The DALYs and the ICIDH contribute to the marginalization of people with disabilities, justify their segregation, encourage eugenics, and deny their rights of equal protection and due process. Both of them further the personal tragedy view of disability. Use of them implicitly and explicitly says that the experience of people with disabilities does not count and is of no value (Brock, 1993; Evans, 1994; Goode, 1994; Hughes, Hwang, Kim, Eisenman, & Killian, 1995; Kaplan, 1994; Kirchner, 1995; Modell & Kuliev, 1991; Nussbaum & Sen, 1993; Parmenter, 1994; Pfeiffer, 1998; Groce, Chamie, & Me, 1999; Rock, 2000).

This view can no longer be tolerated. As set forth at length in Devlieger, Rusch, and Pfeiffer (forthcoming) people with a disability have the right to be different and the right to be treated equally with all other people. They have the right to equal protection and due process in the provision of social services, in everyday life, and in the performance of disability research.

REFERENCES

Albrecht, G. L. (Ed.) (1976). *The sociology of physical disability and rehabilitation*. Pittsburgh, PA: University of Pittsburgh Press.

Albrecht, G. L. (1992). The disability business: Rehabilitation in America. Newbury Park, CA: Sage Publications.

Altman, B. M. (1984). *Examination of the effects of individual, primary and secondary resources on the outcomes of impairment*. Doctoral dissertation, Uni-versity of Maryland, College Park. Unpublished.

Amundson, R. (2000a). Against Normal Function. *Studies in History and Philosophy of Biological and Biomedical Sciences, 31*, 33–53.

Amundson, R. (2000b). Biological Normality and the ADA. In L. Francis & A. Silvers (Ed.), *Americans with disabilities: Exploring implications of the law for individuals and institutions* New York: Routledge, pp. 102–110.

Arnold, D. (1993). *Colonizing the body: State medicine and epidemic disease in nineteenth-century India*. Berkeley, CA: University of California Press.

Barbour, A. (1997). *Caring for patients: A critique of the medical model*. Palo Alto, CA: Stanford University Press.

Barker, R. G. (1948). The Social Psychology of Physical Disability. *Journal of Social Issues, 4*, 28–38.

Barnes, C. (1996). Theories of disability and the origins of the oppression of disabled people in Western society. In L. Barton (Ed.), Disability and society: Emerging issues and insights (pp. 43–60). London: Longman.

Barnes, C. (1999). Disability studies: New or not so new directions? *Disability & Society, 14*, 577–580.

Barton, L. (1996). Sociology and disability: Some emerging issues. In L. Barton (Ed.), Disability and society: Emerging issues and insights (pp. 3–17). London: Longman.

Becker, H. S. (Ed.) (1963). *Outsiders: Studies in the sociology of deviance*. New York: The Free Press.

Beresford, P. (2000). What have madness and psychiatric system survivors got to do with disability and disability studies? *Disability & Society, 15*, 167–172.

Bickenbach, J. E. (1993). Physical disability and social policy. Toronto: University of Toronto Press.

Birenbaum, A. (1975). The disabled as involuntary deviants. In E. Sagarin (Ed.), *Deviants and deviance: An introduction to the study of disvalued people and behavior* (pp. 201–214). Westport, CT: Praeger.

Birenbaum, A. (1979). The Social Construction of Disability. *Journal of Sociology and Social Welfare, 6*, 89–101.

Blaxter, M. (1976). *The meaning of disability: A sociological study of impairment*. London: Heinmann.

Bogdan, R. & Taylor, S. J. (1982). *Inside out: The social meaning of mental retardation*. Toronto: University of Toronto Press.

Branfield, B. (1999). The disability movement: A movement of disabled people—A Response to Paul S. Duckett. *Disability & Society, 14*, 399–403.

Brock, D. (1993). Quality of life measures in health care and medical ethics. In M. C. Nussbaum & A. Sen (Eds.), *The quality of life* (pp. 95–132). Oxford: Clarendon Press.

Brown, S. E. (1994). *Independent living: Theory and practice*. Las Cruces, NM: Institute on Disability Culture.

Burgdorf, R. L. Jr. (1997). "Substantially limited" protection from disability discrimination: The special treatment model and misconstructions of the definition of disability. *Villanova Law Review, 42*, 409–585.

Butler, J. (1990). *Gender trouble: Feminism and the subversion of identity*. New York: Routledge.

Conrad, P. (1992). Medicalization and social control. *Annual Review of Sociology, 18*, 209–232.

Corker, M. (1999). Differences, conflations and foundations: The limits to "accurate" theoretical representation of disabled people's experience. *Disability & Society, 14*, 627–642.

Crossley, M. (2000). Impairment and Embodiment. In L. Francis & A. Silvers (Eds.), *Americans with disabilities: Exploring implications of the law for individuals and institutions* (pp. 111–123). New York: Routledge.

Crow, L. (1996). Including all of our lives: Renewing the social model of disability. In C. Barnes & G. Mercer (Eds.), *Exploring the divide*. Leeds: Disability Press.

DeJong, G. (1983). Defining and implementing the independent living concept. In N. M. Crewe & I. K. Zola (Eds.), *Independent living for physically disabled people* (Chap. 1). San Francisco: Jossey-Bass.

Devlieger, P., Rusch, F., & Pfeiffer, D. (Eds.) (forthcoming). *Disability at the crossroads: Emergent definitions, concepts, and communities*. Ann Arbor, MI: University of Michigan Press.

Eagleton, T. (1983). *Literary theory: An introduction*. Minneapolis, MN: University of Minnesota Press.

Engel, G. L. (1977). The need for a new medical model: A challenge for biomedicine. *Science, 196*(April 8), 129–136.

Evans, D. R. (1994). Enhancing quality of life in the population at large. *Social Indicators Research, 33*(1–3), 47–88.

Finkelstein, V. (1980). *Attitudes and disabled people*. New York: World Rehabilitation Fund.

Foucault, M. (1980). *Power/Knowledge*. New York: Pantheon.

French, S. (1993). Disability, impairment or something in between. In J. Swain, V. Finkelstein, S. French, & M. Oliver (Eds.), *Disabling barriers–Enabling environments*. London: Sage Publications.

Germon, P. (1998). Activists & academics: Part of the same or a world apart? In T. Shakespeare (Ed.), *The disability reader: Social science perspectives*. London: Cassell.

Germon, P. (1999). Purely academic? Exploring the relationship between theory and political activism. *Disability & Society, 14*, 687–692.

Gerstmann, E. (1999). *The constitutional underclass: Gays, lesbians, and the failure of class-based equal protection*. Chicago: University of Chicago Press.

Gewirth, A. (1996). *The community of rights*. Chicago: University of Chicago Press.

Gliedman, J., & Roth, W. (1980). *The unexpected minority: Handicapped children in America*. New York: Harcourt Brace Jovanovich.

Goffman, E. (1963). *Stigma: Notes on the management of spoiled identity*. Englewood Cliffs, NJ: Prentice-Hall.

Goode, D. (Ed.) (1994). *Quality of life for persons with disabilities: International perspectives and issues*. Cambridge, MA: Brookline Books.

Gove, W. R. (Ed,) (1980). *The labeling of deviance*. Beverly Hills, CA: Sage Publications.

Gramsci, A. (1971). *Selections from the prison notebooks*. New York: International Publishers.

Groce, N. E., Chamie, M., & Me, A. (1999). Measuring the quality of life: Rethinking the World Banks's Disability Adjusted Life Years. *International Rehabilitation Review, 49*(1&2), 12–15.

Higgins, P. C. (1992). *Making disability: Exploring the social transformation of human variation*. Springfield, IL: Charles C. Thomas.

Hughes, C., Hwang, B., Kim, J., Eisenman, L. T., & Killian, D. J. (1995). Quality of life in applied research: A review and analysis of empirical measures. *American Journal on Mental Retardation, 99*(6), 623–641.

Humphrey, J. C. (2000). Researching disability politics, or, some problems with the social model in practice. *Disability & Society, 15*, 63–85.

Huyssen, A. (1986). After the great divide: Modernism, mass culture, postmodernism. Bloomington, IN: Indiana University Press.

Illingworth, P., & Parmet, W. E. (2000). Positively disabled: The relationship between the definition of disability and rights under the ADA. In L. Francis & A. Silvers (Eds.), *Americans with disabilities: Exploring implications of the law for individuals and institutions* (pp. 3–17). New York: Routledge.

John, M. E. (1996). *Discrepant dislocations: Feminism, theory, and postcolonial histories*. Berkeley, CA: University of California Press.

Johnson, H. M. (1981). Who is handicapped? Defining the protected class under the employment provisions of Title V of the Rehabilitation Act of 1973. *Review of Public Personnel Administration, 2*, 49–61.

Kaplan, R. M. (1994). Using quality of life information to set priorities in health policy. *Social Indicators Research, 33*(1–3), 121–163.

Kirchner, C. (1995). Economic aspects of blindness and low vision: A new perspective. *Journal of Visual Impairment & Blindness, 89*, 506–513.

Kitchen, R. (2000). The researched opinions on research: Disabled people and disability research. *Disability & Society, 15*, 25–47.

Kuhn, T. (1970). *The structure of scientific revolutions* (2nd ed.). Chicago: University of Chicago Press.

Liachowitz, C. H. (1988). *Disability as a social construct: Legislative roots*. Philadelphia: University of Pennsylvania Press.

Longino, C. F. Jr., & Murphy, J. W. (1999). The old age challenge to the biomedical model: Paradigm strain and health policy. Amityville, NY: Baywood Publishing.

March, J. G., & Simon, H. A. (1958). *Organizations*. New York: John Wiley.

Marks, D. (1999a). Dimensions of oppression: Theorising the embodied subject. *Disability & Society, 14*, 611–626.

Marks, D. (1999b). *Disability: Controversial debates and psychosocial perspectives*. London: Routledge.

Meyerson, L. (1948). Physical disability as a social psychological problem. *Journal of Social Issues, 4*, 95–100.

Modell, B., & Kuliev, A. M. (1991). Services for thalassaemia as a model for cost–benefit analysis of genetics services. *Journal of Inherited Metabolic Disorders, 14*, 640–651.

Moore, C. L., & Feist-Price, S. (1999). Societal Attitudes and the Civil Rights of Persons with Disabilities. *Journal of Applied Rehabilitation Counseling, 30*, 19–24.

Morris, J. (1991). *Pride against prejudice*. London: Women's Press.

Murray, C. J. L., & Lopez, A. D. (1996a). Evidence-Based health policy: Lessons from the global burden of disease study. *Science, 274*, Nov. 1, 740–743.

Murray, C. J. L., & Lopez, A. D. (Eds.) (1996b). *The global burden of disease: A comprehensive assessment of mortality and disability from diseases, injuries, and risk factors in 1990 and projected to 2020*. Cambridge, MA: Harvard University Press.

Nussbaum, M. C., & Sen, A. (Eds.) (1993). *The quality of life*. Oxford: Clarendon Press.

Oliver, M. (1983). *Social work with disabled people*. London: Macmillan.

Oliver, M. (1990). *Politics of disablement*. London: Macmillan.

Oliver, M. (1995). *Understanding disability: From theory to practice*. New York: St. Martin's Press.

Oliver, M. (1996). *A sociology of disability or a disablist sociology?* In L. Barton (Ed.), *Disability and society: Emerging issues and insights* (pp. 18–42). London: Longman.

Osberg, S., Corcoran, P. J., DeJong, G., & Ostroff, E. (1983). Environmental barriers and the neurologically impaired patient. *Seminars in Neurology, 3*, 180–194.

Parmenter, T. R. (1994). Quality of life as a concept and measurable entity. *Social Indicators Research, 33*(1–3), 9–46.

Parsons, T. (1951). *The social system*. Glencoe, NY: Free Press.

Parsons, T. (1957). Illness and the role of the physician: A sociological perspective. *American Journal of Orthopsychiatry, 2*, 452–460. Reprinted in Peter Hamilton (Ed.) (1985). *Readings from Talcott Parsons* (pp. 145–155). New York: Tavistock Publications.

Parsons, T. (1975). The sick role and the role of the physician reconsidered. *Health and Society, 53*, 257–278.

Paterson, K., & Hughes, B. (1999). Disability studies and phenomenology: The carnal politics of everyday life. *Disability & Society, 14*, 597–610.

Percy, S. L. (1989). *Disability, civil rights, and public policy: The politics of implementation*. Tuscaloosa, AL: University of Alabama Press.

Pfeiffer, D. (1992). Disabling definitions: Is the World Health Organization normal? *New England Journal of Human Services, 11*, 4–9.

Pfeiffer, D. (1993). Overview of the disability movement: History, legislative record, and political implications. *Policy Studies Journal, 21*, 724–734.

Pfeiffer, D. (1994). Eugenics and disability discrimination. *Disability & Society, 9*, 481–499. Reprinted in R. P. Marinelli & A. E. Dell Orto (Eds.) (1999), *The psychological & social impact of disability* (4th ed.) (pp. 12–31). New York: Springer Publishing.

Pfeiffer, D. (1996). Understanding disability policy: [A review of] Michael Oliver, *Understanding Disability: From Theory to Practice* (New York: St. Martin's Press, 1995). *Policy Studies Journal, 24*, 157–159.

Pfeiffer, D. (1998). The ICIDH and the need for its revision. *Disability & Society, 13*, 503–523.

Pfeiffer, D. (2000). *The disability paradigm. Disability policy: Issues and implications for the new millennium* (pp. 81–82). Report on the 21st Mary E. Switzer Memorial Seminar, September 1999, L. R. McConnell & C. E. Hansen (Eds.). Alexandria, VA: National Rehabilitation Association.

Ratzka, A. (1999). *What is independent living? Personal Assistance Users' Newsletter*, April.

Rock, M. (2000). Discounted lives? Weighing disability when measuring health and ruling on 'compassionate' murder. *Social Science and Medicine, 51*(3), 407–417.

Safilios-Rothschild, C. (1970). *The sociology and social psychology of disability and rehabilitation*. New York: Random House.

Schriner, K. F., & Scotch, R. K. (1998). Beyond the minority group model: An emerging paradigm for the next generation of disability policy. In E. Makas, B. Haller, & T. Doe (Eds.),

Accessing the issues: Current research in disability studies (pp. 213–216). Dallas: The Society for Disability Studies and The Edmund S. Muskie Institute of Public Affairs.

Schur, E. M. (1971). *Labeling deviant behavior: Its sociological implications.* New York: Harper and Row.

Schur, E. M. (1979). *Interpreting deviance.* New York: Harper and Row.

Scotch, R. (2000). Models of disability and the Americans with Disabilities Act. *Berkeley Journal of Employment and Labor Law, 21,* 213–222.

Scotch, R., & Schriner, K. (1997). Disability as human variation: Implications for policy. *The Annals of the American Academy of Political and Social Science, 549,* 148–160.

Scott, R. A. (1969). *The making of blind men: A study of adult socialization.* New York: Russell Sage Foundation.

Scullion, P. A. (1999). 'Disability' in a nursing curriculum. *Disability & Society, 14,* 539–559.

Shakespeare, T., & Watson, N. (1997). Defending the social model. *Disability & Society, 12,* 293–300.

Silvers, A. (1998). A fatal attraction to normalizing. In E. Parens (Ed.), *Enhancing human traits: Ethical and social implications* (pp. 95–123). Washington, DC: Georgetown University Press.

Society for Disability Studies (2000). *2000 Membership Directory.* Chicago: Author.

Stone, E., & Priestley, M. (1996). Parasites, pawns and partners: Disability research and the role of non-disabled researchers. *British Journal of Sociology, 47,* 699–716.

tenBroek, J. (1966). The right to live in the world: The disabled in the law of torts. *California Law Review, 54,* 841–919.

tenBroek, J., & Matson, F. W. (1966). The disabled and the law of welfare. *California Law Review, 54,* 809–940.

UPIAS. (1976). Fundamental Principles of Disability. London: Union of the Physically Impaired Against Segregation.

U.S. Department of Education, Office of Special Education and Rehabilitative Services, National Institute on Disability and Rehabilitation Research (2000). *Long-Range Plan 1999–2003,* Executive Summary. Washington, DC: Author.

Ustun, T. B., Bickenbach, J. E., Badley, E., & Chatterji, S. (1998). A reply to David Pfeiffer "The ICIDH and the Need for its Revision." *Disability & Society, 13,* 829–831.

Vander Zanden, J. (1972). *American minority relations* (3rd ed.). New York: Ronald Press.

Waddington, L. (1996). Reassessing the employment of people with disabilities in Europe: From quotas to antidiscrimination laws. *Comparative Labor Law Journal, 18,* 62–101.

White House Conference on Handicapped Individuals. May 23–27, 1977, Wasington, DC.

Wikler, D. (1979). Paternalism and the mildly retarded. *Philosophy and Public Affairs, 8,* 377–392.

Wildman, S. (1996). *Privilege revealed: How invisible preference undermines America.* New York: New York University Press.

Williams, G. H. (1983). The movement for independent living: An evaluation and critique. *Social Sciences and Medicine, 17,* 1003–1010.

World Bank (1995). Chile: The adult health policy challenge. Washington, DC: Author.

Wright, B. A. (1983). *Physical disability—A Psychosocial Approach.* New York: Harper and Row.

Zola, I. K. (1982a). *Missing pieces: A chronicle of living with a disability.* Philadelphia: Temple University Press.

Zola, I. K. (1982b). Social and cultural disincentives to independent living. *Archives of Physical Medicine and Rehabilitation, 63,* 394–397.

Zola, I. K. (1989). Toward the necessary universalizing of a disability policy. *Milbank Quarterly, 67*(Supplement 2, Part 2), 401–428.

Zola, I. K. (1993a). Disability statistics, what we count and what it tells us: A personal and political analysis. *Journal of Disability Policy Studies, 4,* 9–39.

Zola, I. K. (1993b). Self, identity and the naming question: Reflections on the language of disability. *Social Science & Medicine, 36,* 167–173.

Zola, I. K. (1994). Towards inclusion: The role of people with disabilities in policy and research issues in the United States—A historical and political analysis. In M. H. Rioux & M. Bach (Eds.) *Disability is not measles: New research paradigms in disability* (pp. 49–66). North York, Ont.: Roeher Institute, York University.

CHAPTER 3

THE ENVIRONMENT OF DISABILITY TODAY: A NURSING HOME IS NOT A HOME*

REIKO HAYASHI

INTRODUCTION

The previous chapters presented historical and theoretical perspectives of disability. This chapter introduces some aspects of the current environment in which people with disabilities now live. Despite the enactment of the Americans with Disabilities Act of 1990 (the civil rights law for people with disabilities), discrimination and prejudice against people with disabilities persist. The historical and theoretical perspectives of discrimination and liberation discussed in previous chapters will help us understand the environment of disability today.

People with disabilities currently face many obstacles in daily life, including inaccessible housing and transportation, employment discrimination, and inadequate health-care services. This chapter focuses on the problem of residential segregation, practiced as a long-term care policy in institutional settings ironically called "nursing homes." With regard to the residential options of people with disabilities, this chapter describes the Medicaid (1965 Title XIX of the Social Security Act) and Medicaid Waiver programs, the Americans with Disabilities Act of 1990, and the Supreme Court 1999 Olmstead decision. Further, the Personal Attendant Services (PAS) program that has been implemented in several states is introduced as a residential alternative to nursing homes. The Medicaid Community Attendant Services and Supports Act (MiCASSA) bill (H.R. 2032/S. 971, pending in Congress as of this writing), which will ensure more residential options to people with disabilities, is also introduced.

The roles of social workers in the long-term care service delivery system are also examined. A key question is, "Are we meeting the needs of the service delivery system or the needs of the consumer?" The gaps are pointed out between

*I gratefully acknowledge members of ADAPT-Utah for their support in writing this chapter.

social work theories and practice regarding services for people with disabilities and between public policies and their implementation (service delivery).

Finally, the real-life stories of four disabled persons who are current and former nursing-home residents are detailed. They were participants in a writing workshop conducted by the partnership of the Community Writing Center and the Disability Rights Action Committee of Utah. These life stories show their diverse backgrounds and their struggles to extricate themselves from the nursing homes in which they were placed. These people provide us with a glimpse of life in nursing homes and the roles of social workers in the service delivery system.

DISABILITY AND POVERTY

A report from the U.S. Department of Commerce (2001) indicates that about half of the nation's nonelderly adults with disabilities are not working, and about 70 percent of those with severe disabilities do not work. Because of the high unemployment rate, people with disabilities are more likely to be in poverty and receive public assistance than the general population. Seven and one half million persons with disabilities are enrolled in the Social Security Disability Insurance program and/or the Supplemental Security Income program, which are the main income-maintenance programs for persons with disabilities (DeJong, Palsbo, & Beatty, 2002). As residential options for people with disabilities in poverty, the Medicaid and Medicaid Waiver programs play critical roles.

Thompson (2001) argues that the society is structured in such a way that power, status, and opportunities are distributed on the basis of social factors such as class, gender, race/ethnicity, age, and disability. Those social factors are interlocking and simultaneously structure the experiences of all people in the society. They create a matrix of domination and oppression. This structural pattern affects individual consciousness, group interaction, and group access to institutional power and privileges (Collins, 2000). Therefore, two persons with the same disability may experience oppression differently in their daily lives depending on other social factors. For a person with a disability from a wealthy family that enjoys privileges regarding residential and other life options, the Medicaid and the Medicaid Waiver programs may not be of interest. But for people with disabilities in poverty who are deprived of life choices in many areas, Medicaid and Medicaid Waiver are the major programs on which they must rely. The following section briefly summarizes the disability paradigm that has affected the enactment of the Medicaid and the Medicaid Waiver programs and other disability-related policies.

THE DISABILITY PARADIGM

The medical model of disability has long enjoyed status as the major perspective on disability in the United States. It treats disability as a personal tragedy, something that should be "cured" by professional intervention. In this view, those who cannot be cured are considered permanently deficient (Mackelprang & Salsgiver, 1998; Gilson & Depoy, 2000; Hahn, 1988; Pfeiffer, previous chapter). The modern disability rights movement started in the 1960s and challenged the medical model (Shapiro, 1993). In Chapter 2, Pfeiffer introduced the disability paradigm that arose out of the disability rights movement. He describes the proceedings of the White House Conference on Handicapped Individuals in 1977 which became a critical point in the history of the disability rights movement. An outgrowth of the conference was the establishment of the National Institute on Disability and Rehabilitation Research (NIDRR), which took a leadership role in research and introduced the new paradigm of disability.

Pfeiffer (1993) asserts that a version of the disability paradigm—the social constructionist model—was well developed in the United States by the mid 1980s. This model emphasizes that environmental factors, not individual disabilities, play a more important role in constructing one's disability identity (Goffman, 1963; Wright 1983; Osberg, Corcoran, DeJong, & Ostroff, 1983). Since then, scholars and advocates have been introducing and discussing other versions, such as the oppressed minority model (Ustun, Bickenbach, Badley, & Chatterji, 1998; Scotch, 2000), the independent living model (Morris, 1991; Williams, 1983), and the discrimination model (Liachowitz, 1988; Illingworth & Parmet, 2000; Bickenbach, 1993). While these versions may differ from one another in some ways, they share the following ideas: Disability is not a tragedy; disability does not mean dependency; disability does not mean a loss of potential, productivity, or social contribution; and disability is a natural part of the human experience. Also it strongly implies that professionals should not be the decision makers regarding the lives of persons with disabilities. The person with a disability should be the one who makes the decisions. It also implies that society, not people with disabilities, has to change by eliminating the attitudinal and institutional barriers that prevent people with disabilities from participating fully in society. The disability paradigm focuses on the whole person functioning in his or her environment while the medical model focuses on the functional limitations of disabled individuals. The disability paradigm has been incorporated in the development of public policies since the 1970s, including Medicaid Home and Community-Based Services (HCBS) waiver programs and the Americans with Disabilities Act of 1990, both of which are described below (Silverstein, 2000).

THE MEDICAID AND MEDICAID
WAIVER PROGRAMS

The Social Security Act Amendments of 1965 (P. L. 89–97) established the Medicaid program, which authorized grants-in-aid to states for the establishment of a medical assistance program for low-income individuals. It included the funding for institutional care for the poor who need personal assistant services. Placement in a nursing home became an entitlement—that is, Medicaid policy mandates that states must provide long-term care services in nursing homes for persons with disabilities who live in poverty. In 1981, Congress passed the Omnibus Budget Reconciliation Act (P. L. 97–35) that authorized the Secretary of Health and Human Services to grant Home and Community-Based Services (HCBS) waivers to states under section 1915(c) of the Social Security Act. These waivers enabled states to provide personal assistance and other services to individuals who, without such services, would require institutional care. If a state chooses to apply for the waivers and create such programs, a disabled person can receive personal care services at home rather than in a nursing home. Home-based care is funded by Medicaid as long as the cost does not exceed the cost of nursing-home care (Miller, 1992; 1997). In 1997, the Medicaid Home and Community Balanced Budget Act (P. L. 105–33) eliminated the requirement of prior institutionalization for services provided under the HCBS waiver (Silverstein, 2000). As a result, a state does not have to institutionalize persons with disabilities living in the community before enrolling them in the HCBS waiver programs.

However, the legislation providing HCBS waiver programs only encourage rather than require states to provide these options. Yet states remain mandated to provide nursing home services, thus creating an "institutional bias." Many people with disabilities living in poverty are still forced into institutional settings, remaining unaware of alternative options, and are thus deprived of the choice to remain in their own homes and receive needed services in the community. Thus, Medicaid HCBS waiver programs have become a focal point of disability advocates who promote independent living in the community as a civil right of people with disabilities. In the Americans with Disabilities Act of 1990, the disability paradigm was explicitly articulated (Silverstein, 2000), and since then, the federal government has begun to encourage the states to implement HCBS waiver programs.

ADA AND THE OLMSTEAD DECISION

The Americans with Disabilities Act (ADA) was enacted in 1990, legislating civil rights for people with disabilities. Congress stated that "the Nation's proper goals regarding individuals with disabilities are to assure equality of opportunity, full participation, independent living, and economic self-sufficiency for such individuals." Title I addresses the issue of employment discrimination for persons with disabilities. Title II prohibits public entities from discriminating against disabled individuals and requires government agencies to assess and eliminate physical barriers in their facilities. It requires that state and local governments give people with disabilities an equal opportunity to benefit from all of their programs, services, and activities. Title III makes discrimination against disabled persons illegal in public accommodations and in commercial facilities. Title IV mandates the establishment of telecommunication's relay services (U.S. Department of Justice, 2002).

The U.S. Supreme Court made a decision based on ADA in the *L.C. & E.W. v. Olmstead* case in 1999. L.C. and E.W. were patients in a state psychiatric hospital in Georgia. They challenged their placement in an institutional setting rather than in a community-based program. The Supreme Court decided that unnecessary institutionalization of individuals with disabilities is discrimination under the ADA, and that the state must provide services in the most integrated setting appropriate to individual clients (Rosenbaum, 2000; National Council on Disability, 2000, 2001, 2002).

Since the passage of ADA and the Olmstead decision, the U.S. Center for Medicare and Medicaid Services (CMS) (formerly the U.S. Health Care Financing Administration) has encouraged state governors and state Medicaid directors to use HCBS waivers to enable individuals to take control over their own lives. CMS acknowledges that there has been institutional bias in Medicaid long-term care funding and service delivery. It offered a grants program to help states develop systems to move nursing-home residents to community settings for residents who choose to do so. A grants program also covered the development of a system to offer community-based alternatives to people who were currently living in the community but were at risk of institutionalization. States were required to do self-evaluations to ensure that their policies, practices, and procedures promote rather than hinder community-based services. CMS also urged state Medicaid directors to seek the active involvement of consumers and their organizations in designing and implementing those programs that promote home and community-based care with a particular emphasis on consumer directed services (Richardson, 1998; Westmoreland, 2000).

The implementation of HCBS waiver programs and other community-based services for disabled people varies from state to state (Buchanan & Alston, 1997; Fox-Grage, Folkemer, & Lewis, 2003). Often the speed of the implementation is too slow from the standpoint of disabled individuals. For example, in Utah, a current nursing-home resident, whose story is introduced as Real-Life Story 2 in this chapter, was told that he was number 28 on the waiting list for the HCBS Brain Injury waiver and that the State moved two to three people a year on the waiting list to a community setting. This meant that his turn would come in ten years if he was lucky. The state of New York, on the other hand, took the initiative to promote the policy. A letter sent by the director of the Office of Health Systems Management in the State Department of Health to nursing home administrators clearly states that every nursing-home resident must be evaluated for the possibility of community re-entry, and that when the placement is feasible and the resident chooses it, the nursing-home staff must work to achieve the placement. Furthermore, the director also informed hospital administrators that hospitals should actively pursue post-hospital placement in the least restrictive setting appropriate for each patient's needs (Osten, 2002). Still in 2000, the vast majority (73 percent) of the total federal Medicaid long-term care expenditures went to institutional care and only 27 percent went to community-based, noninstitutional services (Burwell, 2001).

A NURSING HOME IS NOT A HOME

Given that ADA acknowledged the civil rights of people with disabilities and that the Supreme Court determined that unnecessary institutionalization of individuals with disabilities is discrimination under ADA, we will here explore what is happening in nursing homes.

People who need personal care services prefer to live in their own homes, not in nursing homes (Mauser & Miller, 1994). The deplorable conditions of many nursing homes are well documented (Doty & Sullivan, 1983; Pillemer & Moore, 1990; Uhlenberg, 1997; Thompson & Graff, 1997; Shaw, 1998; Glendenning, 1999; Nolan, 1999). Physical and emotional abuse and neglect are not uncommon in these institutions. Pillemer and Moore (1990) report the results of a telephone survey of 477 nursing-home aides and nurses which revealed that 10 percent of respondents committed physical abuse and 40 percent psychological abuse. The abuse included yelling, insulting, over-restraining, pushing, grabbing, shoving, slapping, kicking, hitting with fists, and threatening to throw or actually throwing something at the resident. Thompson and Graff (1997) estimate that 35,000 Americans die every year prematurely or in unnecessary pain, or both in nursing homes. Many neglected residents develop bedsores, receive poor nutrition and improper medication, and are left in unclean conditions (Glendenning, 1999).

Even those nursing-home residents who have not been subjected to extreme abuse have little control over their own lives. Lachman, Ziff, and Spiro (1994) assert that people who feel in more control of their lives are less depressed, less neurotic, less anxious, more open-minded, and more assertive. Friedman (1997) emphasizes that a sense of control is essential for a person's psychological and physical well-being. When people become disabled, they may be upset over their physical, social, and financial losses. But it is the loss of control over one's life that is most damaging. It causes deep depression and weakens the will to live. In contrast, a survey study (Doty, Kasper, & Litvak, 1996) about Medicaid personal care services in the community in Michigan, Maryland, and Texas shows a strong statistical association between indicators of consumer control of care and indicators of consumer satisfaction among elderly adults who are recipients of those services. Thus control over one's life is an essential component of a high quality of life.

Four real-life stories about former and current nursing home residents are included in this chapter. They are about young persons with disabilities from diverse backgrounds. They describe the loss of control over their own lives as well as the loss of dignity they experienced in nursing homes. John, a former nursing-home resident in Real-Life Story 1, describes his struggle to keep control over his own life while the nursing-home staff tried to teach him his proper role as a docile patient. He was placed in a nursing home after undergoing radical surgery in a hospital. After a year of stay, he left the nursing home voluntarily, even though he still needed medical care, because he could not take the dehumanization he was forced to endure there. Tim, a current nursing home resident in Real-Life Story 2,*

(Text continues on page 59.)

REAL-LIFE STORY 1

"Life is an expression of identity"

John, former nursing home resident

I was born in a rural town in Utah and graduated from a state university in 1972. I could not find a good job there, so I moved to Northern California. While in California I started a custodial service business, but in 1996 I shut it down and decided to move to Wyoming. On the way I visited my sister in Salt Lake City. While there I became sick and I thought I had the flu. Although I didn't know it, I had bleeding ulcers. I was passing out, so my sister took me to the emergency room of a local hospital. I went into a coma from loss of blood. When I came out of the coma, they performed surgery on me. I was bleeding heavily. They took out a third of my stomach and four inches of intestines and bowel. It was a radical procedure. When I came out of surgery, I felt fine. And then they brought my first meal. I remember it because I looked at it and asked, "Are you sure I am supposed to eat this?" It was a meal with meat patty, potatoes, vegetables, Jell-O and juice. I ate it and had a massive hemorrhage. They should have given me a clear liquid. The reason I got solid food right after radical stomach surgery was that I had no insurance. They wanted to save money by not keeping me in the hospital for three days. For a patient who had radical surgery, they should serve a clear liquid for the first day, a milky liquid the second day, then on the third day they should serve soft food. Since I did not have insurance, the doctor ordered solid food for the first day to see if the sutures would hold. They didn't. They shouldn't experiment on people. The doctor still works there.

My kidney and liver were failing too. I became delirious. They didn't know what to do. So, they moved me to the University Hospital trauma center. I was very delirious and confused. They used numerous procedures to save me. But, I was experiencing mental problems. I thought I was kidnapped and tortured. I tried to escape. I was tied in for six weeks there. Then, they released me to a nursing home.

I was very weak. I was in a fetal position and slept and slept. They thought I was terminal. But slowly I gained strength and decided to try to live. Then, I became more and more aware of what was going on there. I stayed there for a year.

My experience at that home was very negative. It was dehumanizing. They want everyone to be docile. They try to take your individuality. You are herded like cattle. They don't take you seriously. When you ask for something, you are treated like a troublemaker. So, I became a troublemaker.

There was a lot of theft going on there since the people who worked there were at the bottom of the labor market and not paid enough. People who value their jobs would not steal. I reported theft from my closet and asked for a lock. I was told that to get a lock I had to submit a work order and go through the procedure. I did. Still I did not get the lock. This is just one example of how I was treated there. They say they will do things for you, but they never do. I realized that it was their game.

They don't care about your diet restrictions, either. I was not fed what I was supposed to be fed. Diet was very important for me because of the surgery and the liver damage. I was not supposed to eat those things they served. But everyone was fed the same thing. I talked to the nutritionist and administrators. Their hands were tied, I guess. They could not make

continued

changes. Fortunately, I had some money in the bank, so I started to go out and eat nutritious meals. That made me a troublemaker. And I could not afford to go out and eat every time.

As soon as I could, I started walking. There was no rehabilitation for me at the facility. Because I had hepatitis C, they said that I was dangerous to others and they could not provide rehabilitation. I used to be athletic when I was young, so I knew what I should do. I did my rehabilitation myself.

Medication was another problem. I talked with my doctor at the University Hospital and he told me that I didn't have to take some medication that I was ordered to take at the nursing home. I didn't take them, and they put on my record that I was noncompliant. One of those medications was a depression medicine. I watched what happened to other people who took the medication. Every morning, they go down and stand in a line to take medication. By the time they finish their breakfast, the drug kicks in. It takes their spirit away and they become automatons. The staff wants you drugged up. I told them that everyone was depressed there. In that situation, being depressed was normal.

Life is an expression of identity. You need to express your individuality, making independent choices about your life, being creative. If you take that away, you might as well be dead. I watched people come in there fine. But they deteriorated rapidly, and in three months, they didn't know who they were. They were dead in a year. Being treated like a non-person will erode you. It takes your desire to live.

Another thing that infuriated me was that they were making a huge profit on the residents. Once, a guy's feet became purple. So two aides and I tried to get socks to protect his feet. We worked hard but it took two weeks to get a pair of socks. I calculated how much the facility was making and how much they paid to their employees. It was a for-profit agency. It made me angry that the owner makes hundreds of thousands of dollars of profit, and he could not afford a pair of socks immediately for a patient? We had hot dogs for supper because the Medicaid pays only $1.25 to feed people there. Something was wrong and I told them that.

I saw feces on the floor one night. In the morning the feces were still there. They left it all night. The agency is making all that money, and cannot afford to have a night cleaning person? An attendant was joking that he had to put on rubber boots to come to work. Something is wrong. They are greedy. I'd say that I hoped they lived long enough and got sick enough to experience this.

I had also seen that residents were injured because the staff were not trained well to assist them. Those incidences were never reported. I did not have a good experience with social workers while I was in the nursing home. They work for the system. They don't work for you. They are part of the brain police. They try to make you accept the patient's role. The ombudsman for the nursing home was a social worker too. I called her many times and reported incidences. But nothing changed.

You had to stand in line for everything there. You had to stand in line to get permission to go for a walk. By the time you get permission you are tired and your time is up. So, I left without permission and went for walk. I needed to go out and see flowers and go to a park and meditate. I was trying to live. Of course I got a noncompliance record for that. I also went out to get a cup of coffee just across the street. First they chased me but they eventually gave up. They again marked me as non-compliant. They tried to force me to play the role of docile patient, but I refused.

I stayed there about a year and they got a new CEO. Her goal was to have 100 percent occupancy rate, and tighter control of the residents. By that time I had a refrigerator in my room for my special diet. She took the privilege away from me. I learned that the game would get worse. I felt that my self-respect was deteriorating by staying in the nursing home and by playing their game. And I knew it would get worse. "I won't let you kill me" I told them. I

continued

had my van, so I put in as much as I could carry. Even an aide helped me load things. They understood that they could not stop me. Then they made me sign a paper and I left.

I had no place to live, so I lived in the van. It was hard. But it made me stronger, more able. At that time, I still had a hole in the side of my body and it was draining. But, I could not take more dehumanization and de-self-actualization in that nursing home. I studied herbs and took care of myself.

I then got involved in the national health-insurance campaign and living-wage campaign. I met members of a disability advocacy group and I got involved with their activities too. I believe that people were born to fulfill the purpose of universe, becoming who we are. I feel more and more that my life has purpose and meaning. My involvement with the disability-rights movement is a part of the process of becoming. I am living a far more rewarding and fulfilling life. I am happy the way things are going now. I will never stop to working to reform this system.

REAL-LIFE STORY 2

"Are you my parole officer?"

Tim, current nursing-home resident

I was a boxer for 8 years in my twenties in Detroit. I was married and had a boy. About 20 years ago, I went to Las Vegas to box and met an attractive woman. I stayed there with her. We had a girl. I fell in with a bad crowd there, and thought I was having a good time, but looking back I wasn't. I was young and I didn't know what I was doing. I am now following my religious teaching. I am a Moslem. I was not at that time. One day I used drugs with a friend, and the next thing I knew I was waking up in a hospital. I don't know how long I was unconscious or how long I was in the hospital. I was told that the drugs went to my brain. I could not walk in the hospital, so I was discharged to a nursing home in Vegas. One day, Nevada's Medicaid sent me to a nursing home in Salt Lake City. They sent many of us here. It was not my choice.

I've lived in the nursing home in Salt Lake City for ten years. It's a concentration camp. They treat you like a number, not a person. Nevada's physical therapists were good. They were real physical therapists. Here, they don't have a real certificate. They only have a job title but they don't know what to do. I am not getting muscle exercises at all.

It's really a concentration camp. Social workers here should be helping us to get out of here. But they don't because we are their paychecks. It's just a job for them so they don't care. And they don't stay very long. We had three different administrators in two years. But, they want us to stay. Once, I invited the governor to visit our nursing home. He should know what it is like to live in here.

In the nursing home, they control my life. I can't go to bed when I want to. They decide when I go to bed. I can't have food in my room. Once, I wanted to go out but they didn't let me go out. They said that it was my punishment because I had bad behavior that day.

The only good things that happen is having visitors like Tamara and Tammy [members of a local disability rights group]. The first time Tamara visited me I joked, "Are you my parole

continued

officer?" They told me about getting out of the nursing home. Tammy shows there is another life. She invited me to visit her apartment. They take me out of the nursing home and take my mind away from the dumb stuff. If you don't have anyone who cares, you'll die in that nursing home. Tammy shows me there's life outside. I know my life is more than a nursing home. I want to be going out and doing different things. She gives me hope. She also shows me respect, so I can trust her. The staff treat you like a number. But when other people outside care about you, they show some respect. They know that if they treat you wrong you'll let others know about it. In the nursing home, I learned that no one will respect you if you don't respect yourself. The nursing home needs more volunteers like Tammy, not just paid employees. We need people who do the job they love to do. I want to meet more people like Tammy, people who really care. I pray sometimes, not so much about me, but for people like Tammy, that they'll be rewarded in real life for helping people who are less fortunate.

I met Hank in the nursing home. He lived there with me. With his family and hard work, he got out and now he has his own place. That was a good lesson for me. Things can be better. I have to get out of here and be a good lesson for someone else in the nursing home. I want to prove not only to other people but to myself that I'm not a loser.

When I get out of the nursing home, I want to go back to school to get a GED. The nursing home gives me no chance to get education. It is understaffed. I have no chance to study in there. You need to get education to learn good from wrong, and you get respect or you will be lost in the system. You got to find a way to get out of the nursing home. They try to keep you here. It's their income. I am their paycheck. It's true.

When I get out of the nursing home, I want to become a counselor. I want to work with kids and teach them about drugs, gangs, and safe sex. I want to teach them if you do right things, you don't have to worry about things. Education is important.

When I am out of the nursing home, I will see People of Islam on a regular basis. Malcolm X opened lots of doors. He taught that you have to respect women like queens. He taught that just praying gets you nowhere. You need to put action in your prayer. If you want to get out of the nursing home, you need action. I learned in the nursing home that I have no one to rely on but Allah. Allah blessed me to meet people like Tammy.

I pray five times a day—in the morning, afternoon, evening, late at night, and before going to bed. I can keep on because Allah gave me life to carry on.

There's so much more I'd like to say. But I'm not good at expressing my thoughts in words, only in action. I'm going to end this, hoping my story can make life better for someone else.

REAL-LIFE STORY 3

"My road to and out of the nursing home"

Chani, former nursing-home resident

I was born in 1962, and adopted by a dysfunctional family. I know nothing about my biological parents. My mother was mentally ill and father was alcoholic. In the adoptive family, I was neglected and abused. While I was growing up I did not get any support, so I had to learn to live to survive on my own. I suppressed lots of things. I didn't like myself, and still I

continued

don't. So, I am now in counseling dealing with my childhood issues. I went to school and I was a straight A student till 8th grade. After that my grades dropped because of my family life. We moved a lot, and I was also placed in foster care several times by the Child Protective Services. My experiences in foster care were both good and bad. Each foster home was different. If I were in a foster home for a long time, I would have been better off. But I was returned to my parents each time. They were still dysfunctional. I was unhappy when I grew up. I have no good memories in my childhood. I just survived.

Finally, I moved out and got my own apartment. Although I use a wheel chair, at that time I could take care of myself without personal attendants. I received public assistance and lived on my own till 1999. My mother died in 1989, and my father died in 1995 [adoptive parents].

In early 1999, I got really sick and ended up in a hospital. They decided not to release me back to my own place. I was on Medicaid. The doctors and nurses told me that they would release me either to a mental hospital or a nursing home. So, I chose the nursing home. It wasn't much of a choice.

I was devastated. I cried two weeks straight. I was also very angry. They don't like an argumentative patient, and I was one. I hated the nursing home. Did you ever see Hogan's Heroes? The nursing home felt like a German concentration camp. I had no choice at all. They—social workers and nursing staff—made all choices. They run your life. You do it the way they want you to do it. They schedule the day. They decide what's good behavior, what's bad behavior. They decide if you are overweight or not. They put you on a diet, without your consent. If they decide you have bad behavior, depending on the "bad behavior" you either get chastised about it or have your activities restricted. I was always chastised for standing up for myself. I had feelings of frustration and anger. They treated me like a kid. I lost my dignity and freedom. They were taken. They make you live by their rules, not yours. It's like being a herd of cattle. It's totally demoralizing.

A typical day in a nursing home: They wake you up at about 6:30 A.M. I had to be ready to go to breakfast by an hour later. I had to have help. It was humiliating. I didn't have any say about when I ate breakfast, when I ate dinner. If you miss a meal, you had to wait till the next meal. Food didn't taste worth anything. Breakfast was a bore, lunch was a bore, dinner was a bore. Sometimes they offered activities: blackjack, movies, arts and crafts. Once in a while I did that stuff to keep from going crazy. Late afternoon they did what's called "walk and roll." It's their exercise time, up and down the halls. Every once in a while they'd have a van ride. And every once in a long while we'd go to Chuck-a-Rama or Wendover. The only time I went for a walk outside was when my friends came. My friends would take me for a walk or pizza or a ride but they couldn't come that often. In the evening, I'd have a shower. If I weren't having a manic episode I'd be asleep by 10:30 P.M. If I was having a manic episode, I might be asleep by 4 A.M. My roommates sometimes woke me up with buzzers and lights.

Once they wanted me to get rid of my checking account. They did not want me to have any ties to the outside. I refused to do it. They wanted me to get rid of my ID card too. There was nothing good about the nursing home. I had lots of arguments there.

The cruelest thing was that they told me that I would never leave the nursing home. My social worker told me, "You must stay here for the rest of your life." I said, "But you are my social worker, you have to help me get out of here." She said, "All staff think that you should stay here. And I agree with them." She was supposed to be my social worker, but she worked for the nursing home, not for me. They said that to lots of people. I told them, "you watch me." Each person represents $36,000 a year. A good portion of it goes to the nursing home as profit. Every person in the nursing home is business material.

continued

I am a private person. I need a quiet life, but there were too many people in the nursing home. Too many. The dining room was ugly and noisy. There were so many people around. It meant lots of germs, and I got sick often.

Neglect and abuse? The nursing home is abusive in nature. Its existence itself is abuse. There is no such thing as quality of life in the nursing home. In my opinion, everyone in a nursing home just "exists" in it—they're not "living."

I met people from DRAC [Disability Rights Action Committee, a grassroots organization]. They were rolling up and down the hall. They started helping me get things together. I was able to get out through a program of DRAC. But it does not mean that I got out without problems. A doctor evaluated me as capable of living in the community if I get home health aides at home and take medication regularly. When I was leaving the nursing home, they refused to give me my medication. That's my medication. DRAC advocates had to negotiate with them and got my medication back.

I've lived in my apartment since November 1999. My apartment isn't the Taj Mahal, but it's mine. This is my home, my room, my reality. Nobody else rules, nobody bosses me around. I can't have it any other way. I will never go back to a nursing home in my lifetime. Here, I do what I want to do when I want to do it. I still get up at 6:30 A.M., but now it's because I want to, not because I have to. My breakfast, lunch, and dinner are chosen by me. So if they're boring, at least it's my fault. I'm sometimes still awake at 4 A.M. No one makes decisions for me anymore. They're mine, and my responsibility. Now, if I want to I can go to Chuck-a-Rama or Wendover on my own accord. I hated the exercise program in the nursing home and now if I don't want to exercise, I don't. When it comes to taking showers, I am now the mistress of my domain.

I have good personal attendants. DRAC got me on a PD waiver [Physical Disability waiver, one of the Home and Community-Based Services (HCBS) waivers].

I hired my attendants. I trained them. I have my personal attendant twenty-nine hours a week and a home health aide two hours a day. I am satisfied with them. I trained them well. My attendant calls me her boss. She treats me as boss. I am the person who makes decisions about my life. I am satisfied with the arrangement. But the state does not pay them enough. They are paid only $9.11 an hour. The state needs to pay more to personal attendants. They do a lot of work. Their work should be recognized.

Because I am disabled, some people think that living alone in my apartment is risky. But, everybody takes risks in their life. I have the right to choose to take a risk. No one else has rights to make decisions for me. I, as an adult woman, as long as I am able to understand what the risks are and how to deal with those risks, I should be permitted to take those risks. Risk is part of life and part of quality of life too. Some people may think that quality of life is the absence of the risk, but I think that life itself is impossible without risks.

I think that the state means well, but they don't understand that they are not responsible for everything. They think they are. They think they should be able to tell you whether or not you can take the risk to live your own life. The state wants to decide for you. For example, the state has taken the decision of marriage out of my hands. If I marry I can lose my medical benefits, if I marry I can lose my financial benefits. I would have to marry someone quite rich for those things not to matter. If I lost my medical benefit, it would cost over $1,000 a month. Without my medical benefits, I couldn't afford my medication. Without Medicaid, I can't have aides come in and get me up every day. So the state has already decided for me that marriage is out of question. I don't believe in sex outside of marriage. It is frustrating that the state still tries to control my personal life.

I had a difficult childhood and had hard time in the nursing home. But I made a best of it. I still have problems with the state social services, but as far as quality of life is con-

continued

cerned, I am having it now. I have friends, and I see them more often than I did in the nursing home. We also have a get together in the apartments. I am independent, quiet, and content. Also, I have a cat and I love her. After getting out of the nursing home, I worked as a VISTA volunteer. Because of my health problems I quit the job. But I'm hoping to do another VISTA year and go to school. I was a sophomore, and I would finish my bachelors and probably go into a graduate school. I would love to be a writer. I also think about becoming a social worker. It may sound strange because I had such bad experiences with social workers. I value my freedom and dignity. I have a future.

REAL-LIFE STORY 4

"There were no groups to tell you about independent living"

Steve, former nursing-home resident

I was born in Detroit, Michigan. My dad was an engineer. We traveled around the country. We lived in many places. When I was a kid I had many problems. I think I had a learning disability. At the beginning of 6th grade, I was diagnosed to have ADHD and got on lots of medications. In the 7th grade I was hospitalized for the first time and by the 8th grade I had numerous hospitalizations. Then, we moved to Utah. During 9th and 12th grade, I was under private practice care and I was hospitalized a few times. I had difficulties with my family and medications. It was a nightmare. But my grades were good in school and I had good friends.

When I was about twenty, I went into the first nursing home. I had been living out of my parents' home at that time and I was hanging out with people around the county building and I didn't have skills for living on my own. A social worker told me to go to the nursing home. At that time it was the only option. There were no group homes or home-care services. No one comes to your home to help you out. There were no groups to tell you about independent living. If you can't take care of yourself, you go to a nursing home.

It was a bad experience. In the nursing home, they tell you when to get up, they tell you when to go to the bathroom, they tell you when to eat, they tell you when to take a nap, they tell you when to go to bed. There was very little independence. There was a strong smell of urine. It was not a place to live. You don't have a life there. A very frustrating thing for me was that one aide tells you one thing, another aide tells you another thing, and the nursing supervisor overrules everything. You don't know what to do. I was accused of starting fires and all kinds of things. You see, I was taking lots of medications and I was in the bed all the time. I had never had problems with the law. I would never do such a thing. I lived there for six or seven months.

One morning in November 1979, I went to Mental Health and was told that I could not go back to the nursing home. They didn't explain why. So, I slept on the floor of the Rescue Mission. I was kicked out of the nursing home and kicked out of SSI. So, I ended up joining the Navy. It was very hard and many people were passing out during the boot camp. But I wanted to succeed. I graduated from the boot camp. But I was discharged in three or four months because I could not make the running around the track.

continued

After getting out of the Navy, I got an apartment and got a job as an orderly in a nursing home in Salt Lake. But I had to quit because the job pressure was too much. I went to Mental Health and I got medicine and they helped me apply for welfare, medical assistance, and food stamps. Around that time, I traveled around on freight trains in Colorado and Idaho. Mental Health in Colorado got me a bed at the Salvation Army, and I also got in a group home. One day I called my sister from Denver. I was sleeping on a floor in front of a bank on newspapers at that time. She sent me a bus ticket to go back to Salt Lake.

That was around 1982. My social worker told me to take advantage of the system and go to a nursing home to get my weight stabilized. I was not eating right. He referred me to a nurse who was a coordinator of a nursing home. I've known her since I was fourteen. She put me in a nursing home on Medicaid. I stayed in the second nursing home for nine to ten months. It was a good nursing home. I visit nursing homes now, so I know that a good nursing home is one in million. The administrator there decided that instead of taking my Social Security money she would let me have it. She wanted to make sure that I would look nice when I got out of the nursing home. They treated me like a person. As part of going to a nursing home I had to attend group sessions and day treatment. It was fine with me. They made sure that I went to Mental Health. Once I had a problem and I called my social worker on a Friday night and he called me back immediately to solve the problem. While I was there, I joined a group—a kind of a social club—at a Mental Health day treatment unit. We had a coffee shop, a thrift shop, and a beauty shop. We worked there and financed the club. I also got some experience in talking with newspaper reporters. They came to interview us. I got my weight back and I left the nursing home. Even though it was a good nursing home, it is still much better living independently in the community. The nursing home does not exist anymore because it was sold to a different company.

I found a low cost apartment and I was there for two, three years. Then, everyone there was threatened to be kicked out. I called an administrator at Mental Health and explained the necessity of low-cost apartments for people who need mental health services. Together, we started an apartment project managed by Mental Health. I was there in the project for thirteen years.

Fifteen or twenty years ago I was diagnosed as having manic depression. So, I had been misdiagnosed and had been taking the wrong medications till then. Since, I got on the right medications and I've been doing good. I've been in a day treatment. I've been a member of Disability Rights Action Committee (DRAC) for close to 10 years and on the board of DRAC for a few years. I'm also part of other organizations, advocacy groups. But there's no advocacy group like DRAC. I am just sold on DRAC. We get things done rather than sitting back and waiting for the change of government to happen. Sometimes things move fast, sometimes slow. But at least we have an organization of disabled people. It is not run by social workers. It is run by us, people with disabilities. When we mess up, we mess up. But we usually correct the mess very quickly. I am very proud of being a DRAC member. We've been successful getting people out of nursing homes.

I visit nursing homes. I think that 90 percent of the people in nursing homes don't have to be there. If they have places in the community where they have access to services, they can live in the community, which we have been saying since day one. We go visit someone in a nursing home, try to hook them up with food stamps and welfare and other services. Even though most people don't have to live in nursing homes, the nursing homes have lobbyists that they pay a huge amount of money. Our lobbyists are ourselves, people with disabilities across the country. We don't have money to pay someone half a million dollars.

continued

I met my current girl friend 5 years ago. Now, I live with her and our biggest focus is on taking care of ourselves and each other. So if I have problems with driving she drives. When she gets tired, I drive. So, we share. When we clean our apartment, she cleans one room and I clean another room. Then we sit down and take a break. Then, I clean one room and she cleans another. Because I also have a physical disability, it is very painful. I have spinal stenosis in my back, I have no cartridge in my left knee, which makes it extremely hard to walk. I can't stand more than a few minutes. I had two back surgeries and four knee surgeries. Now I understand well that curb cuts are very important. They make a big difference for people with physical disabilities.

Still I feel that I am happier living in a community. If I was put back in a nursing home, I would take off the next day. I have learned that we as an organization can help people get out of nursing homes. As an individual it is very difficult. I am looking forward to seeing many people moving out of nursing homes. I figured out how to move out so anyone can move out. I am on the citizen's commission of the Utah Transit Authority. I will continue to be active in DRAC.

and Chani, a former resident in Real-Life Story 3, describe nursing homes as "concentration camps." Tim was also discharged from a hospital to a nursing home. He has lived in a nursing home more than ten years and is on the waiting list of the HCBS Brain Injury waiver program. He does not know, however, when and if the state will let him out of the "concentration camp." Chani was also placed in a nursing home after a hospital stay. Even though the nursing-home social worker told her that she would never leave there, she left the nursing home in a year to a community setting with the help of a grass-roots disability advocacy group. While Tim is still in a nursing home, and the nursing-home experiences of John and Chani are recent (having left in the late 1990s), Steve, in Real-Life Story 4, stayed in nursing homes in the late 1970s and early 1980s. He left on his own at that time, when there were no other options for people who needed personal attendant services in Utah. The three former residents are content with their lives in the community. John and Steve are actively involved in a grassroots disability advocacy group that helps nursing-home residents move to community settings. John, Tim, and Chani have not had good experiences with social workers in nursing homes. They perceive social workers as those professionals who try to control their lives. They do not feel that social workers cared about their lives. In their view, social workers work for the benefit of the nursing homes, not for the benefit of the clients. Steve, on the other hand, found the social workers in his second nursing home to be responsive to his needs and to care about his future. Still he was happy to leave the nursing home. [Pseudonyms are used in the real-life stories].

In response to the public outcry on the situation in nursing homes, the U.S. Department of Justice (DOJ) has investigated several nursing homes in the country. In April 2003, the DOJ published the result of the investigation of the Laguna Honda Hospital and Rehabilitation Center, a nursing home in San Francisco. The DOJ states that the City and County of San Francisco were violating Title II of the Americans with Disabilities Act of 1990 by failing to ensure that the nursing-home residents were being served in the most integrated setting appropriate to meet their needs. The investigation found that Laguna Honda did not have appropriate assessment procedures to evaluate the needs of individuals at admission or on an on-going basis. The nursing home also failed to provide individualized care plans, and its discharge process was unduly cumbersome. Consequently, many residents remained in the facility long after they could have moved into the community. The report also points out that San Francisco's public agencies had not taken adequate steps to expand housing and residential services for nursing-home residents with a desire to move to community settings (U.S. Department of Justice, 2003).

GAP BETWEEN PUBLIC POLICIES AND SERVICE DELIVERY

The question must be asked, "Where were we social workers all these years while the new disability paradigm was developed and influenced the enactment of public policies?" Many social workers have close contact with people with disabilities in their work. The definition of the disability paradigm should be very familiar to social workers. It is synonymous with the social work practice paradigm "person-in-the-environment." Yet few social workers have learned and practiced the disability paradigm. While lawmakers pass legislation that is based on the disability paradigm, the medical model remains pervasive among social workers and other helping professionals in the long-term care area.

Policy enactment and policy implementation are two different matters (Lipsky, 1980). Congress may enact the ADA and other civil rights laws, and federal departments under the executive branch may interpret those laws and encourage states to implement them. However, the front-line workers of local governmental and social-service agencies, including social workers, are the people who directly implement those policies and affect the everyday lives of people with disabilities. Although schools of social work teach their students the roles of social workers as facilitators, planners, brokers, advocates, mediators, activists, catalysts, teachers, and trainers who work for the benefit of their clients (Miley, O'Melia, & DuBois, 2001), many people with disabilities perceive them very differently. In the real day-to-day lives of people with disabilities, social workers are often seen as those who try to control and restrict their lives. For many people with disabilities, social workers are representatives of the system that oppresses them.

Many people with disabilities who want to live in a community setting often find their social workers to be impediments to the implementation of the ADA and the Olmstead decision. If social workers are embracing the empowerment theory (Solomon, 1976), the strengths perspective (Saleebey, 1997), and the resiliency model (Bernard, 1991; Wolen & Wolen, 1993) as a framework for practice, why is this happening? Do those theories remain in the classrooms while different perspectives replace them in practice settings with people with disabilities? Thompson's (2000) discussion about formal and informal social work theories and Lipsky's (1980) analysis of street-level bureaucracies may provide some answers to this subject of the gap between education and practice.

FORMAL AND INFORMAL THEORIES OF SOCIAL WORK PRACTICE

Thompson (2000) discusses the distinction between formal and informal theories of social work practice. Formal practice theories are considered "official" since they are formally documented in academic literature and publications of professional organizations. Those are also the theories taught in schools of social work. Informal practice theories are not officially recognized. They constitute the "practice wisdom" of the social work profession. Informal knowledge and assumptions are built up through actual practice and are "culturally transmitted" to new generations of social workers in agencies and in the field. While formal theory is open to debate and counter-argument, informal theory tends to be protected because it is covert and implicit. It is often seen as "common sense" among social workers in their practice culture. Thompson (2000) argues that common sense is ideological and deters critical thinking. Furthermore, it serves to reinforce traditional values and inequalities, and in the long-term care field may be the medical model. Thompson further asserts that formal academic knowledge for those who practice social work is simply not required. Thus, even if the disability paradigm may be discussed and promoted in social work schools, and while it may influence public-policy enactment, in the front line of policy implementation, which is service delivery, it is not often practiced. According to Thompson (2001), since social workers occupy positions of power and influence, there are abundant opportunities for discrimination and oppression, whether intentional or by default.

SOCIAL WORKERS AS STREET-LEVEL BUREAUCRATS

Lipsky (1980) introduces public-service workers, such as teachers, police officers, and social workers, as "street-level bureaucrats" who deliver governmental services to the public. In real life, the individual decisions of those workers represent public policies for those who receive their services. Most citizens encounter government not through meetings with members of Congress but through the teachers of their children, police officers patrolling the streets, or social workers from welfare offices. Lipsky defines street-level bureaucrats as public employees who execute governmental policies at the every-day level. However, from the standpoint of citizens who receive those services, they are indistinguishable from the employees of the organizations that receive government funding to provide services. For example, for a disabled person living in poverty, the difference between a social worker who works for a local government as a case manager and a social worker who is assigned to him or her by a private home health-care agency that accepts Medicaid clients may not be obvious. A social worker is a social worker. Both social workers carry out public policies. Therefore, the functions and characteristics of street-level bureaucrats described below, according to Lipsky, could be extended to social workers who work for private organizations that accept governmental funds to provide public services.

Lipsky (1980) regards street-level bureaucrats as policymakers because of their relatively high degrees of discretion and relative autonomy from organizational authority. Social workers who work under medical professionals in the tight control of the managed-care workplace may object to this viewpoint. However, it is true that social workers often deal with complicated human situations that cannot be reduced to standardized procedures. Discretion allows them to make decisions to suit each condition they deal with in their practice. Also, discretion promotes a social worker's self-regard as a professional, and that professional self-regard encourages their clients to believe that social workers possess power over their well-being. In this way, public policy regarding service delivery is made every day by social workers. Worker discretion is in fact a necessity of the agency's function to provide public services. But the fact of discretion does not mean that social workers are free from the rules and regulations of their agencies. On the contrary, political and administrative officials determine the major dimensions of public policy, including the level of benefits, categories of eligibility, nature of rules and regulations, and services. With all those restrictions, social workers are expected to exercise discretionary judgment in the field. Therefore, discretion is a relative concept.

Another important aspect of the street-level bureaucrat's job is the nonvoluntary nature of their clients. The poorer a person is, the more likely she or he is to be a nonvoluntary client of social workers. Government may not monopolize an essential service, but it often provides the only service available for the poor. For example, personal care attendant service at home can be obtained privately but only at relatively high cost. A disabled individual living in poverty who needs personal attendants has no choice but to become a client of a social worker of a governmental agency or of a private agency that provides public services. Therefore, those clients with whom social workers regularly interact are not among their primary reference group. They cannot discipline social workers, and social workers usually have nothing to lose by failing to satisfy clients. They can be neglectful or impose inconveniences on their clients without concern for retaliation. If clients refuse to continue interacting with social workers, clients are always considered at fault (Lipsky, 1980).

The nonvoluntary nature of disabled clients receiving social services creates a power difference between them and their social workers. Social workers communicate the proper client role to them verbally or nonverbally. Most clients comply in response to the superior power of social workers. When clients do not accept their proper role, they are reprimanded. We can see examples in our real-life stories. In the case of Tim (Real-Life Story 2), he was not allowed to go out with a friend one day as punishment because his behavior was considered unacceptable that day. Let me emphasize that Tim and the others who provided these real life stories were adults. John (Real-Life Story 1) received "noncompliance" reports many times in his nursing home's record while he fought for his rights. He now worries that his record will affect him negatively in the future when he needs Medicaid's medical services.

Social workers may also convey to clients that they should expect few services. They may imply in a friendly and not-overtly-confrontational way that clients should give up their own interests. Social workers may tell nursing-home residents that nothing can be done to help them move to a community setting. However, it is often obvious to nursing-home residents that more could be done. Grassroots disability-rights organizations such as ADAPT. (Formerly known as Am. Dis. for Accessible Public Transportation. Since 1990 stands for Am. Dis. for Attendant Program Today.) have successfully moved disabled individuals from nursing homes to community settings in which people with disabilities were already entitled. (See http://www.adapt.org for more information.) When the social worker says "Nothing can be done" often she or he really means, "I don't intend to change my priorities in your case, although they could be changed" (Lipsky, 1980). In Real-Life Story 3, a nursing-home social worker told Chani that nothing could be done and that she would have to stay in the nursing home for the rest of her life. The Disability Rights Action Committee, a grassroots disability rights organization, arranged for her to get out of the nursing home. She now lives in an apartment with a cat and receives personal attendant services.

Social workers as street-level decision makers have power over nonvoluntary nursing-home residents. While formal social work practice theories may embrace the idea of client empowerment, the practice wisdom and the practice culture may reinforce the medical model that focuses on clients' limitations. Although social workers have the option to play the role of advocates to help their clients take control over their own lives and live with dignity, many social workers fail in this endeavor.

PERSONAL ATTENDANT SERVICES

While many people with disabilities live in nursing homes without knowing of other residential options, there are others who live in community settings utilizing HCBS waiver programs and other state-funded programs. Many people who live in the community receive services from personal attendants who visit their homes and provide services such as housekeeping and personal care. Currently, most paid supportive home services are provided by certified home-care agencies. The case managers, usually social workers who are employees of local government or home-care agencies, assess clients' needs, determine service tasks and hours necessary, and arrange personal attendants to visit the clients. Those personal attendants are employed by the home-care agencies. This service model is called the case management model or the agency-directed model (Kane & Degenholts, 1997; Kapp, 1999).

The other model whose utilization has increased recently is called the "consumer-directed model," because clients themselves organize and direct their own home-based services. Consumer-directed home care was first tested in public programs in the 1970s. It is now offered in about thirty states. Those services are authorized under Medicaid, either under the optional personal assistance benefit or the HCBS waiver, or under state-funded programs (Miller, 1997). In this model, clients are responsible for hiring, training, supervising, and firing personal attendants. Because consumer direction reduces the need for home care agencies and case managers, service costs are expected to be lower (Glickman, Stocker, & Garo, 1997; Feder, Komisar, & Niefeld, 2000; Benjamin & Matthias, 2000; Benjamin, 2001).

Currently, only a few research reports on the consumer-directed model and its comparison with the case-management model have been published. Doty, Kasper, and Litvak (1996) summarized consumer-directed services that were offered in several states where the definition of "consumer direction" varies somewhat. They reported the findings of a survey of client choice and satisfaction among older persons with disabilities receiving in-home attendant services in Michigan, Maryland, and Texas. They concluded that higher levels of consumer satisfaction are associated with greater consumer involvement in hiring and firing, scheduling, supervising, and paying personal attendants. Glickman, Stocker and Garo (1997) interviewed a random sample of more than 800 elderly home-care consumers in the Massachusetts Home Care Program and reported that while the majority of clients showed high levels of satisfaction with their traditional home-care services and personal attendants, a quarter to a third of the respondents reported their willingness to assume more responsibility for supervising home-care workers. Benjamin and Matthias (2000) compared consumer-directed and traditional agency-directed models of California's in-home supportive services program. Telephone interviews of a random sample of 1,095 clients out of 200,000 Californians were conducted. They found that clients of the consumer-directed service reported feeling no less safe than the clients of the agency model, while being more empowered in their service relationship, more satisfied with the technical and interpersonal aspects of services, and more positive about the quality of their lives. The authors also reported that these outcomes are found across age groups.

> As the consumer-directed model of home care services is expanding, there are various issues which continue to be discussed, including a number of questions (Kapp, 2000; Benjamin, 2001). Who should be enrolled in the programs that are based on the consumer-directed model? Should people with cognitive impairments be included? How can consumers' rights be protected? How can service quality be insured? Who can be hired as a personal attendant? How can personal attendants' rights be protected? The cost-effectiveness of consumer-directed programs is also an issue to be discussed. Benjamin, Mattias, and Franke (1998) report that, in some states, consumer-hired personal attendants earn lower wages and fewer benefits than agency employed workers. Are the savings accomplished by shifting costs to hired personal attendants or unpaid helpers such as family members? As the paradigm shifts away from the traditional agency model toward the consumer-

directed model within which the consumer is empowered to control the who-what-where-when and how details of the service plan, relationships among parties involved also change. New relationships will be created and new legal concerns about rights and responsibilities will be raised. (Kapp, 2000)

As only 27 percent of Medicaid's long-term care expenditures went to community-based services in 2000, the percentage will likely increase (Burwell, 2001). Further research on personal attendant services should provide information on a model (or models) of service that will contribute to the increased quality of life of the clients.

MiCASSA

As disability advocates seek the expansion of personal attendant services and HCBS waiver programs in each state, they are also pursuing the passage of the Medicaid Community Attendant Services and Supports Act (MiCASSA) bill (H.R. 2032/S. 971) at the federal level. The bill is pending in Congress as of this writing. If MiCASSA passes, Medicaid will be amended to give people with disabilities more residential options. MiCASSA allows all individuals eligible for institutional care the opportunity to choose a community living arrangement with attendant services. Medicaid money follows the individual. Personal attendant services, currently provided as Medicaid waiver programs or state funded programs, will be expanded, ending the long waiting lists for the programs. The MiCASSA bill promotes the consumer-directed model of home care services. A summary of the bill is provided below.

Federal and state officials concerned about the costs of long-term care are now more receptive to community-based services, which are considered less costly. As of May 2003, eleven Senators and twenty-three House Representatives are cosponsoring the bill. Furthermore, in his FY 2004 budget, President Bush proposed a "Money Follows the Person Rebalancing Initiative" that would provide assistance to help states develop more community-based service options (Centers for Medicare & Medicaid Service, 2003). This initiative would ensure that Medicaid money paid to nursing homes for resident care would follow the client when he or she decides to move out of a nursing home and receive necessary services in a community setting. That is exactly what disability advocates have lobbied for in Congress. Various national and local organizations also have joined in to support the MiCASSA bill. As of September 2002, eighty-six national organizations had declared their support. They include the National Association for the Advancement of Colored People, Families USA, the American Association on Mental Retardation, the Brain Injury Association, the National Council on Aging, the National Council on Independent Living, and the National Spinal Cord Injury Association. Additionally, hundreds of local and state-level organizations support the bill. Among social work institutions, however, only the Texas NASW chapter officially supports MiCASSA.

■ ■ ■ ■ ■ ■

A BRIEF SUMMARY OF MiCASSA

THE MEDICAID COMMUNITY ATTENDANT SERVICES AND SUPPORTS ACT S. 971 AND HR 2032

MiCASSA gives people real choice in long term services. Amending Title XIX of the Social Security Act (Medicaid), it creates an alternative service called Community Attendant Services and Supports. MiCASSA allows individuals eligible for Nursing Facility Services or Intermediate Care Facility Services for the Mentally Retarded (ICF-MR) the choice to use these dollars for "Community Attendant Services and Supports." The money follows the individual!

Specifically what does this bill do?

1. Provides community attendant services and supports which range from assisting with:
   - activities of daily living (eating, toileting, grooming, dressing, bathing, transferring).
   - instrumental activities of daily living (meal planning and preparation, managing finances, shopping, household chores, phoning, participating in the community).
   - health-related functions.
2. Includes hands-on assistance, supervision and/or cueing, as well as help to learn, keep, and enhance skills to accomplish such activities.
3. Requires services be provided in *the most integrated setting* appropriate to the needs of the individual.
4. Provides community attendant services and supports that:
   - are based on an assessment of functional need.
   - are provided in home or community settings like schools, workplaces, or recreation or religious facilities.
   - are selected, managed, and controlled by the consumer of the services.
   - are supplemented with backup and emergency attendant services.
   - are furnished according to a service plan agreed to by the consumer.
   - include voluntary training on selecting, managing, and dismissing attendants.
5. Allows consumers to choose among various service delivery models including vouchers, direct cash payments, fiscal agents and agency providers, all of which must be consumer controlled.
6. For consumers who are not able to direct their own care independently, MiCASSA allows for "individual's representative" to be authorized by the consumer to assist. A representative might be a friend, family member, guardian, or advocate.
7. Allows health-related functions or tasks to be assigned to, delegated to, or performed by unlicensed personal attendants, according to state laws.
8. Covers individuals' transition costs from a nursing facility or ICF-MR [Intermediate Care Facilities for Persons with Mental Retardation] to a home setting, for example: rent and utility deposits, bedding, basic kitchen supplies and other necessities required for the transition.
9. Serves individuals with incomes above the current institutional income limitation—if a state chooses to waive this limitation to enhance the potential for employment.

continued

■ ■ ■ ■ ■

A BRIEF SUMMARY OF MiCASSA   (*continued*)

10. Provides for quality assurance programs, which promote consumer control and satisfaction.
11. Allows states to limit the aggregate amount spent on long-term care in a year to that amount the state would have spent on institutional services for such eligible individuals in the year.
12. Provides a maintenance-of-effort requirement so that states can not diminish more enriched programs already being provided.

REAL CHOICE SYSTEMS CHANGE INITIATIVES

MiCASSA also provides grants for Real Choice Systems Change Initiatives to help the states transition from current institutionally dominated service systems to ones more focused on community services and supports. Each state will create a consumer task force to develop a plan for transitioning services into a more community-oriented system. A majority of the members must be people with disabilities or their representatives.

The Secretary of Health and Human Services, along with the National Council on Disabilities, will review regulations and report to Congress on how to reduce excessive use of medical services. The Secretary will also establish a task force to examine financing of long-term care services.

Adapted from ADAPT (2003). *Free our people.* Retrieved May 29, 2003 from http://www.freeourpeople.org/MiCASSA/default.htm#sum

CONCLUSION

The answer to the chapter question, "Are we, social workers, meeting the needs of the service delivery system or the needs of the consumer?" is obvious. At least in the long-term care field for people with disabilities, regardless of all our good intentions, many clients see social workers as working for the oppressive system. Hiranandani asserts in Chapter 4 that there is no single repressive power in modern societies. Instead, liberal institutions such as health and welfare services tend to be instruments of domination. Social work professionals exercise power over people with disabilities through welfare policies and services. There are contradictions between the practice reality of social workers and the practice ideal of client empowerment and self-determination. One explanation is that social workers are often employed by medical facilities. These host agencies typically follow the medical model causing a dilemma for social workers. While disability rights advocates now direct their efforts toward implementation of PAS programs and passage of the MiCASSA bill, what roles are we social workers going to play in the environment of people with disabilities?

REFERENCES

Americans with Disabilities Act (ADA) of 1990, P.L. 101–336, 42 U.S. Code Section 12101.

Benjamin, A. E. (2001). Consumer-directed services at home: A new model for persons with disabilities. *Health Affairs,* Nov./Dec., 80–95.

Benjamin, A. E., & Matthias, R. E. (2000). Comparing consumer- and agency-directed models: California's in-home supportive services program. *Generations,* Fall, 85–87.

Benjamin, A. E., Mattias, R. E., & Franke, T. M. (1998). *Comparing client-directed and agency models for providing supportive services at home: Final report to the U.S. Department of Health and Human Services.* Los Angeles: UCLA School of Public Policy.

Bernard, B. (1991). *Fostering resiliency in kids: Protective factors in the family, school, and community.* San Francisco: Western Regional Center.

Bickenbach, J. E. (1993). *Physical disability and social policy.* Toronto: University of Toronto Press.

Buchanan, R. J., & Alston, R. J. (1997, July, August, September). Medicaid policies and home health care provisions for persons with disabilities. *Journal of Rehabilitation,* 20–34.

Burwell, B. (2001). *HCBS waiver data.* Presented at the 19th Annual National Home and Community Based Services Waiver Conference, Arlington, VA. Retrieved May 21, 2003 from *http://www.hcbs.org/search.php?glbSearchBox= HCBS+waiver+data&glbSearchGo.x=6&glb SearchGo.y=5*

Centers for Medicare & Medicaid Services (CMS) (2003). "Money follows the individual" rebalancing initiative. Retrieved May 29, 2003 from *http://cms.hhs.gov/newfreedom/0303mfir.pdf*

Collins, P. H. (2000). *Black feminist thought: Knowledge, consciousness, and empowerment.* New York: Routledge.

DeJong, G., Palsbo, S. E., Beatty, P. W. (2002). The organization and financing of health services for persons with disabilities. *The Milbank Quarterly, 80*(2), 261–301.

Doty P., Kasper, J., & Litvak, S. (1996). Consumer-directed models of personal care: lessons from Medicaid. *The Milbank Quarterly, 74*(3), 377–409.

Doty, P., & Sullivan, E. W. (1983). Community involvement in combating abuse, neglect and mistreatment in nursing homes. *Milbank Memorial Fund Quarterly/Health and Society, 61*(2), 222–251.

Feder, J. , Komisar, H. L., & Niefeld, M. (2000, May/June). Long-term care in the United States: An overview, *Health Affairs,* 40–56.

Fox-Grage. W., Folkemer, D., & Lewis, J. (2003). The states' response to the Olmstead decision: How are states complying? National Conference of State Legislatures. Retrieved May 21, 2003 from *http://www.ncsl.org/programs/health/ forum/olmsreport.htm*

Friedman, M. I. (1997). *Improving the quality of life: A holistic scientific strategy.* Westport, CT: Praeger.

Gilson, S. F., & Depoy, E. (2000). Multiculturalism and disability: A critical perspective. *Disability & Society, 15*(2), 207–218.

Glendenning, F. (1999). Elder abuse and neglect in residential settings: The need for inclusiveness in elder abuse research. *Journal of Elder Abuse & Neglect, 10*(1/2), 1–11.

Glickman, L. L., Stocker, K. B., & Garo, F. G. (1997). Self-direction in home care for older people: A consumer's perspective. *Home Health Care Services Quarterly, 16*(1/2), 41–55.

Goffman, E. (1963). *Stigma: Notes on the management of spoiled identity.* Englewood Cliffs, NJ: Prentice-Hall.

Hahn, H. (1988). The politics of physical differences: Disability and discrimination. *Journal of Social Issues, 44,* 39–47.

Illingworth, P. & Parmet, W. E. (2000). Positively disabled: The relationship between the definition of disability and rights under the ADA. In L. Francis & A. Silvers (Eds.), *Americans with disabilities: Exploring implications of the law for individuals and institutions.* New York: Routledge.

Kane, R. A. & Degenholts, H. (1997). Case management as a force for quality assurance and quality improvement in home care. *Journal of Aging & Social Policy. 9*(4), 5–27.

Kapp, M. B. (1999). Home health care regulation: Is

it good for the patient? *Care Management Journals, 1*(4), 251–257.

Kapp, M. B. (2000, Fall). Consumer direction in long-term care: A taxonomy of legal issues. *Generations*, 16–21.

Lachman, M. E., Ziff, M. A., & Spiro, A. (1994). Maintaining a sense of control in later life. In R. P. Abeles, H. C. Gift, & M. G. Ory (Eds.), *Aging and quality of life* (pp. 216–219). New York: Springer.

Liachowitz, C. H. (1988). *Disability as a social construct: Legislative roots.* Philadelphia: University of Pennsylvania Press.

Lipsky, M. (1980). *Street-level bureaucracy: Dilemmas of the individual in public services.* New York: Russell Sage Foundation.

Mackelprang, R. W., & Salsgiver, R. O. (1998). *Disability: A diversity model approach in human service practice.* Pacific Grove, CA: Brooks/Cole Publishing.

Mauser, E., & Miller, N. A. (1994). A profile of home health users in 1992. *Health Care Financing Review, 16*(1), 17–33.

Miley, K. K., O'Melia, M., & DuBois, B. (2001). *Generalist social work practice: An empowering approach.* Boston: Allyn and Bacon.

Miller, N. (1992). Medicaid home and community-based care waivers. *Health Affairs, 11*(4), 162–171.

Miller, N. (1997, Winter). Patient centered long-term care. *Health Care Financing Review*, 1–10.

Morris, J. (1991). *Pride against prejudice.* London: Women's Press.

National Council on Disability (NCD) (2000). National disability policy: A progress report (November 1998–November 1999). Retrieved April 10, 2003 from *http://www.ncd.gov/newsroom/publications/pdf/policy98-99.pdf*

National Council on Disability (NCD) (2001). National disability policy: A progress report (November 1999–November 2000). Retrieved April 10, 2003 from *http://www.ncd.gov/newsroom/publications/pdf/progressreport2000.pdf*

National Council on Disability (NCD) (2002). National disability policy: A progress report (December 2000–December 2001). Retrieved April 10, 2003 from *http://www.ncd.gov/newsroom/publications/pdf/progressreport_07-26-02.pdf*

Nolan, M. (1999). Enhancing the quality of care in residential and nursing homes: More than just a professional responsibility. *Journal of Elder Abuse & Neglect, 10*(1/2), 61–77.

Osberg, S., Corcoran, P. J., DeJong, G., & Ostroff, E. (1983). Environmental barriers and the neu-

rologically impaired patient. *Seminars in Neurology, 3*, 180–194.

Osten, W. M. (22 July, 2002). Letters to nursing home and hospital administrators. State of New York, Department of Health.

Pfeiffer, D. (1993). Overview of the disability movement: History, legislative record, and political implications. *Policy Studies Journal, 21*, 724–734.

Pillemer, K. A., & Moore, D. W. (1990). Highlights from a study of abuse in nursing homes. *Journal of Elder Abuse & Neglect, 2*(1/2), 5–29.

Richardson, S. K. (28 May, 1998). Letter to state Medicaid director. Center for Medicare & Medicaid Services. Retrieved January 8, 2003, from *http://cms.hhs.gov/states/letters/smd52898.asp*

Rosenbaum, S. (2000, Sept/Oct). The Olmstead decision: Implication for state health policy. *Health Affairs*, 228–232.

Saleebey, D. (Ed.). (1997). *The strengths perspective in social work practice* (2nd ed.). New York: Longman.

Scotch, R. (2000). Models of disability and the Americans with Disabilities Act. *Journal of Employment and Labor Law, 21*, 213–222.

Shapiro, J. P. (1993). *No pity: People with disabilities forging a new civil rights movement.* New York: Times Books.

Shaw, M. M. (1998). Nursing home resident abuse by staff: Exploring the dynamics. *Journal of Elder Abuse & Neglect, 9*(4), 1–21.

Silverstein, R. (2000). Federal disability policy framework. *The Iowa Law Review, 85*, 1691–1798.

Solomon, B. B. (1976). *Black Empowerment.* New York: Columbia University Press.

Thompson, M., & Graff, J. (1997). Fatal neglect. *Time 150*(17), 34–38.

Thompson, N. (2000). *Theory and practice in human services.* Buckingham, England: Open University Press.

Thompson, N. (2001). *Anti-discriminatory practice.* Hampshire, UK: Palgrave Macmillan.

U.S. Department of Justice (2002). P.L. 101–336: Americans with Disabilities Act of 1990. Retrieved May 23, 2003 from *http://www.usdoj.gov/crt/ada/pubs/ada.txt*

U.S. Department of Commerce (2001). *Americans with disabilities: Household economic studies.* Washington, DC: Bureau of the Census.

U.S. Department of Justice (2003). Investigation of Laguna Honda Hospital and Rehabilitation Center. Retrieved May 28, 2003 from *http://www.usdoj.gov/crt/split/Findsettle.htm*

Uhlenberg, P. (1997). Replacing the nursing home. *Public Interest, 128*(Summer), 73–84.

Ustun, T. B., Bickenbach, J. E., Badley, E., & Chatterji, S. (1998). A reply to David Pfeiffer "The ICIDH and the Need for its Revision." *Disability & Society, 13,* 829–831.

Westmoreland, T. M. (11 January, 2000). Letter to state Medicaid director. Center for Medicare & Medicaid Services. Retrieved January 8, 2003, from *http://cms.hhs.gov/states/letters/smd11100.asp*

Williams, G. H. (1983). The movement for independent living: An evaluation and critique. *Social Sciences and Medicine, 17,* 1003–1010.

Wolen, S. J., & Wolen, S. (1993). *The resilient self: How survivors of troubled families rise above adversity.* New York: Villard.

Wright, B. A. (1983). *Physical Disability—A Psychosocial Approach.* New York: Harper and Row.

CHAPTER 4

RETHINKING DISABILITY IN SOCIAL WORK: INTERDISCIPLINARY PERSPECTIVES

VANMALA S. HIRANANDANI

INTRODUCTION

Historically, individuals with disabilities have had to struggle to live full and productive lives as independently as possible in a society fraught with stigma, discrimination, and environmental barriers. Just as the cultural presence of race and gender was either invisible or imagined as narrow marginal concerns in the academic world prior to the 1970s, disability is still often considered a specialized area or a medical issue marginal to social sciences. Throughout history, legislation, policies, and practices have regarded persons with disabilities as unfit for society, as sick, as a minority group, and as functionally limited (Brooks, 1991; Brzuzy, 1997; Mackelprang & Salsgiver, 1996; Quinn, 1995a).

In recent years, the notion of disability as an individual problem has been challenged as not concurring with the experience of people with disabilities (Asch & Fine, 1988; Barton, 1988; Fleischer & Zames, 2001; Oliver, 1983; Priestley, 1999; Sapey & Hewitt, 1991). The growth of self-organization of people with disabilities since the 1970s has led to redefinition of disability as a social construct: Societal, cultural, political, and environmental barriers have been repeatedly suggested as more disabling than physical or cognitive disabilities (Oliver, 1996; Priestley, 1999). Concurrently, emerging disability scholarship in humanities and social sciences has put forth alternative analyses that view the construction of disability from a critical lens. These developments challenge traditional notions of disability in social work and call the profession to examine alternative ways of knowing disability.

SOCIAL WORK AND THE MEANING
OF DISABILITY

The dominant view of disability in social work and social services has been the medical model, which views disability as a functional limitation, as an individual "problem," "pathology," "dysfunction," or "deviance" (Brzuzy, 1997; Finkelstein, 1991). Oliver (1996) emphasized that the individual model locates the "problem" of disability within the individual and considers functional limitations or psychological losses to arise naturally from the individual deficit. This view is also called the "personal tragedy theory of disability," which posits that disability is a natural disadvantage suffered by disabled individuals when placed in competitive social situations. Instead of viewing disability as inextricably linked to social, cultural, and political milieus, the medical or personal tragedy framework infers that the disabled individual is plagued by deficits and is in need of medical "fixing" (Quinn, 1995b).

Social work also addresses the issue of grief, loss, and bereavement associated with mental and physical disability. Disabled individuals are commonly depicted as suffering subjects, characterized by the devastating changes and crises for both themselves and their families. Recognizing, accepting, and coming to terms with the disability are viewed as the targeted outcomes of social work intervention (e.g., Hartman, Macintosh, & Engethardt, 1983; Krausz, 1988; Parry, 1980).

The concept of disability has also been addressed from an ecological or psychosocial perspective within the field of social work. For example, Mackelprang and Hepworth (1987) suggested the importance of extending the medical perspective of disability to social factors, such as stigma, architecture, and awareness of a social structure constructed by the able-bodied. Under this framework, the extent of disability is reciprocally determined by transactions between people and their environments rather than within the individual alone. Social workers have, indeed, voiced interest in inclusion and accommodation for individuals with disabilities; however, they have largely stayed away from active involvement in the disability rights movement, which has been initiated by people with disabilities and their advocates. Most epistemological factors, such as the conceptual framework and pedagogy of disability as a functional deficit, have been left unchallenged in the field of social work. The profession has done little to promote disability rights; social work literature, research, and practice on disabilities have lagged behind other topical areas dealing with oppressed groups (Gilson, Bricout, & Baskind, 1998; Mackelprang, 1993; Mackelprang & Salsgiver, 1996).

The impact of the individual model of disability is evident in policy analysis research, which is synonymous with a lack of consultation with people having disabilities, lack of emphasis on the social and political forces impacting the lives of people with disabilities, and a reduction of disability to simplistic "objective" criteria that measure functional limitations. To the extent that disability policies rely on disability-as-individual-problem framework, they marginalize the possibility of more enabling modes of human welfare that are based on participation, social integration, and equal citizenship (Priestley, 1999).

ALTERNATIVE PERSPECTIVES ON DISABILITY

Challenges to the traditional medical model of disability have emerged from a variety of theoretical starting points in various fields of humanities and social sciences, such as anthropology, political science, rhetoric, history, literary and cultural criticism, and disability studies (Barnes, Mercer, & Shakespeare, 1999). In this book, salient critical themes emanating from these disciplines are highlighted that can inform social work practice, pedagogy and research on disability. Key issues raised are the relationship between disability and the emergence of industrial society (Oliver, 1990, Stiker, 1982); the role of social and cultural factors in the development of the category of disability (Ingstad & Reynolds-Whyte, 1995; Priestley, 1999; Stiker, 1982); the emergence of a social model of disability (Barnes, Mercer & Shakespeare, 1999; Oliver, 1996; Priestley, 1999); and a critique of the discourse of normalcy (Davis, 1997; Amundson, 2000), the discourse of measurement (Cintron, 1997), and professional domination experienced by people with disabilities (Foucault, 1973, 1977; Sapey & Hewitt, 1991).

It should be noted that the histories of people recognized to have different disabilities, such as various physical disabilities, developmental disabilities, and mental health problems, are not homogeneous. Nevertheless, once a human condition is labeled as "disabled," many similarities emerge that comprise the overall experience of disability in our culture.

Historical Materialist Accounts of Disability in Western Countries

Karl Marx believed an understanding of human societies must begin with the material conditions of human existence, or the economics of producing the necessities of life. The economic mode of production, because of its importance, influences other aspects of life, such as political organization, ideology, religion, and culture: "The ideas of the ruling class are in every epoch the ruling ideas: that is, the class which is the 'ruling material force' of society, is at the same time its ruling intellectual force" (Marx & Engels, 1994, p. 15).

Marxist writers analyze disability as a social problem that is directly linked to the changing mode of production: Definitions of disability and other social problems are influenced by both the economic and social structures and the core values of particular modes of production existing in a historical time period (Oliver, 1990; Priestley, 1999). For Oliver (1990), the individualized and medicalized approach to disability emerged from the functional necessities of capital, mainly the requirement of a workforce that is physically and intellectually able to meet the demands of industrialization.

Oliver further posited, "historical materialism is not just about placing social relationships within a historical setting. It also attempts to provide an evolutionary perspective on the whole of human history, and of particular relevance here are the transitions from feudal through capitalist to socialist society" (1990, p. 26). Oliver asserted feudal society did not exclude disabled people from participation in the process of production; even in cases where they could not fully participate, their contributions were still included, and they were not segregated from the rest of society. The development of capitalism led to economic changes in the organization of labor, leading to profound implications for social relations, family life, and attitudes. While disability, of course, did not emerge with the rise of capitalism, it clearly took a different form of social relations: Industrial capitalism excluded disabled people from equal participation in the labor force (Priestley, 1999). World War I led to the development of rehabilitation efforts in Europe and in the United States. It is at this point that a broad paradigm shift occurred in dealing with disability, as Western societies attempted to cope with large numbers of those mutilated by war (Stiker, 1982). Disability, in modem times, raised technical problems to be dealt with by medical and legal specialists, social workers, and vocational trainers with the underlying concern to "integrate" disabled people into "ordinary" life and work. These circumstances led to the growth of institutional welfare arrangements to serve the new needs of disabled people.

The emergence of rehabilitation as a medical and paramedical specialization, beginning in the struggle for professional control over damaged bodies of World War I led to the development of disability as a concern of the state (Gritzer & Arluke, 1985). Rehabilitation implied the general notions of replacement, substitution, and compensation, which over time were applied to all congenital and acquired impairments. The development of rehabilitation and intervention by the state has been accompanied by legislation, administrative procedures, welfare institutions, medical diagnoses, professional specializations, and business interests (Ingstad & Reynolds-Whyte, 1995).

Habermas (1987) argued that welfare capitalism leads to new forms of domination and subordination as the "life world" becomes increasingly "colonized" under the control of rationalized bureaucracies. The state assigns to medical professionals the task of determining who is entitled to the rights of financial support and services. The political issue of redistribution, that involves separating the deserving from the undeserving, becomes a clinical problem. In an analysis of the history of disability in United States as an administrative classification, Stone (1984) examines the dispositions towards expanding the category. Flexibility in disability definitions and incorporation of new conditions (e.g., chronic fatigue syndrome, fibromyalgia) reflects various interests. Although cast in biomedical terms, the determination of disability involves political decisions about the distribution of social goods. However, as Stone suggests, ongoing discourse in most disability research and policy is about "objective criteria" and measurements of incapacity that leads to the perception that the state is distributing "scarce goods" in a "fair" and "systematic" way.

With the expansion of federal legislation on disability, an aging population, an increase in chronic diseases, and the growth of the health-insurance industry, disability has become big business (Albrecht, 1992; Finkelstein, 1991). Disability has been institutionalized and rehabilitation goods and services have become commodified in an ever-expanding market. As a result, people with disabilities have become consumers, who now have an identity and have formed groups as users of services.

In sum, it can be argued that, "in late-capitalist countries disability exists and is produced by the state, legal, educational, economic, and biomedical institutions. A person's identity, notions of citizenship, value lost through impairment and added through rehabilitation are shaped by these institutions" (Ingstad & Reynolds-Whyte, 1995, p.10). The meaning of disability must therefore be understood as a construct related to prevailing economic organization, institutions, bureaucratic structures, and political contexts in a particular historical period.

Disability As a Social and Cultural Construction

In recent years, there has been a move towards the application of a social constructionist framework to disability. For instance, an analysis of the functions of language (Brzuzy, 1997), epistemology and positivism (Ringma & Brown, 1991), meaning-making processes, linguistic subjugation and constraints (Borden, 1992), and social interaction (Birenbaum, 1979) have been introduced under generative frameworks of inquiry to expand our thinking and perceptions about the construct of disability. Social constructionist theory embraces a wide range of ideas stemming from professional and academic disciplines such as philosophy, anthropology, history, literary criticism, and social psychology (Epston, White, & Murray, 1992). Implicit in social constructionism is the idea that knowledge is not an objective entity, but rather a social creation (Levine, 1997). Described as a theory that attempts to "elucidate the sociohistorical context and ongoing social dynamic of descriptions, explanations, and accountings of reality" (Witkin, 1990, p. 38), constructionism devotes particular attention to the ways in which knowledge is historically situated and embedded in cultural values. Rather than taking theory and the dominant forms of understanding as definite conclusions, constructionists uphold that what can be known is bound by cultural assumptions, historical precedents, sociocultural rules, and language (Patterson, 1997). Subsequently, constructionism as an epistemology contributes a liberating quality to the social sciences by way of alteration to the monolithic landscape of positivism and scientific inquiry (Witkin, 1990)

Social constructionism can offer significant insight to contemporary conceptualizations of disability. Constructionism posits that language serves as a method for producing meaning and generating knowledge rather than as a reflection or representation of objective "truth." Most individualistic (personal-tragedy) accounts of disability fail to recognize that even the most objective of disorders, such as visual impairment, do not exist independent of culture and society. Nor do these accounts recognize that the delineation of difference in and of itself is a cultural and linguistic expression.

The cultural construction of disability is suggested by a large number of ethnographic studies undertaken by anthropologists (e.g., Groce & Scheer, 1990;

Ingstad & Reynolds-Whyte, 1995; McDermott & Varenne, 1996). Social work in an increasingly multicultural United States poses the question of how disability is understood in different cultures. How are deficits of the body and mind interpreted and dealt with in different societies? How is an individual's identity as a person affected by the cultural connotations of disability? How do processes of cultural transitions shape local understanding of disability? Definitions of disability in terms of measurable functional limitations fail to recognize that culture permeates the variations of the human condition with consequences much deeper than the simple ability to perform a given task (Ingstad & Reynolds-Whyte, 1995). Objective criteria of functional limitations do not answer the question of how important individual ability is as a source of social identity in different cultures.

The experience of disability, too, varies across cultures. For example, Edgerton (1985) showed attitudes toward people with impairments varied greatly in non-Western cultures, from negative discrimination, to acceptance, and to positive attribution of supernatural powers. Locust (1985) explores the differences in Native American beliefs about "unwellness" across cultures such as the Hopi, Apache, Yagui, and Navajo. One telling example is that of Piki Maker, an expert bread maker whose physical differences in back structure and arm length are promoted by her community as assets that allow her to produce bread at a more efficient rate than anyone else in the tribe.

Disability is, therefore, hardly a unitary concept: In many cultures one cannot be "disabled" because "disability" as a distinct category does not exist. The term "disabled" does not translate into many languages, although there are terms for people with visual, hearing, and cognitive impairments (Ingstad & Reynolds-Whyte, 1995). The lack of a universal definition of disability throughout history indicates a tenuous relationship between the disabled individual and society.

The perspective of disability as a social and cultural construct brings into question the assumptions and values that inform social work practice with disabled populations at the levels of treatment, counseling, rehabilitation, service provision, case management, research, and policy analysis. Most of the theoretical leanings that undergird social work in the arena of disability have been borrowed from medicine and psychiatry; as such they may often lack conformity between our code of ethics and an agenda of human rights/social justice (Brzuzy, 1997). In this regard, constructionism provides a theoretical framework to rethink disability in liberating and empowering terms.

A Social Model of Disability

The social and political focus on disability has attracted increasing attention across a range of academic disciplines, resulting in an unprecedented growth of "disability studies" courses and journals in America (Linton, 1998; Pfeiffer & Yoshida, 1995). This new, humanities-oriented approach to disability borrows from many fields and movements, including cultural studies, area studies, feminism, race-and-ethnic studies, and so on. It is extensively informed by literary and cultural criticism inasmuch as it pulls apart concepts about disability to critically examine what cultural politics, antagonisms, and insecurities went into shaping them. Many writers have advanced the approach known as "body criticism," the study of the ways in which cultures impose various meanings and conditions on the human body (Woodill, 1992). According to Barnes, Mercer, and Shakespeare (1999), the main factor in the growth of disability studies is an ever increasing community of academics and researchers with disabilities.

A hallmark of the field of disability studies is that it articulates disability as a particular form of social oppression. This framework has been termed "the social model of disability" (Oliver, 1996; Corker, 2000). Instead of a narrow focus on functional limitations, the social model emphasizes society's failure to provide appropriate services and adequately ensure that the needs of people with disabilities are fully taken into account in the social organization. Disability, according to the social model, encompasses all factors that impose restrictions on people with disabilities, ranging from negative social attitudes to institutional discrimination, from inaccessible public buildings to unusable transport systems, from segregated education to exclusion in work arrangements, and so on. It can be seen that the social model of disability derives from a social constructionist approach discussed earlier. The difference is the social model of disability has been put forth by people with disabilities themselves, mainly activists and academics with disabilities.

While it is acknowledged that the relationships of people with disabilities to their bodies involve elements of pain and struggle that perhaps cannot be eliminated or mitigated, yet many of the barriers that people with disabilities face are the consequences of having those physical impairments under existing social arrangements. These social systems could but do not accommodate disabled people's physical conditions or integrate their struggles into the cultural concept of everyday life (Asch & Fine, 1988).

The Discourse of Normalcy: The Discourse of Measurement and Disciplinary Power

Foucault's version of social constructionism has given fresh impetus to recent studies to examine the medicalization of social problems and the impact of professional power. Under Foucault's influence, medical concepts of disease and "madness" have been analyzed in terms of historically specific ways of viewing the body (Foucault, 1970, 1973, 1977). Foucault argued that the new scientific medicine, which took root in the eighteenth and early nineteenth centuries, assumed a "normalizing gaze" of the human body, defining novel boundaries between the "normal" and the "abnormal." Medicine served a moral as well as a clinical function: "It claimed to ensure the physical vigor and the moral cleanliness of the social body; it promised to eliminate defective individuals, degenerate and bastardized populations. In the name of biological and historical urgency, it justified the racism of the state. . . . It grounded them in "truth" (Foucault, 1977, p. 54). The value-laden normalizing gaze of biological sciences became a device for the scaling and measuring of physical and mental capacities against standardized norms. Solomos and Back (1996) explain that during the late eighteenth century, the obsession with measurement and statistics generated a conception of hierarchies of physical, psychological, and cultural differences: "People could be conveniently divided and classified not merely in terms of geographical origin or color but equally by virtue of cranial capacity and shape" (p. 34). More specifically, the measurement of bodies relative to biological norms became the primary mechanism through which social norms of acceptance were also defined. Thomson (1997) demonstrates how there are hierarchies of embodiment which decide valued and devalued identities: "In this economy of visual difference, those bodies deemed inferior become spectacles of otherness while the unmarked are sheltered in the neutral space of normalcy" (p. 8). A critical analysis of the discourse of normality and measurement, therefore, would serve to illuminate and expose power inequities. Just as recent scholarship on race (e.g., Hartigan, 1999) suggests that instead of focusing on the person of color in the study of race, we must turn our attention to whiteness in order to understand how race works in specific contexts, contemporary disability theorists (e.g., Davis, 1997; Amundson, 2000) assert that instead of focusing on a disabled person as the object or subject of study, it is necessary to focus on the construction of normalcy in order to understand the ways in which the ubiquity, power, and value of the normative image resonate in our culture.

From a different premise, Cintron (1997) posits the discourse of measurement is concerned with the creation of precise orderings and emergence of an expert class that is skillful in applying these ordering schemes to individual and social life in order to better manage both spheres. Discourses of measurement, thus, are "practices but also ways of speaking and thinking that create order, coherence, and sets of rules to organize the otherwise random motions of daily life" (p. 211). Consequently, specific disciplines of knowledge and technologies have emerged that have the ability to monitor, control and, in certain cases, change the conditions of the bodily organ. This has led to the emergence of the "expert" class that wields the power of that knowledge and technology.

Foucault (1977) emphasized the power of scientific knowledge inherent in the medicalization of illness and that impairment creates a contrast between sovereign and disciplinary power. In modern societies there is not necessarily an easily identified, single authority, or oppressive sovereign power. Instead, liberal institutions such as education, health, and welfare services and the production and distribution of consumer goods are all instruments of domination (Foucault, 1980). Disciplinary power is about hierarchical observation, or the ways in which bodies are understood, monitored, and regulated. In tracing the history of "madness," Foucault argues that the reasons underlying the development of a more humane medicine were less "progressive" than imagined (Foucault, 1973). While psychiatry was viewed as a key part of the apparatus of regulation and control, new specializations, such as rehabilitation medicine and epidemiology, emerged and claimed chronic illness as their domain of authority. The significance of discourses in various disciplines, such as medicine, psychiatry, social work and rehabilitation, is that it legitimizes the ability of professional elites to maintain relationships of power and gaze over disabled people in the production of welfare policies and services. These relationships of power and surveillance, that are inconsistent with social work principles of client empowerment and self-determination, call for critical reflections on social work pedagogy.

CONCLUSION

In sum, alternative frameworks drawn from humanities, social sciences, and disability studies can form the foundations of a powerful critical theory of disability that questions the entrenched notion of disability as necessarily a personal tragedy, and reveals how the category of disability is socially reproduced. This chapter calls for rethinking of disability: Specifically, social work should endeavor to challenge extant notions of disability, to re-narrate disability, and to re-vision it as a part of human experience and history. Further, social work needs to contest existing "expert" discourses on disability by actively collaborating with people with disabilities and their advocates. To this end, social work, and the people with disabilities that it serves, can benefit immensely by developing interdisciplinary collaborations with humanities and social sciences in which the new disability scholarship is more robust.

REFERENCES

Albrecht, G. L. (1992). The disability business: Rehabilitation in America London: Sage Publications.

Amundson, R. (2000). Biological normality and the ADA. In L. P. Francis & A. Silvers (Eds.), *American with disabilities: Exploring implications of the law for individuals and institutions* (pp. 102–110). New York: Routledge.

Asch, A., & Fine, M. (1988). Shared dreams: A left perspective on disability rights and reproductive rights. In M. Fine & A. Asch (Eds.), *Women with disabilities: Essays in psychology, culture and politics.* Philadelphia: Temple University Press.

Barnes, C., Mercer, G., & Shakespeare, T. (1999). *Exploring disability: A sociological introduction.* Malden, MA: Blackwell.

Barton, L. (Ed.) (1988). *The politics of special needs.* Brighton, MA: Falmer Press.

Birenbaum, A. (1979). Social construction of disability. *Journal of Sociology and Social Welfare,* 6(1), 89–101.

Borden, W. (1992). Narrative perspectives in psychosocial intervention following adverse life conditions. *Social Work, 37*(2), 135–141.

Brooks, N. (1991). Self-empowerment among adults with severe physical disability: A case study. *Journal of Sociology and Social Welfare,* 18(1), 105–120.

Brzuzy, S. (1997). Deconstructing disability: The impact of definition. *Journal of Poverty, 1 1, 81–91.*

Cintron, R. (1997). *Angels' town: Chero ways, gang life, and rhetorics of the everyday.* Boston: Beacon Press.

Corker, M. (2000). The U.K. Disability Discrimination Act: Disabling language, justifying inequitable social participation. In L. P. Francis & A. Silvers (Eds.), *Americans with disabilities: Exploring implications of the law for individuals and institutions* (pp. 357–370). New York: Routledge.

Davis, L. J. (1997). Constructing normalcy. The bell curve, the novel, and the invention of the disabled body in the nineteenth century. In L. J. Davis (Ed.), *The disability studies reader* (pp. 9–28). New York: Routledge.

Edgerton, R. B. (1985). *Rules, exceptions, and social order.* Berkeley, CA: University of California Press.

Epston, D., White, M., & Murray, K. (1992). A proposal for re-authoring therapy:

Rose's revisioning of her life and commentary. In S. McNamee & K. Gergen (Eds.), *Therapy as a social construction* (pp. 97–115). Newbury Park, CA: Sage Publications.

Finkelstein, V. (1991). Disability: An administrative challenge? In M. Oliver (Ed.), *Social work: Disabled people and disabling environments.* London: Jessica Kingsley.

Fleischer, D. Z., & Zames, F. (2001). *The disability rights movement: From charity to confrontation.* Philadelphia: Temple University Press.

Foucault, M. (1970). *The order of things.* New York: Random House.

Foucault, M. (1973). *Madness and civilization: The history of insanity in the age of reason* (R. Howard, Trans.). New York: Vintage Books. (Original work published 1961 in French.)

Foucault, M. (1977). *Discipline and punish.* New York: Vintage Books.

Foucault, M. (1980). *Power/knowledge: Selected interviews and other writings 1972–1977.* Brighton: Harvester Press.

Gilson, S. F., Bricout, J. C., & Baskind, F. R. (1998). Listening to the voices of individuals with disabilities. *The Journal of Contemporary Human Services, 79*(2), 188–196.

Gritzer, G., & Arluke, A. (1985). *The making of rehabilitation: A political economy of medical specialization. 1890–1980.* Berkeley, CA: University of California Press.

Groce, N., & Scheer, J. (1990). Introduction. *Social Science and Medicine, 30*(8), v–vi.

Habermas, J. (1987). The theory of communicative competence: *Lifeworld and system* (vol. 2). Boston: Beacon.

Hartigan, J. (1999). *Racial situations: Class predicaments of whiteness in Detroit.* Princeton, NJ: Princeton University Press.

Hartman, C., Macintosh, B., & Englehardt, B. (1983). The neglected and forgotten sexual partner of the physically disabled. *Social Work, 28,* 370–374.

Ingstad, B., & Reynolds-Whyte, S. (1995). Disability and culture: An overview. In B. Ingstad & S. Reynolds-Whyte (Eds.), *Disability and culture* (pp. 3–31). Berkeley, CA: University of California Press.

Krausz, S. (1988). Illness and loss: Helping couples cope. *Clinical Social Work Journal, 16*(1), 52–65.

Levine, J., (1997). Re-visioning attention deficit hyperactivity disorder. *Clinical Social Work Journal, 25*(2), 197–211.

Linton, S. (1998). Disability studies: Not disability studies. *Disability and Society, 13,* 525–541.

Locust, C. (1985). *American Indian concepts concerning health and unwellness.* Unpublished Manuscript, supported by the National Institute on Disability and Rehabilitation Research, U.S. Department of Education.

Mackelprang, R. W., & Hepworth, D. (1987). Ecological factors in rehabilitation of patients with severe spinal cord injuries. *Social Work in Health Care, 13*(1), 23–38.

Mackelprang, R. W., & Salsgiver, R. (1996). People with disabilities and social work: Historical and contemporary issues. *Social Work, 41*(1), pp. 7–14.

Mackelprang, R. W. (1993). *Social work education and persons with disabilities: Are we meeting the challenges?* Paper presented at the annual program meeting of the Council of Social Work Education, New York.

Marx, K., & Engels, F. (1994). History as class struggle. Excerpts reprinted in R. Collins (Ed.), *Four sociological traditions.* New York: Oxford University Press.

McDermott, R. P., & Varenne, H. (1996). Culture, development, disability. In R. Jessor, A. Colby, & R. A. Shweder (Eds.), *Ethnography and human development* (101, 126). Chicago: University of Chicago Press.

Oliver, M. (1983). *Social work with disabled people.* Basingstoke, U.K.: Macmillan.

Oliver, M. (1990). *The politics of disablement: A sociological approach.* New York: St. Martin's Press.

Oliver, M. (1996). *Understanding disability: From theory to practice.* Basingstoke, U.K.: Macmillan.

Parry, J. (1980). Group services for the chronically ill and disabled. *Social Work with Groups, 3*(1), 59–67.

Patterson, K. A. (1997). Representations of disability in mid twentieth-century southern fiction: From metaphor to social construction. Doctoral Dissertation, University of California at Santa Barbara. *Dissertation Abstracts International, 38,* PS 261.

Pfeiffer, D., & Yoshida, K. (1995). Teaching disability studies in Canada and the USA. *Disability and Society, 10,* 475–500.

Priestley, M. (1999). *Disability politics and community care.* London: Jessica Kingsley.

Quinn, P. (1995a). Social work education and disability: Benefiting from the impact of the ADA. *Journal of Teaching in Social Work, 12*(1), 55–71.

Quinn, P. (1995b). Social work and disability management policy: Yesterday, today, and tomorrow. *Social Work in Health Care, 20*(3), 67–82.

Ringma, C., & Brown, C. (1991). Hermeneutics and the social sciences: An evaluation of the function of hermeneutics in a consumer disability study. *Journal of Sociology and Social Welfare, 18*(3), 57–73.

Sapey, B., & Hewitt, N. (1991). The changing context of social work practice. In M. Oliver (Ed.), *Social work: Disabled people and disabling environments*. London: Jessica Kingsley.

Solomos, J., & Back, L. (1996). *Racism and society*. New York: St. Martin's Press.

Stiker, H. (1982). *A history of disability*. Paris: Aubier Montaigne.

Stone, D. (1984). *The disabled state*. Philadelphia: Temple University Press.

Thomson, R. (1997). *Extraordinary bodies: Figuring physical disability in American culture and literature*. New York: Columbia University Press.

Witkin, S. L. (1990). The implications of social constructionism for social work education. *Journal of Teaching in Social Work, 4*, 37–48.

Woodill, G. (1992). *Independent living and participation in research: A critical analysis* (discussion paper). Toronto: Center for Independent Living.

CHAPTER 5

CHANGING THE FUTURE OF DISABILITY: THE DISABILITY DISCRIMINATION MODEL

GARY E. MAY

INTRODUCTION

The Disability Discrimination Model is designed to give professional social workers a way to conceptualize disability so that their work can play a role in the transformation of how people with disabilities are treated in our society. The guiding principle of this text is that disability-related impairment is a social construction rather than an immutable, objective reality. Impairment operates as a set of beliefs supported by theories and practices within society so that deviations from normative expectations in physical and biological makeup and function are defined as limiting and excluding. The Disability Discrimination Model proposes a theoretical model along with a set of practice principles upon which social workers can restructure their practices.

The model is based on Pfeiffer's conceptualization of the disability paradigm (Chapter 2), that includes the following components:

> The disability paradigm states that the study of the experience of people with disabilities focuses on the following variables which impinge on the phenomenon of disability and interact with each other and other human characteristics: (1) the process in which the performance of social roles and tasks produces discrimination; (2) the discriminatory treatment of people with disabilities produced by the organization of society; (3) the recognition that an impairment does not imply tragedy and a low quality of life; (4) the stark reality that people with disabilities are an oppressed minority which experiences discrimination; (5) the need of all people including people with disabilities for various services in order to live independently; (6) the realization that all people have agendas so that the unstated assumptions of disability policy must be revealed; (7) the knowledge that people over time move on a continuum from non-disabled to disabled so that eventually

everyone experiences disability; (8) the rejection that there is "normal" human behavior on which social policy can be based; and (9) the all pervasiveness of discrimination against persons with disabilities (May & Raske, 2004, p. 80).

This chapter will introduce social work students, educators, and practitioners to the Disability Discrimination Model and show how this alternative view of disabilities can transform how our society interacts with persons with disabilities. The authors believe that it is through the daily acts of social work practice that social change takes place. However, individual workers need a fully constructed model of practice to compete with the power of the accepted paradigm—the medical model. If social workers are to transform their work with persons with disabilities they need a theory, supported by clear practice examples, that guides their use of the strengths and empowerment perspectives.

This work follows a long tradition of social work reform. For generations, social workers and other scholars have used theories to transform practice (Brzuzy, 1997; Cummerton, 1986; Daly, 1973; Fraser & Gordon, 1994; James & Thomas, 1996; Merrick, 1994; and Ringma & Brown, 1991). In recent years, for example, empowerment theory has helped social workers develop partnerships with marginalized groups such as persons of color and persons living in poverty (Fisk, Rowe, Brooks, & Gildersleeve, 2000; and Kosciulck, 1999). Unfortunately, empowerment theory has limited impact on practice with populations more affected by the mainstream medical model (Bucaro & Kapfstein, 1999; Goodley & Moore, 2000; Linton, 1998; Morris, 1991; Moxley, 1992). This is most evident in work with persons with physical and mental disabilities (Allison, 1999; Brooks, 1991; Brown & Ringma, 1989; Felske, 1994; Thapar & Bhardwau, 1999; Ward & Meyer, 1999; and Zola, 1989).

The implications of this new lens for assessment will be discussed along with the implications of traditional views for social work and social workers. Normality will be looked at as a limiting concept in our thinking about disabilities; and finally, a case study will be used to exemplify the consequences of the traditional view of disability and the dramatically different consequences when a more comprehensive, accommodating perspective is adopted. The reader will be able to appreciate the contribution of the Disability Discrimination Model in furthering understanding, acceptance, and shared responsibility for corrective interventions.

DISABILITY DISCRIMINATION MODEL

The Disability Discrimination Model necessitates acceptance of an understanding of disability where "disability" and "impairment" are not inherently linked. This theory asserts that the concepts of disability and impairment are socially constructed, and that the "facts" concerning the consequences of disability are not immutable, objective realities, but merely affirmations of a pejorative and stereotypic perspective.

Pfeiffer, in Chapter 2, (May & Raske, 2004) in critiquing the Human Variation Model of Disability, attributed this axiom to that model: "In a flexible social
system which fully accommodates a person with a disability, the disability disappears." This view precludes the simultaneous existence of a disability—which may
be defined as the presence of an appearance or functional characteristic that is a
departure from normative expectations—and positive connotations that might be
associated with the label "disabled." Seemingly, one cannot have a disability and
feel good. Thus, this perspective implicitly validates the traditional medical model
where a disability is a negative aberration that becomes the focus of preventive or
remedial intervention.

The Disability Discrimination Model contends that being labeled "disabled" is
no different from being labeled "female," "African American," "Hispanic," or any
other nominal distinction, but for the consequences of the label. Historically, people with disabilities, unlike these other groups, have not been socialized to experience pride and associate a positive connotation with the label "disabled." We
believe that proud, positive connotations can and do accompany the label "disabled," even under conditions when the consequences of the label are constructed
as negative, limiting, and pejorative. For example, the fact that I have bilateral
above-the-knee amputations (a deviation from appearance and functional norms)
does not mean that I cannot be proud of my total being, including that portion of
my body and functionality that is appropriately labeled "disabled."

As Pfeiffer (Chapter 2) suggests, a hospitable environment that accommodates my appearance and functional deviations (read "disability") is desirable, but
the absence of such an accommodating environment does not meant that I move
from a nondisabled state to a disabled state. The absence of such necessary and
desirable accommodations merely suggests that the socially constructed environment *causes* impairment. I may still proudly maintain the label "disabled" in either
instance.

In the previously cited examples of women, African Americans, Hispanics,
and others, we do not insist that they relinquish identity or proud adherence to
the labels that connote their group's deviation from the majority. Nor do we suggest that they no longer occupy a role and status within their labeled group if they
experience an accommodating social system. Indeed, great effort is expended to
ensure that everyone understands the value of diversity (read "deviation") in contemporary U.S. culture. Not so when disability is the issue. Here, the focus is on
"restoring" the person who is labeled "disabled" so he or she no longer deviates
from normative expectations. There is no systematic effort to identify sources of
pride or to instill positive connotations on being "disabled."

The implications for social workers and other intentional helpers are profound and require a "working with" orientation with the disabled client versus a
"working on" orientation. From this "working with" perspective, the client system
is not merely the collection of difficulties or clinical symptomatology, but is one
component of an interactive system that may produce impairment. Solutions,
then, are not to be found solely in the person with the disability, but in the larger
social environment.

Decisions about what needs to be done and who should do it are reached through collaboration and consultation, not merely clinical practice or psychotherapy. The Disability Discrimination Model asserts that the "client" system is victimized by poor quality social interaction, not by the client's personality or behavioral characteristics.

As noted earlier, the Disability Discrimination Model makes an essential distinction between disability and impairment and views impairment as a socially constructed phenomenon. From this perspective, disability becomes disabling, or impairment, where an observed or perceived atypical appearance or functional characteristic intersects with a negative, stereotypic, limiting set of expectations. Typically, the possessors of the atypical appearance or functional characteristics are labeled "disabled," and the holders of the negative, stereotypic, limiting expectations are labeled "non-disabled." Such a depiction allows the person with a disability to continue to "own" and even celebrate the disability, and implicitly, membership in the disability culture, and explains deferential treatment and limiting elements associated with disability as consequences of the social and physical environment.

From the Disability Discrimination Model, interventions are enacted in a broader field and necessarily include all important elements of the client's experience. Important human elements, such as family and friends, will need to be educated about the important contributions they can make to the quality of life of the person with a disability. Resistance to this novel perspective that shifts responsibility from the identified client to the milieu as the insidious influence of traditional victim-blaming perspective is substantial. The shift from "working on" to "working with" may not be easy.

Normality As a Limiting Concept

The modern concept of normality—ostensibly denoting the average, usual, and ordinary—has its origins in the mid-nineteenth century in the pervasive belief in progress. It enjoyed cultural popularity in the advent of evolutionary theory. Normality was ". . . a dynamic concept for a changing and progressing world, the premise of which was that one could discern from the observation of human behavior the direction of human progress, or evolution . . ." (Baynton, 1997, p 83) Normality, in actual usage, generally excluded only those defined as below average, even though the term denotes the average, usual, and ordinary. In this era, physical and mental abnormalities were depicted as instances of atavistic reversions to earlier stages of evolutionary development. For example, Down syndrome was originally called mongolism by the doctor who first identified it in 1866 because he believed it to be a biological reversion of Caucasians to the Mongol racial type (Baynton, 1997). More recently, the contiguous displays of "defectives" and "primitives" at the 1904 World's Fair confirmed the intersection of classification schemes for both individuals and races seen as inferior (Baynton, 1997, p. 85).

This comparison led to the emergence of the eugenics movement to combat the threat to human progress by identifying and eliminating undesirable characteristics. Disability has represented a danger to progress and evolution and thus one of the greatest threats to the progress-defined "modern era" (Baynton, 1997, p. 84). In the late nineteenth century, progress was depicted as a phenomenon of increasing purity, where the world is rid of imperfection and "contaminants." Consequences of this view have included withholding life-saving surgical interventions from disabled infants (a practice referred to as "the Greater Surgery"—the surgery that cuts away the bad and leaves only the good, pure, sweet, and clean), "pure oralism" for the deaf, sterilization and eugenic euthanasia in the United States and mass killings of "defective" individuals in Germany (the first to die in Nazi Germany were people with disabilities) (Baynton, 1997, p. 85).

As the concept of never-ending progress has waned, so has the concept of normality lost some of its cultural potency. The rebellions of the 1960s against an oppressive conformity, sameness, and anonymity moved American culture away from the sense of normality as defined in the modern era. Indeed, the concept of normality has been the target of serious, sustained challenge in most areas of popular culture. In spite of changes, the ideology of normality, as applied to people with disabilities, is still represented as binary oppositions, with one side held as a universal norm and the other side as a deviation from that norm.

Challenges to the conceptualization of normality became a prominent feature early in the women's rights movement. Women were depicted as strong, capable, and upright, in contrast to weak, "degenerate" men who were identified as "idiots" or "lunatics" (Baynton, 1997, p. 86). The argument was then made that it was unconscionable to place women in the same category with those who were *justifiably* denied social and political rights. Obviously, these comparisons did nothing to challenge the assumptions about normality as applied to people with disabilities.

The successes of the women's movement, efforts to extend civil rights protections to people of color, and an emerging cadre of well-educated, assertive people with disabilities in the social environment of the 1960s, which encouraged tolerance and acceptance, provided a rich impetus for the emergence of a disability rights movement. This movement refutes the assumptions of the medically-oriented model, which classified, people with disabilities on the basis of functional limitations.

Disability Content in Social Work Education

The revised Educational Policy and Accreditation Standards (EPAS) of the Council on Social Work Education (CSWE) took effect on July 1, 2002. According to the standards, social work educators are to prepare students for work with persons with disabilities "without discrimination, with respect, and with knowledge and skills" (correspondence from CSWE to deans and directors of CSWE member programs on June 30, 2001, p. 6). Thus, along with age, class, color, culture, ethnicity, family structure, gender, marital status, national origin, race, religion, sex, and sexual orientation, disability must be a core issue in BSW and MSW degree programs throughout the United States. Social work educators need tools, such as the proposed text, to comply with these new standards.

Gilson and DePoy (2002) argue that viewing disability from a social constructionist perspective has more utility for social workers than the more traditional, deficit-oriented, diagnostic perspective. The implications for viewing disability from a social constructionist perspective are reflected in disability-related content in key elements of professional social work texts (p. 158, Table 1). The essential differences are the aperture through which disability is defined and the environment in which change is sought. In the diagnostic (medical) model, disability—and the related impairment—are an objective condition in the person with a disability. The constructionist perspective asserts that a disability-related impairment comes from the relationship of the person with a disability to the social environment. This perspective shifts intervention targets to the person with a disability and his or her environment and establishes shared "ownership" of the disability-related impairment. Consequently, interventions to remediate disability-related impairment must be shared and require accommodations in the individual with the disability *and* his or her environment. This stands in sharp contrast to the nominal position taken by the academy relative to the education of social workers regarding disability (Gilson & DePoy 2002), where the emphasis is on rehabilitation and mitigation.

The Council on Social Work Education's 1992 Curriculum Policy Statement and the 1994 *Handbook of Accreditation Standards and Procedures* are ambiguous regarding disability definition and content requirements (Gilson & DePoy 2002). Most commonly, disability is defined diagnostically so that persons with disabilities are aggregated in the "populations at risk" category. Thus, pedagogy, limited though it is, is confined to diversity content courses, already chock full of mandates and advocacy for including numerous discrete populations thought to be "at risk" as a consequence of their membership in identified "out" groups. A consequence of this reality is that disability content is irregular and education sometimes superficial. Some instructors report that there isn't enough time to "cover" the plethora of specifically identified populations in such diversity courses. The consequences include some sad confessions by diversity instructors, as reflected in the following account.

During a conversation between the first author and a diversity instructor, the instructor was lamenting the lack of interest by his graduate students in his diversity course. The course is among the last required prior to the completion of graduate studies. "They've had about all the diversity content they can stand," he opined. He then listed the topics and populations that had been the focus of his instruction during the term. Somewhat sheepishly, he apologized for "not getting around to disabilities" because there "just wasn't enough time." Interestingly, a student with blindness was enrolled in this section of the course. The instructor hastened to add, "I apologized to him, too."

It was as if confessing excused not teaching. In the absence of clear standards and consistent direction from the Council on Social Work Education, it is likely this sad scenario will play itself out in other CSWE-sanctioned programs. What's needed is leadership on this issue and support for instructors and students who strive for an understanding of disability and disability-related impairment that is consistent with social work's values and that facilitates effective intervention by social work practitioners at all levels.

Payne (1997) identified three views of social work: reflexive–therapeutic, socialist–collectivist, and individualist–reformist. The *reflexive–therapeutic* view sees social work as a reactive therapeutic response aimed at achieving "the best possible well-being for individuals, groups, and communities in society by promoting and facilitating growth and self-fulfillment" (p. 4). The *socialist–collectivist* view sees social work as seeking "cooperation and mutual support in society so that the most oppressed and disadvantaged people can gain power over their own lives" (p. 4). Finally, the *individualist–reformist* perspective sees social work as individually therapeutic as well as improving service delivery systems—"It meets the individuals' needs and improves services of which it is a part, so that social work and the services can operate more effectively" (p. 4).

Gilson and DePoy (2002) advocate for a combination of the diagnostic and constructionist viewpoints in disability content in social work education. "The knowledge, theory, and skills that would emerge from this complex, multifaceted, and contemporary treatment of disability would reflect social work's professional commitment to social justice and locate discussions of disability within the larger discourse on diversity" (p. 163). This would seem to place it within the socialist–collectivist view of social work in Payne's typology (1997).

Payne (1997) advanced the premise that social work itself is socially constructed. This construction includes creating the need for a social worker. Thus, social workers are defined by occupational expectations in encounters with clients. Social and political forces and perceptions about need shape the response to needs. The organization of services and agencies within the broader culture reflect legislative and popular sanction for social workers and their services. These definitions, based on occupational expectations, perceptions about needs and responses and the existence of services and agencies in the context of the broader culture, expose areas of actual or potential conflict (p. 16). In the area of disability, such conflicts, actual or potential, may center on the role of social workers in the lives of individual persons with disabilities.

Should the social worker strive for rather passive "acceptance" of the disability by the owner? To what extent do the worker's definition and understanding of disability influence what roles they enact? What is the social worker's obligation regarding client education and in broadening horizons regarding self-advocacy, empowerment, or self-actualization? What is the role for social work when social and political forces devalue or narrowly reframe needs and responses to needs? How does social work rise to the challenge when the consumers of our services are defined as "undeserving" and "unworthy" by the public? Finally, what should social work's position be when the definition of the "problem" of disability is narrowly crafted and leads to a one-dimensional response?

These questions suggest that social work is but a component in a network of related professions and occupations. Thus, our understanding of theories that explain and predict human behavior and our subsequent adoption of practice models and intervention strategies need to be seen as reflective of the assumptions and beliefs that we accept. Gilson and DePoy (2002) seem to suggest that, as it pertains to disability, many of the assumptions and beliefs we accept do not serve the broad, long-term interests of persons with disabilities. Acceptance of the medical model, especially when not critically examined, and assuming a diagnostic framework for understanding and intervening in disability, is limited and limiting.

Hiranandani (2002) has suggested that social work would be well served by a more critical perspective regarding disability. Relevant questions from this critical perspective include, "How are deficits of the body and mind interpreted and dealt with in different societies? How is an individual's identity as a person affected by the cultural connotations of disability? How do processes of cultural transitions shape local understanding of disability?" (p. 10). Definitions of disability constructed around measurements of functional limitations fail to address these cultural and contextual issues.

So, constructing and defining clients with disabilities as composites of impairments *caused* by their disabilities predicts a narrow, reflexive–therapeutic (Payne 1997) approach by the social worker. This linear depiction minimizes and suppresses the full range of possible social work responses. Conversely, defining *impairments* of clients as *caused* by the broader sociocultural construction of disability unleashes the inclusive, dynamic social system orientation that characterizes social work.

Discrimination Model

Pfeiffer (Chapter 2) has suggested that a new disability paradigm is necessary. He identified limitations in the traditional medical model for understanding disability and for policy formation. Similarly, Pfeiffer cited deficiencies in the social constructionist and oppressed minority models of disability. In the former, the "problem" is defined as judgments made about people with disabilities by those with no disabilities on the basis of a departure from normative expectations. In the case of the oppressed minority, the model is lacking because it does not explain the variation in experiences by persons with disabilities.

For example, one would be hard pressed to defend the assertion that Christopher Reeve (the contemporary U.S. actor, whose most prominent role was "Superman" in movies, and who is now a quadriplegic as a result of an accident) is oppressed. He has sufficient resources to ensure his life in the community, to continue his work—albeit in a different primary role—and to provide for his family. Neither the medical model, with its individualistic, deficit-oriented definition of disability and related impairment, nor the social constructionist model, with its "eye of the beholder" orientation, nor the oppressed minority model fully explains Reeve's experience. At various times, however, Reeve surely faces impairment in functioning and access that is related to his disability.

Pfeiffer (2000) suggests that disability exists where discrimination exists. As noted earlier, he opined, "In a flexible social system which fully accommodates a person with a disability, the disability disappears" (May & Raske, 2004). This model seems wanting also, however. It suggests that the experience of and with disability is mediated by the external environment. For example, would such a model suggest that a person with amputations is *not* disabled if they are in a "flexible social system which fully accommodates" them? If the answer is affirmative, how is this reconciled with the "disability pride" movement? Doesn't this model contain the major limitations of the constructionist model, to wit, relinquishing to others the matter of *defining* disability? Recent advocates have asserted that there is a disability culture (*Vital Signs*) and that membership in this culture is not anathema to feeling pride and a strong identity with this culture.

What is necessary is the construction of a theory that is responsive to the broad range of experiences of persons with disabilities. The challenge is to capture the disparate disability-related experiences, which range from abject deferential treatment and exploitation to empowerment and enlightenment. For example, see Cleland's (2000) description of the positive, transformative implications of his disability as he describes his adjustment to his very serious injuries in Vietnam. The construction of such a theory in social work seems best built on the foundation of methods, values, and philosophies that underpin the field of social work.

CONSTRUCTIONISM

Witkin (1990) describes constructionism as a theory that seeks to "elucidate the sociohistorical context and ongoing social dynamic of descriptions, explanations, and accountings of reality" (p. 38). Particular attention is devoted to the historical and cultural contexts of knowledge. Constructionists view theory and the dominant forms of understanding as shaped and limited by cultural assumptions, history, sociocultural mores and norms and language (Patterson, 1997).

From the constructionist perspective, language is a method for generating meaning and knowledge rather than a representation of an intrinsically objective "truth." The contemporary language and rhetoric of disability, with its individualistic portrayals of personal tragedy, then, suggest that disability and impairment exist independent of cultural, historical, or other contexts. Contrary to the dominant emphasis on cultural influences on human behavior in other arenas, social workers, as well as other professional helpers, seem to accept the intrinsic objective "realities" of disability and impairment, thereby overlooking environmental factors.

"Disability," from the constructionist perspective, is not a singular, concrete concept. There are cultural and individual differences in definition, evaluation, perception, and expression of "disability." Taxonomical expediency, rhetorical limitations, patterned, circular discourse, and an unwillingness to challenge disability "truths" perpetuate the antithesis of this reality.

For social workers operating from this "reality," their assessment of "problems," "solutions," "strengths," and "weaknesses," will be skewed, and ultimately serve to perpetuate the dominant, unchallenged medical depiction of disability. The burden for change will be borne disproportionately by the person with the disability, as he or she is made to conform to the expectations of others. "Failures" will be attributed to personal attributes (read "limitations"); the explicit expectation that success includes "overcoming" so-called "real" barriers will endure. The sad consequence for people with disabilities is the poor showing on quality-of-life standards (N.O.D./Harris Survey of Americans with Disabilities, 2000).

Understanding disability as a constructed phenomenon, rather than an intrinsic objective reality calls into question the assumptions that are the foundation of social work involvement with this population. Most of the knowledge in this area is from medicine. Medical concepts and perspectives are assimilated and operationalized. The Disability Discrimination Model provides a theoretical framework from which to rethink disability in empowering, positive, self-actualizing terms (as discussed in the case later in this chapter)—a perspective true to social work's heritage.

ASSESSMENT

Assessment is a key component in social work intervention. It both represents the biases of the examiner and directs the nature, focus, and methods of intervention. Over the past several years, attention has been focused on assessment as it is applied to persons with disabilities. The interest seems focused on identifying an alternative to the traditional medical model of assessment.

This model is a deficit-oriented, pathology-based, individualistic, static approach that is predicated on the assumption that the physical condition is an irrefutable objective reality. From this stance, the purpose of assessment is to define the disability as a departure from objective normative expectations. These variations are typically depicted as deficiencies or inadequacies. The intervention that is suggested by this assessment is remedial and corrective in nature. The deficit, having been identified, becomes the target for intervention and the person possessing the deficit is little more than the vessel containing the deficit. Intervention is narrow, deficit oriented, restorative, and administered by trained professionals, who are identified as possessing all necessary and helpful information. The role for client self-determination is minimized, as treatment professionals administer their "cures" of the identified deficits. Trieschmann (1980, p. 24) pointed out that in this model, behavior (B) is seen as ". . . a function of treatments to the organic variables (O) unless hindered by underlying personality problems" B = F(O x p) (Mackelprang & Salsgiver, 1999, p. 214).

In recent years, challenges to the medical model have emerged from a variety of theoretical perspectives (Barnes, Mercer, & Shakespeare, 1999; Pfeiffer, 2000; Handbook of Disability, 2001; Hahn 2000). These challenges have come from a variety of academic fields, including anthropology, political science, history, rhetoric, and disability studies. Unfortunately, social work and social workers have not been in the forefront of this charge.

The rethinking of the medical model and its implications should find a comfortable home in social work, with its commitment to the broad systems perspective, the focus on social and economic justice and a pervasive empowerment perspective for most other oppressed populations.

Social work's increasing clinical orientation and the fact that social work is rarely the primary profession in organizations and institutions employing social workers seem to conspire to suppress assertiveness and critical thought in the area of disability awareness and assessment. In this and other instances, the activist social work perspective is muted by the influence of more powerful medical-model driven professional perspectives and by the influence of funding sources that favor rehabilitation and mitigation-focused approaches.

An alternative, identified by Trieschmann (1980) (Mackelprang & Salsgiver, 1999, pp. 214–215), is a learning model. This model introduces the additional variables, or targets for evaluation, of the person and the environment, both largely absent in the medical model. In this model, *person variables* include personality style, coping mechanisms, and internal and external loci of control. *Organic variables* include age, health, and severity of disability. *Environmental variables* include family support, finances, and public policies. The assessment range is expanded to include the psychological and environmental variables, but the individual remains the primary focus of the assessment. The outcome of assessment from the learning model is the identification of knowledge deficits that the client needs to function independently. In this model, behavior (B) is seen as a function of the person (P), the organism (O), and the environment (E): $B = F(P \times O \times E)$. (Mackelprang & Salsgiver, 1999, p. 215).

Other models include the economic model (Condeluci, 1995), which emphasizes the inability of the person with the disability to earn a living (either because of the limitations of the disability or because of the limited expectations of the evaluators) and the minority group model (Hahn, 1991), which stresses a broader social versus individual approach, where social stigma is the major problem facing people with disabilities.

Marxist analysts view disability as a social problem that is directly linked to the changing mode of production. The mode of economic production influences other important institutions, such as political organizations, ideology, religion and culture: "the ideas of the ruling class are in every epoch the ruling ideas; that is, the class which is the 'ruling material force' of society, is at the same time its ruling intellectual force" (Marx & Engles, 1994, p. 15). From this perspective, the individualized and pathologized approach to disability is a consequence of the functional necessity for a workforce that is physically, intellectually, and emotionally able to serve the demands of industrialization. In short, standards more suited to machines were applied to people with disabilities. If the machine was determined to not serve the interests of production, it was judged to be of little or no use. In this model, modifying the mode of production is not considered. This is a very durable model that exists today, in spite of employers' insistence that they distinguish between fixed mechanical assets and human capital.

A more recent paradigm for assessment is the social model. In this model the roles in the traditional medical model are reversed. The person with the disability becomes the expert, while professionals occupy the role of responding to the needs or wishes of the person with the disability. This model does not presume that the knowledge or opinions of professionals are superior or that they trump the knowledge of the person with the disability. It is predicated on the assumption that the person with the disability is the expert in his or her own life.

The social model, more than most others, introduces the important role played by the environment. For example, from this perspective, wheelchair users are not "confined to the wheelchairs," but use wheelchairs because of environmental obstacles that impede their mobility. This model also emphasizes people's strengths and other assets, a refreshing departure from the deficit-oriented medical model. It also addresses the role of pervasive institutional oppression and devaluation to which people with disabilities have been subjected (Mackelprang & Salsgiver, 1999, p. 217).

Because of its expanded universe of elements for examination, and because it recognizes the knowledge and control of the person with the disability, the social model is offered as the preferred model for social workers (Mackelprang & Salsgiver, 1999, p. 218). While the social model does represent an improvement, a major deficiency is its emphasis on the responsibility of the person with the disability to correct identified barriers to inclusion and appropriate interdependence.

Assessment Using the Disability Discrimination Model

The Disability Discrimination Model demands an additional element in evaluation and remediation, which shifts the burden from the person with the disability to a shared responsibility between him or her and the socially constructed environment. Corrective actions are not the sole province and in the sole interest of the person with a disability. They are accepted as a beneficial consequence for all, including those *without* disabilities. In assessment from a Disability Discrimination Model perspective, behavior (B) is a function of the interaction of the person (P), the organic (O) (age, health, and severity of disability), and the environment (E), as expressed in ongoing interaction with society (S): $B = F(P \times O \times E)S$. Evaluation must include examination of social forces (versus personal forces) that mediate behavioral outcomes. The essential element is that the origin and maintenance of impairment is not singularly of interest to the person who is marginalized by such impairment, but it is understood to be a shared responsibility. Interventions must include a macro perspective.

ANALYSIS

Andrea was able to transition to the community and realize the U.S. middle-class dream of home ownership because she and her mother experienced an environment that was supportive of her and her atypical needs. This is what Gray (2002) referred to as "environmental receptivity." According to this perspective, a receptive environment supports participation by a person in the community with

CASE STUDY

BACKGROUND

Andrea is a thirty-seven-year-old female with multiple severe disabilities, including a grand mal seizure disorder since age three, profound mental retardation, and hyperactivity. Her siblings, a thirty-five-year-old brother with learning disabilities, and a thirty-year-old sister with no known disabilities, are settled into adult roles. Andrea's mother is a fifty-eight-year-old executive in a disability service organization. She and Andrea's father divorced nineteen years ago, as the number, severity, and extent of Andrea's physical conditions were becoming more apparent.

Andrea was institutionalized at a state-funded developmental center for the first time at age five. The principal purpose for the admission was because of her uncontrollable seizures, and the impact of family-provided home care. Andrea's brother was three at the time. Mother reports that there was little support for home care from the medical establishment or from the community.

At age ten, Andrea was removed from the developmental center by her family. They were dissatisfied with the level and quality of care there and Andrea was very unhappy there.

From age ten to twelve, Andrea was cared for in the family home. After two years, she was admitted to a private children's home at state expense. Medical professionals advised her parents to "forget about Andrea and take care of the family." There were few supports for Andrea while she was at home and for the family after she went to the children's home. While there, she attended school. She remained at this private children's home until she was eighteen, at which time her discharge was required, as the state would not fund additional services because of her age. She was then readmitted to the state developmental center from which she was previously removed by the family. She was discharged from the state developmental center in 1998 when the facility was closed by the state.

She moved to a rental home with two roommates from the state developmental center. The closure of the developmental center triggered access to a broad range of services and supports for former residents. Andrea's mother became aware of these community-based services, many of which had not existed earlier in Andrea's life, and still others of which were available but not known to the mother. Andrea now has a vagus nerve stimulator to mitigate the seizures. She still experiences daily seizures, but they are less severe than in the past.

Andrea was assisted in finding a residence in the community. She has a roommate who also has developmental disabilities. Andrea and the roommate maintain their own residence with assistance from a personal care attendant. Andrea's mother is her guardian. Andrea was recently approved for a mortgage and is in the process of buying a home near her mother. She and her roommate will live in their new home.

Over the years, what was initially a supportive network for Andrea's mother disintegrated. She lost her husband through divorce. The faith community of her church dismissed her because she would not heed the medical advice to "forget about Andrea" and concentrate on her other children. Similarly, the medical community abandoned the family and did not pursue or consider options other than palliative treatments predicated on low expectations of Andrea.

Mother is now committed to sharing her experiences with other families so that they will not have to repeat the heart-wrenching experiences she has had. The agency for which she works supports people with disabilities in the community by providing services consistent with a person-centered plan. Her guiding motto is, "The community just needs to understand that we're all just people and to be more accepting. We need to make all people part of the community."

disability labels. No demand was made on Andrea to relinquish her "disabled" label, nor was any expectation imposed that negated the pride she might experience in association with the label. She did not become nondisabled when she experienced an accommodating environment. What she experienced may be more appropriately thought of as her extrication from the limiting consequences of her previously socially constructed reality. She still has cognitive, behavioral, and physical characteristics that are departures from norms *and* she has a much better quality of life (read "reduced" or "eliminated impairment") because of a more hospitable environment as a direct consequence of a different construction of the consequences of her disabilities.

Components of such a receptive environment include the natural environment, which includes the physical surroundings, the climate, the weather, and built elements, including universal design. The receptive environment also includes human changes to the environment, such as modifications to the landscape, access accommodations, environmental controls for temperature, humidity, and so on. Human relationships, supports, and attitudes are another element in the Gray (2002) paradigm. This includes the understanding and support of the social environment. In Andrea's case, much of her support, including her father, the church, and the medical establishment, turned their backs on her and her mother.

Services, systems, and policies, the absence of which led to Andrea's institutionalization at various points in her life, are critical components of a receptive environment. Early in her life, the services that might have benefited Andrea were not available; nor were there systems or policies that challenged the "wisdom" of institutionalization for persons like her. Finally, products and technology need to be present in a receptive environment. In Andrea's case, such technological advances included the development of a more effective method for mitigating her seizures, which made it possible for her to achieve a level of independence that she must not have even imagined before. The synergy and complementarity suggested in this depiction of a receptive environment is apparent. All components must be present to constitute a receptive environment.

Andrea and her family experienced the influence of medical technology and linear thinking when they were offered advice relative to institutionalization. The advice, predicated on the apparently accepted premise that caring for Andrea at home would have a deleterious effect on the overall functioning of the family, in effect, created a self-fulfilling prophecy. Such advice did not include any good faith offer of support or assistance in caring for Andrea at home. The absence of such support, in the form of modifications to the environment, human support through relationships and attitudes, and services, systems, and policies, almost guaranteed that Andrea's family would not be successful. The absence of success then, became "proof" of the premises upon which the advice was built. The net effect for Andrea was spending the majority of her life in large institutional settings away from her family.

Community participation, on the other hand, is a complex construct with temporal, personal evaluation and receptive environment qualities. The temporal aspect includes the frequency of a person's engagement in a preferred activity and the amount of preparation time. Personal evaluation involves the importance, choice and satisfaction that the person attaches to the element of participation.

Applying this community participation construct to Andrea's life, one could surmise that, from a temporal perspective, she had little choice relative to frequency or preparation time for participation in the nominal community while she was institutionalized. Choices were made by others. Similarly, because Andrea exercised very little choice, the degree of importance and satisfaction that she derived from the choices made for her by others was negligible. Indeed, her mother reported that one of the agonizing elements of her institutional life was the family's realization that she was fundamentally unhappy and felt trapped in the institutional environments. The conclusion that the institutions did not, in any significant way, represent receptive environments seems inescapable.

CONCLUSION

From the Disability Discrimination Model perspective, then, the extent to which impairment is associated with disability is mediated by the quality of the interaction between the "disabled" person and the "nondisabled" person. Because of the low status and pejorative views of disability and the lack of socialization into the role, persons with disabilities often hold the same negative, stereotypic, and limiting expectations as the nondisabled. The Disability Discrimination Model necessitates challenging the hegemony of the medical model, while recognizing that it has its use in limited, mostly acute, applications.

In the areas of race and gender relations, the presence of an objective characteristic, such as skin color or gender, is not the primary predictor of the quality of life experience. Instead, it is the nature and quality of interaction with others. So, too with disability, the quality of life experience is mediated by interaction.

But in stark contrast to the areas of race and gender relations, where the possessors of the "atypical" characteristics—as defined by deviation from a white, middle-class male standard—are socialized to view their "difference" as nominal or as a source of pride, persons with disabilities, the vast majority of whom have adventitious disabilities, are socialized to view disability negatively, and not as a source of pride. In the former examples, the default view is either neutral or positive. For persons with disabilities, the default view is a deficit-defined negative. This reality blunts efforts to understand and depict disability as a source of pride by either the possessors of disabilities or the nondisabled.

Depictions of causality and explanations of impairment typically state or imply a direct, linear causality from the atypical characteristics to impairment. The presence of an atypical characteristic (disability) is thought to cause impairment. This paradigm influences policy, practice, leadership, quality of life, and opportunities for people with disabilities as well as for the nondisabled. It is the essence of primary prevention campaigns and policy and practice initiatives.

The effort by professionals is to mitigate the atypical characteristics rather than focus on the broader implications of the quality of understanding and interaction between the disabled and nondisabled, where a major obstacle to be overcome initially is the negative, stereotypic and limiting expectations of the nondisabled. Persons with disabilities, who are the focus of interventions because of their low status, become the targets for corrective actions to improve their lives, when attention should be focused on the role of the nondisabled.

Ironically, this approach, that may be termed "benevolent victim blaming," serves to reinforce and perpetuate the very dynamic which, the Disability Discrimination Model asserts, causes poor comparisons on quality-of-life standards for persons with disabilities. By focusing policy, practice, research, and structural and representational interventions on the qualities possessed by the person with the disability, attention is diverted not only from the quality of the interaction between the disabled and the nondisabled, but also from the responsibility to contribute to corrective efforts by the nondisabled. The result is the reinforcement of the simple, linear paradigm that predicts outcome from the presence of a disability. This reinforcement predicts that subsequent attempts at corrective action will substantially resemble previous ones. That this predictive model is wanting is substantiated by the consistently poor comparisons of people with disabilities with the nondisabled on objective measures of quality of life in the United States (Harris Survey, 2000).

REFERENCES

Albrecht, G. L., Seelman, K. D., & Bury, M. (2001). *Handbook of Disability Studies*. Thousand Oaks, CA: Sage Publications.

Allison, C. E. (1999). Disability as diversity: A sociolinguistic construct for the new millennium. *Reflections, 5*(4), 47–51.

Barnes, C., Mercer, G., & Shakespeare, T. (1999). Exploring disability: A sociological introduction. Malden, MA: Blackwell.

Baynton, D. C. (1997, Spring). Disability. A useful category of historical analysis. *Disability Studies Quarterly, 17*(2).

Brooks, N. A. (1991). Self-empowerment among adults with severe physical disability: A case study. *Journal of Sociology & Social Welfare, 18*(1), 105–120.

Brown, C., & Ringma, C. (1989). The myth of consumer participation in disability services: Some issues for social workers. *Australian Social Work, 42*(4), 35–40.

Brzuzy, S. (1997). Deconstructing disability: The impact of definition. *Journal of Poverty, 1*(1), 81–91.

Bucaro, T., & Kapfstein, R. (1999). Coming out: Claiming disability in and out of the classroom. *Reflections, 5*(1), 71–81.

Cleland, M. (2000). *Strong at the Broken Places: A Personal Story*. Longstreet Press.

Condeluci, A. (1995). *Interdependence: The route to community* (2nd ed.). Winter Park, FL: GR Press.

Cummerton, J. M. (1986). A feminist perspective on research: What does it help us see? In N. Van Den Bergh & L. B. Cooper (eds.). *Feminist visions for social work.*

Daly, M. (1973). *Beyond God the Father*. Boston: Beacon Press.

Epi-Hab (1998). Evansville, IN: Epi-Hab Brochure.

Felske, A. W. (1994). Knowing about knowing: Margin notes on disability research. In M. H. Rioux & M. Bach (Eds.). *Disability is not measles*. North York, Ontario: L'Institut Roeher, 181–194.

Fisk, D., Rowe, M., Brooks, R., and Gildersleeve, D. (2000). Integrating consumer staff members into a homeless outreach project: Critical issues and strategies. *Psychiatric Rehabilitation Journal, 23*(3), 244–252.

Fraser, N., & Gordon, L. (1994). A genealogy of dependency: Tracing a keyword of the U.S. welfare state. *Signs: Journal of Women in Culture and Society, 19*(2), 309–336.

Gilson, S. F., DePoy, E. (2002, Winter). Theoretical approaches to disability content in social work education. *Journal of Social Work Education, 38,* (1).

Goodley, D., & Moore, M. (2000). Doing disability research: Activist lives and the academy. *Disability & Society, 15*(6), 861–882.

Gray, D. B. (2002). "Assistive technology: Enhancing participation through new research and changing old policy" [PowerPoint presentation]. Society for Disability Studies, Oakland, CA.

Hahn, H. (1991). "Alternative views of empowerment: Social services and civil rights" [Editorial]. *The Journal of Rehabilitation, 57*(4), 17(3).

Hahn, H. (2000). "Accommodations and the ADA: Biased reasoning or unreasonable bias?" *Berkeley Journal of Employment and Labor Law, 21*(1), 166–192.

Hiranandani, V. S., (2002). "Rethinking disability in social work: Interdisciplinary perspectives." Manuscript submitted for publication. *Social Work.*

James, P., & Thomas, M. (1996). Deconstructing a disabling environment in social work education. *Social Work Education, 15*(1), 34–45.

Kosciulek, J. F. (1999). The consumer-directed theory of empowerment. *Rehabilitation Counseling Bulletin, 42*(3), 196–213.

Linton, S. (1998). *Claiming disability.* New York: York University Press.

Mackelprang, R., & Salsgiver, R. (1999). *Disability: A diversity model approach in human service practice.* New York: Brooks/Cole.

Marx, K., & Engles, F. (1994). *History as class struggle.* Excerpts reprinted in R. Collins (Ed.), *Four sociological traditions.* New York: Oxford University Press.

May, G. E., Raske, M. B., Eds. (2004). *Ending disability discrimination: Strategies for social workers.* Boston: Allyn & Bacon.

Merrick, L. (1994). The disability triage: Denial, marginalization, and legislation. *Journal of Religion in Disability & Rehabilitation, 1*(1), 39–45.

Morris, J. (1991). *Pride against prejudice.* Philadelphia: New Society Publishers.

Moxley, D. (1992). Disability policy and social work practice. *Health and Social Work, 17*(2), 99–103.

National Organization on Disability (2000). N.O.D./Harris Survey of Americans with Disabilities. Washington, DC.

Patterson, K. A., (1997). *Representations of disability in mid twentieth-century southern fiction: From metaphor to social construction.* Doctoral Dissertation, University of California, Santa Barbara. *Dissertation Abstracts International, 38,* PS 261.

Payne, M. (1997). *Modern Social Work Theory* (2nd ed.). Chicago: Lyceum Books.

Pfeiffer, D. (2000, Fall). The disability paradigm, (Invited guest reaction paper.) *Journal of Disability Policy Studies, 11*(2).

Ringma, C., & Brown, C. (1991). Hermeneutics and the social sciences: An evaluation of the function of hermeneutics in a consumer disability study. *Journal of Sociology & Social Welfare, 18*(3), 57–73.

Snyder, S., & Mitchell, D. (Directors). 1996. *Vital Signs: Crip culture talks back* [Video]. Marquette, MI: Brace Yourself Productions.

Thapar, N., & Bhardwaj, S. M. (1999). Overcoming the tyranny of space: Experiences of multiple sclerosis patients. *Reflections, 5*(4), 64–70.

Trieschmann, R. B. (1980). *Spinal cord injuries: Psychosocial, social, and vocational adjustment.* New York: Pergamon.

U. S. Department of Commerce, Census Bureau, (1997). *Current population reports: Household economic studies; Americans with disabilities: 1994–1995.* U. S. Department of Commerce, Washington, DC.

Ward, M. J., & Meyer, R. N. (1999). Self-determination for people with developmental disabilities and autism: Two self-advocates' perspectives. *Focus on Autism and Other Developmental Disabilities, 14*(3), 133–139.

Witkin, S. L. (1990). The implications of social constructionism for social work education. *Journal on Teaching in Social Work, 4,* 37–48.

Zola, I. K. (1989). Toward the necessary universalizing of a disability policy. *The Milbank Quarterly, 67*(2), 401–428.

CHAPTER 6

THE DISABILITY DISCRIMINATION MODEL IN SOCIAL WORK PRACTICE

MARTHA RASKE

INTRODUCTION

In recent years social workers and others have recognized the limitations of the medical model in work with persons with disabilities (Brzuzy, 1997; Mackelprang & Salsgiver, 1996; Pfeiffer, 2000). Theoretical perspectives have emerged to bolster practice to guide the work needed to change people's lives (Allison, 1999; Payne, 1991, 1997; Simpson, 1995; Turner, 1996). Concepts such as the strength perspective, empowerment, and resiliency have been among the most useful (Burack-Weiss, 1991). Although each has played a key role in work with persons with disabilities, no theories or perspectives have the transformational power to alter societal and individual views about disability and whether or not impairment has any relationship to disability. None have incorporated the notion that disability must be redefined to sever its socially constructed link with functional impairment and subsequently, with discrimination. Pfeiffer said, "In a flexible social system which fully accommodates a person with a disability, the disability disappears" (2001). Social work lacks a conceptual model to show practitioners that even when impairment persists, disability could, given a flexible, inclusionary social system and physical environment, disappear. In this chapter, the Disability Discrimination Model is utilized as the framework in which the strengths perspective, empowerment, resiliency, and the medical model are blended to support individual, relationship, and societal change in the hopes that social work can play a role in creating that more flexible social system.

As Hayashi stated in Chapter 3, social workers are often seen not as advocates and champions of self-determination for persons with disabilities, but as "those who try to control or restrict their lives." Why, she asked, are theories of empowerment not transferable to social work practice? In part the answer to this question lies in the nature of the social work culture. One reason is that formal and informal practice activities, rules, and regulations constrain social workers to act as agents of social control (Payne, 1997). Rules that regulate placement of clients in various levels of residential services typically require differing sets of functional limitations. How often does a worker tell a client seeking services, "I wish I could help, but my hands are tied." When clients reject the restricted menu of service options that agencies provide, clients are often described as uncooperative or noncompliant (Pfeiffer, 2000). Once social workers internalize institutional rules and regulations they become agency-centered rather than client-centered. Thus, the challenge for any model that seeks to transform disability practice is to create an agency culture that focuses more attention on diagnosing and treating oppressive agency practices than diagnosing the problems and deficiencies of clients. Because such a cultural change will require social workers to think differently about every aspect of their daily work, transformational concepts that are already widely accepted form the framework for the Disability Discrimination Model of practice.

A FRAMEWORK OF TRANSFORMATIONAL THEORIES AND PERSPECTIVES

Practice based on the Disability Discrimination Model blends theoretical perspectives. The strengths perspective, empowerment theory, and the resilience model have demonstrated efficacy in work with social work client groups, including people with disabilities (Cook, Cook, Tran, & Tu, 1997; Fisk, Rowe, Brooks & Gildersleeve, 2000; Gilson, Bricout, & Baskind, 1998; Lee, 1996; Rapp, 1998; Saleebey, 1997; Thapar & Bhardwaj, 1999; Turner, 1996).

The strengths perspective is the lynchpin for transforming daily social work practice. Strengths include talents, capacities, knowledge, and resources. This perspective assumes that strengths are present in all individuals and communities. The strength's perspective was developed at a time when "our culture was obsessed with and fascinated by psychopathology, victimization, abnormality, and moral and interpersonal aberrations" (Saleebey, 1997, p. 4). The perspective has been applied to persons with substance abuse, older adults, persons with serious mental illness, and schools. Rapp (1998) applied the strengths perspective to case management with persons with serious mental illness and then proposed and tested a theory of strengths. The aim of social work practice, then, is to help clients discover and use their strengths to create more satisfying lives. Interaction with clients, however, is more than simply developing a list of strengths and attributes.

The relationship between social worker and client focuses on learning what the client wants. It is about helping clients change in ways that match "their hopes and aspirations" (Saleebey, 1997, p. 17). Partnership is emphasized as client and social worker discuss the client's view of life, discover how the client has learned to deal with challenges, and frame a working relationship with hope and change.

Using the strengths perspective, disability is viewed as an opportunity for growth as well as a source of impairment. Practice with peoples with disabilities focuses service assessment, planning, and delivery on abilities instead of disabilities and related impairments. In most settings diagnosis is a requirement of the intake process. However, in these cases social work encounters with clients should begin by focusing on the client's strengths, hopes and aspirations.

Based primarily on the work of Solomon (1976), social work embraced empowerment theory as a framework to ensure that practice helps clients achieve control over their own lives. "Empowerment refers to a process whereby persons who belong to a stigmatized social category throughout their lives can be assisted to develop and increase skills in the exercise of interpersonal influence and the performance of valued social roles" (1976, p. 6). This model stresses the need to deal with power imbalances in each person, in interpersonal relationships, and in society. Designed for social work in oppressed communities, particularly as related to racial inequality, empowerment theory has been extended to fit all forms of powerlessness including the oppression and discrimination experienced by persons with disabilities (Brooks, 1991; Kosciulek, 1999; Simon, 1994; Ward & Meyer, 1999). Empowerment theory places expert knowledge in the hands of those who experience oppression and discrimination. Personal and social changes are equal partners.

The resiliency model contributes to practice with persons with disabilities by highlighting individuals and families who have overcome societal and personal barriers in spite of trauma, oppression, and discrimination (Bernard, 1991; Wolen & Wolen, 1993). People with disabilities may be viewed as survivors who overcame adversity. Social work practice focuses attention on points of survival, victory, and success instead of limitations and impairments.

The strengths, empowerment, and resilience perspectives are transformational in nature. All are built on the assumption that to affect change, client experiences, assets, choices, and leadership comes first. Each perspective builds upon the insights of the others. The strengths perspective extends empowerment to arm clients with the power of their talents and accomplishments. The resilience model makes strength out of adversity by changing victimization into survival.

In addition to the transformational perspectives, the practice application of the Disability Discrimination Model incorporates the traditional medical model. Clearly, the medical model cannot be viewed as a transformational perspective. It is instead widely considered to be one component of current practice that oppresses and marginalizes persons with disabilities. In other chapters of this text the authors have argued that the medical model is the basis of many acts of discrimination. However, in spite of the oppressive nature of some of its practices, the medical model remains central to planning, delivering, and reimbursing disability services. No population, including persons with disabilities, should be denied access to medically based services, such as prosthetics or post-injury medical interventions that repair damaged bodies. Social workers must continue to advocate for essential medical services. Because social workers are ethically obligated to work with their clients to secure all needed services and resources, and many social workers are employed by agencies that adhere to the medical model, it is neither ethical nor practical to present a practice chapter that excludes it. The reality of practice today is that essential resources are embedded in a medically oriented delivery system. If practitioners are forced to give up the medical model in order to embrace transformational theories, they risk the loss of assets beneficial to clients with disabilities.

The medical model, based on the logic of the scientific method, brings clarity and focus to the assessment and treatment of disease. Using a set of rigorously defined and standardized concepts, medical diagnosis hypothesizes the causal connection between symptom and disease. Signs and symptoms include sleep, appetite, lab results, physical examination, observations made while the patient is engaged in activities, and patient complaints. Standardized treatment protocols are based on each patient's observed and reported signs and symptoms. The aim of treatment is to eliminate or reduce symptoms. In some cases medical science has traced the cause of symptoms and developed ways to eliminate disease. The polio vaccine is one example. Because the diagnostician is dealing with thousands of diseases listed in the international classification system for medical disorders, the main task is to settle on the disease or disorder that fits each client's particular cluster of signs and symptoms. The complexity of this diagnostic task, combined with the invasive and dangerous nature of many medical treatments, forces the diagnostician to focus attention on accurate identification of the patient's disease process. It is little wonder that strengths, talents, and skills get little attention. By participation in services that provide persons with disabilities with vitally important medical care, social workers operate in a system that encourages attention to pathology to the exclusion of strengths, power, and resiliency. In creating a model for transforming social work practice, one cannot ignore the contradictions and inconsistencies experienced in the practice community, including the fact that social workers are compelled to structure services to fit the medical model.

The Disability Discrimination Model establishes a socially constructed view of disability-related impairment that sets the framework in which the medical model, the strengths perspective, empowerment, and resiliency can be blended to set the stage for individual, relationship, and societal change for persons with disabilities. For such a blend to have transformational power, specific strategies and techniques are needed. The social work practice strategies outlined in this chapter show how this blended model transforms daily practice for social work with people with disabilities.

Four assumptions underlie the new practice strategies introduced in this chapter:

1. The practice of discrimination related to disabilities makes the distinction between disability-related impairment and disability. Discrimination occurs in the routine, daily interactions between people with disabilities and the relationships and environments in which they live. Thus, intervention strategies must call into question daily events and routine practices that may be

acts of discrimination and oppression that go unnoticed. It is daily work that must be scrutinized and transformed.

2. Disability and related impairment is an individual, relational, and societal problem. Therefore, intervention strategies must be aimed at change in all three levels of the system. Individual work may include identifying and bolstering strengths and talents as well as securing medical or rehabilitation interventions to address pain or disease. Relational work may include securing, strengthening, or modifying important relationships, including work that alters the way social workers and agencies relate to persons with disabilities. Societal work includes changing organizations, communities, and policies to eliminate stigma and marginalizing social policies. In all settings in which social workers engage in work for and with persons with disabilities, all three systems levels are included as targets for change.

3. The key interventions that will have the most lasting impact are those that target oppression and discrimination as experienced by each individual. Discrimination and oppression affect the lives of each person labeled disabled. Thus, no individual treatment plan or organization policies can exclude assessments and interventions that remedy discrimination.

4. The practice of discrimination against a person with a disability takes place within social service organizations in which social work practice occurs, including the unwitting attitudes and behaviors of social work administrators, supervisors, and practitioners. Thus the targets of change include social workers who work for and with people with disabilities and the organizations that provide disability services.

DISABILITY DISCRIMINATION MODEL APPLIED TO SOCIAL WORK PRACTICE

The Disability Discrimination Model's guiding principle is that impairment related to disability is socially constructed (see Chapter 5 for a detailed explanation of the Disability Discrimination Model). Disability is not a physical or mental limitation, but a set of beliefs shared by a society and supported by policies and professional practices so that differences in physical and biological construction are redefined as limiting or excluding. Thus, people with disabilities are placed outside the "norms" of society and the meaning attached to normalcy constitutes the basis of exclusion and discrimination.

According to the Disability Discrimination Model, specialized social services, such as group homes and special education, define and perpetuate the discrimination and oppression of persons with disabilities. In order to apply discrimination theory to social work practice, intervention strategies must be reorganized so that persons with disabilities can take charge of defining, organizing, and challenging the terms and conditions of disability and impairment.

Practice based on the Disability Discrimination Model, however, is not designed to supplant existing theories or intervention models that help reduce or remove pain or impairments that may be associated with disability. The Disability Discrimination Model acknowledges that social workers, supervisors, and administrators in disability organizations must adapt any new practice strategies to fit current policies and procedures. Social workers who use the medical perspective focus attention on client limitations and pathology. Yet impairment may be associated with disability, and the nature of the impairment must be examined to establish and deal with any resulting limitations or challenges. It would be remiss to advocate a model of practice that ignores this aspect of a client's life and refuse to utilize a model of practice, namely the medical model, which was specifically designed to deal with impairment and disease. Further, it is hoped that social workers, who believe their livelihood and their client's well-being hinges on embracing the medical model, will be more likely to adopt some of the Disability Discrimination Model's new practice strategies because they can see how the transformational model can join the traditional medical model. Admittedly, the strategies derived from this unlikely combination of transformational and traditional perspectives are likely to be incremental in nature. While this may be viewed by some as a weakness of the Disability Discrimination Model, it is an attempt to create change within the existing system of social work practice.

Practice Strategies

Putting forth a transformational model lays the groundwork to change disability services, but it fails to provide the road map needed to negotiate a practice world embedded with subtle forms of oppression and discrimination. Practitioners will face many challenges. Service providers, like everyone else, are socialized into a world that pities disability and categorizes persons with disabilities. Then, as if that was not enough, we are socialized to our professions to carry out procedures that institutionalize oppression and discrimination (Payne, 1997). During training we are given a new language, new theories, and codes of conduct that define how we are to act with our clients and with each other. Our language includes terms like "patient," "client," "consumer," or "participant." In any case, whatever we call people with disabilities, we have defined them as different from ourselves.

Additional barriers to change are constructs that shape what organizations do to help people with disabilities. Diagnostic procedures make us search for disability, disorder, and disease. Lengthy intake forms insure that the initial assessment considers every possible diagnostic category or disease. Using checklists and an international diagnostic coding system, service providers worldwide share a common language. However, the laborsaving, scientifically validated instruments leave little room to note individual distinctions or talents. In this case, what we do not look for, namely ability, order, and well-being, we eventually do not see. What we do not document, we eventually do not remember. The focus of our attention becomes the focus of the client's attention. If we fail to see and remember client abilities and well-being, it is not surprising that the client eventually identifies with the limitations said to be caused by the disability.

Because of scarce economic resources, we limit ourselves to a fairly standard menu of treatment options. We can order certain types of therapy sessions, offer specific types of housing, and pay for limited types of training or employment options. Modern technology can give us preset treatments that are linked to predetermined outcomes.

And finally, we are pressed for time. As resources diminish and work loads increase, there is little time in the workday to reflect, little time to be creative, and little time to develop innovative treatment plans. Therefore, the Disability Discrimination Model must be linked to daily social work behaviors by embedding transformational strategies in everyday work tasks.

The Disability Discrimination Model transforms daily work by: (1) providing a discrimination framework to blend all relevant theoretical perspectives; (2) encouraging flexibility in worker/client roles, including role reversal; (3) expanding collaborative partnerships to include advocates and critics beyond client family and friends and organizational staff; (4) setting an intervention triad that includes individual, relationship, and societal targets for all clients in all organizations, and (5) providing cultural and clinical supervision for practitioners, supervisors, and administrators to address issues of oppression and discrimination in addition to clinical services.

BLENDED PERSPECTIVES

Work under the umbrella of the Disability Discrimination Model blends perspectives. It is not exclusive, but inclusive. Most particularly, it is inclusive of the strengths perspective, empowerment, resilience, and the medical model. In blended perspectives all other theories are inside, blended with, and supportive of ending discrimination. The strengths perspective helps focus service delivery on abilities, not limitations. The empowerment model stresses the need to address power imbalance in each person and in society. Resilience locates those attributes that any of us possess that help us overcome adversity. The medical model provides access to traditional medical and rehabilitative care.

Table 6.1 summarizes the contribution of each perspective, and the following case illustrates how the perspectives are blended in practice.

CASE STUDY 1

BACKGROUND
Jeff is thirty-five years old. Diagnosed with cerebral palsy as a child, he was raised in a mid-sized town where he received speech, and physical and occupational therapies at the local rehabilitation agency and attended regular classes in the public school. With support from his family, Jeff graduated from a nearby public university with a major in political science. An extensive job search resulted in one offer as a full-time data-entry clerk for the local

continued

rehabilitation agency. He was advised that his speech and mobility impairments limited his career choices.

At the time Jeff met with the social worker he was living at home with his parents and remained at the data-entry job he had accepted twelve years earlier. "I'm here because I want to try living on my own," he said.

INTERVENTION

Using blended perspectives the social workers *began* by focusing the discussion on Jeff's accomplishments and resources, which include effectively managing a regular classroom education in the public schools, using a wheelchair to enhance his mobility, using public transportation throughout his university education, and learning to communicate his needs and assignments even though others were not equipped to cope with his speech. Then, Jeff described his desire to live independently and advance to a job with more responsibility and authority. Jeff and the social worker talked about the challenges he felt might be blocking the achievement of his aspirations, such as his parents' concerns the he would be in danger if they were not nearby, his employer's apparent belief that his speech and mobility impairments would interfere with more challenging work assignments, and the community's lack of identified accessible housing.

SUMMARY

Noting Jeff's survival skills the social worker asked him to describe how he had coped with the challenges of school, work, and family. The social worker invited Jeff to join an independent-living advocacy group led by persons with disabilities and health-care professionals. Before the meeting ended, the worker completed the biopsychosocial assessment using the standard agency form.

TABLE 6.1   BLENDED THEORIES IN DISABILITY PRACTICE

MODEL	KEY CONCEPTS	BASIC PRINCIPLES	PRACTICE STRATEGIES
Strengths Perspective	Hope Transformation	1. People/communities have capacities, talents, and resources. 2. Trauma/impairment viewed as potential opportunities/challenges.	1. Strengths first in assessment. 2. Client dreams documented.
Empowerment	Oppression Power	1. People are experts regarding their own conditions. 2. Problems are located in the structure of society/organizations. 3. Focus of attention on oppression & marginalized groups.	1. Collaborative problem solving. 2. Consciousness raising. 3. Targets of change = individuals & society. 4. Group work.

TABLE 6.1   Blended Theories in Disability Practice *(Cont.)*

MODEL	KEY CONCEPTS	BASIC PRINCIPLES	PRACTICE STRATEGIES
Resiliency	Survival	1. People with disabilities have found ways to master their own life experiences. 2. Focus on client survival techniques.	1. Make resiliency part of client's self-concept. 2. Reframe negative into pride of survival.
Disability Discrimination Model	Discrimination Impairment	1. Disability is socially constructed. 2. Disability is a diverse experience.	1. Develop receptive environments. 2. End discrimination. 3. Focus on pride/accomplishment.
Medical Model	Diagnosis Scientific Method	1. Medical care is part of holistic services. 2. Systematic review of signs and symptoms shape diagnosis and treatment.	1. Assess and treat for acute care needs. 2. Differential diagnosis and prescribed treatment protocols.

Flexible and Interchangeable Roles

The second way in which the Disability Discrimination Model transforms daily work with persons with disabilities is the creation of flexible and interchangeable roles. The social worker may act as advocate, case manager, counselor, guide, and then shift or switch roles with the client, or a family member. Then, at another time, roles may shift again—all aimed at achieving a partnership that recognizes that at different times each person has different strengths and needs. The following case example illustrates flexible and interchangeable roles.

CASE STUDY 2

BACKGROUND

Jamie is eleven years old. Diagnosed with Down syndrome, she is a special education student in a large metropolitan public school. At the time Jamie visited the social worker she had entered the fifth grade. "I want to be a ballerina and they won't let me take dance lessons," she said. Jamie's mother explains that she had not been able to find an instructor who would include Jamie in regular dance classes. Jamie had begun to act out her frustration by disrupting her classroom at school.

continued

INTERVENTION

Using flexible and interchangeable roles, the social worker began in the counselor role. The worker listened and responded empathically as Jamie and her mother described details of their search for a dance class, and verbalized their feelings of anger, frustration, and sadness. The worker described personal experiences in advocating for new programs and offered to provide guidance in locating additional resources. Jamie, her mother, and the social worker talked about expanding the search for dance instruction.

SUMMARY

The social worker learned about a dance troop in a nearby city organized for students with developmental disabilities. The social worker located phone numbers and addresses and asked Jamie and her mother if they would be willing to interview the director and one of the students to learn about how the troop was organized. Jamie and her mother visited the troop and took pictures of rehearsals and a performance. With help from her mother and the social worker, Jamie took on the role of advocate and prepared a presentation for local dance instructors and school officials to spark their interest in forming a dance troop in her city.

Expanded Partnerships

The third way daily work is transformed is in expanded partnerships that emphasize egalitarian relationships with persons with disabilities and traditional service providers. Other partners include families, friends, housing providers, political figures, or any other persons identified as important to helping the person lead a satisfying life.

CASE STUDY 3

BACKGROUND

Brian is twenty-six years old. He has been diagnosed with a developmental disability and has been living in a residential group home for five years. Aquariums and tropical fish fascinate him. During his annual care conference, attended by the case manager, residential staff, teachers, family, and the social worker, one of the residential staff commented about Brian's interest in tropical fish. Brian affirms his interest as he laughs and smiles at the mention of tropical fish.

INTERVENTION

Using expanded partnerships, the social worker offered to lead a group that would find a way to bring an aquarium into Brian's life. The group, which included Brian, his sister, the case manager, a residential staff member, and the agency safety officer, met to discuss and agree on safety and care issues related to placing an aquarium in Brian's residential facility. The group discussed additional partners needed to make the aquarium a success.

continued

SUMMARY

Later the social worker contacted an acquaintance who collected tropical fish. Together they recruited several aquarium owners, including a deputy in the mayor's office, who were willing to take Brian along on shopping trips to pet shops and help him begin to stock his own aquarium.

THE INTERVENTION TRIAD: INDIVIDUAL, RELATIONAL, COMMUNITY

Daily work will be expanded to three arenas of intervention: work with the individual client, work on the client's relationships, and work in the client's community. The model ignores the traditional and false dichotomy between clinical work and community work. In other words, in addition to utilizing standard assessment and diagnostic procedures, workers must use the strengths model and resiliency to go beyond clinical syndromes and use the Disability Discrimination Model to break down the isolation and social stereotypes experienced by many persons with disabilities. Work will include interventions that target individual and community change and will include open discussions of oppression and bias.

CASE STUDY 4

BACKGROUND

Willa is sixty-two years old. She is diagnosed with spina bifida and major depressive disorder. Willa has lived in a nursing home since her parents died fifteen years ago. Because there are many days she remained in bed or in her room, her primary contacts were with her roommate, who did not speak to her or the aides who brought medication, meals, and assist with showering and dressing. She did not participate in the nursing home's social and activity programs. Prior to living in the nursing home, Willa attended church, went shopping, and belonged to several community service organizations. At the first meeting with the social worker Willa stated she hated the nursing home and the other residents, and wanted out.

INTERVENTION

Using the intervention triad, the social worker began with a review of Willa's symptoms and medical treatments, including her symptoms of depression. Willa and the worker discussed how the nursing home handled her mobility strengths and limitations. They talked about Willa's accomplishments while living in the community and the impact of her parents' deaths. Willa described her sense of isolation and hopelessness.

SUMMARY

In addition to talking with Willa about depression, social isolation, and loss, the social worker invited Willa to accompany her out for lunch and a visit to a nearby shopping center. With

continued

Willa's permission the social worker contacted the community service organizations to which she formerly belonged. The social worker spoke to the organizations about conditions in the nursing home and challenged the organizations to find ways to support and encourage memberships among the home's residents. Then, the social worker arranged meetings with community service organization leaders and nursing-home staff. She kept Willa informed and invited her to attend and participate in each meeting. As Willa expressed interest, the social worker helped her attend community service organization meetings and events.

CULTURAL AND CLINICAL SUPERVISION

The key to transforming daily practice is to maintain the focus on the Disability Discrimination Model's framework and make sure that social work practice is self-reflective. Supervision provides for reflective practice. Clinical supervision provides workers with opportunities to think critically about engaging clients in services and helps them evaluate all the processes of daily practice with people with disabilities, from assessment and diagnosis through intervention and evaluation.

Cultural supervision is equally important. If we seek change, we operate outside accepted practices and expose ourselves to criticism and condemnation. Workers, supervisors, and administrators will need support and opportunities for their own consciousness raising in order to see how discrimination affects us all. Cultural supervision is a group technique that invites workers to share observations and insights about the experience of being agents of social change. In a nonjudgmental atmosphere workers will need to expose their fears, yet challenge each other's biases.

Supervisors and social workers need tools to help them expand their thinking about clinical work so that issues of discrimination as well as individual client strengths remain central to case planning. To assist with this process, Table 6.2 shows the Guide to Developing Disability Discrimination Model Service Plans. The guide offers a checklist that will help the treatment planner document community, relational, and individual barriers to goal attainment. The guide reinforces the need for clinical social workers to target community attitudes and barriers (economic, architectural, sensory, cognitive) as well as client challenges (impairments due to diagnosis, relationship issues, perceived personal barriers), and client strengths (pride in disability, personal strengths, relationship strengths). Community economic barriers mean lack of resources to help clients meet their goals. Architectural barriers mean lack of access to community structures. Sensory barriers mean lack of sensory options to assist persons with visual or auditory disabilities. Cognitive barriers mean a lack of alternative guidelines to assist persons with cognitive impairments. The Guide to Service Plan will help supervisors and social workers consider targets and strategies for changing community, relationship, and individual barriers, as well as assign leadership roles (change agents) to various members of the team, including the client, the family, and persons in the community.

TABLE 6.2   GUIDE TO DEVELOPING DISABILITY DISCRIMINATION MODEL SERVICE PLANS

TARGETS OF CHANGE (CIRCLE ALL THAT APPLY)	CHANGE STRATEGIES	CHANGE AGENT ASSIGNED BY TEAM	PROJECTED OUTCOMES	FIELD NOTES & OBSERVATIONS
Community Barriers:				
a. Attitudinal				
b. Architectural				
c. Sensory				
d. Cognitive				
e. Economic				
Community Capacities:				
a. Attitudinal				
b. Architectural				
c. Sensory				
d. Cognitive				
e. Economic				
Relationship Barriers:				
Relationship Capacities:				
Individual Barriers:				
Individual Capacities:				

CONCLUSION

Practice breathes life into theory. When social work fully engages blended perspectives, flexible roles, expanded partnerships, the Intervention Triad, and cultural supervision in daily practice we can test the power and potential of thousands of social workers and clients engaged in interventions for social change. Research will be needed to examine the impact of this transformational model on social work practice and persons with disabilities.

REFERENCES

Allison, C. E. (1999). Disability as diversity: A sociolinguistic construct for the new millennium. *Reflections, 5*(4), 47–51.

Bernard, B. (1991). *Fostering resiliency in kids: Protective factors in the family, school, and community.* San Francisco: Western Regional Center.

Brooks, N. A. (1991). Self-empowerment among adults with severe physical disability: A case study. *Journal of Sociology & Social Welfare, 18*(1), 105–120.

Brzuzy, S. (1997). Deconstructing disability: The impact on definition. *Journal of Poverty, 1*(1), 81–91.

Burack-Weiss, A. (1991). In their own words: Elders' reactions to vision loss. *Journal of Gerontological Social Work, 17*(3/4), 15–23.

Cook, P., Cook, M., Tran, L., & Tu, W. (1997). Children enabling change: A multicultural, participatory, community-based rehabilitation research project involving Chinese children with disabilities and their families. *Child & Youth Care Forum, 26*(3), 205–219.

Fisk, D., Rowe, M., Brooks, R., & Gildersleeve, D. (2000). Integrating consumer staff members into a homeless outreach project: Critical issues and strategies. *Psychiatric Rehabilitation Journal, 23*(3), 244–253.

Gilson, S. F., Bricout, J. C., & Baskind, F. R. (1998). Listening to the voices of individuals with disabilities. *Families in Society, 79*(2), 188–196.

Kosciulek, J. F. (1999). The consumer-directed theory of empowerment. *Rehabilitation Counseling Bulletin, 42*(3), 196–214.

Lee, J. A. B. (1996). The empowerment approach to social work practice. In F. J. Turner (Ed.) *Social work treatment* (4th ed.) (pp. 218–249). New York: Free Press.

Mackelprang, R. W., & Salsgiver, R. O. (1996). People with disabilities and social work: Historical and contemporary issues. *Social Work, 41*(1), 7–14.

Morris, J. (1991). *Pride against prejudice.* Philadelphia: New Society Publishers.

Payne, M. (1991). *Modern social work theory.* Chicago: Lyceum Books.

Payne, M. (1997) *Modern social work theory* (2nd ed.). Chicago: Lyceum Books.

Pfeiffer, D. (2001). The conceptualization of disability. In S. N. Barnartt & B. M. Altman (Eds.), *Exploring theories and expanding methodologies: Where we are and where we need to go* (pp. 29–52). New York: Elsevier Science.

Pfeiffer, D. (2000). The disability paradigm. *Journal of Disability Policy Studies, 11*(2), 98–99.

Rapp, C. A. (1998). *The strengths model: Case management with people suffering from severe and persistent mental illness.* New York: Oxford University Press.

Saleebey, D. (Ed.). (1997). *The strengths perspective in social work practice* (2nd ed.). New York: Longman.

Simon, B. L. (1994). *The empowerment tradition in American social work.* New York: Columbia University Press.

Simpson, M. K. (1995). The sociology of "competence" in learning disability services. *Social Work & Social Science Review, 6*(2), 85–97.

Solomon, B. B. (1976). *Black Empowerment.* New York: Columbia University Press.

Thapar, N., & Bhardwaj, S. M. (1999). Overcoming the tyranny of space: Experiences of multiple sclerosis patients. *Reflections, 5*(4), 64–70.

Turner, F. J. (Ed.). (1996). *Social work treatment: Interlocking theoretical approaches* (4th ed.). New York: Free Press.

Ward, M. J., & Meyer, R. N. (1999). Self-determination for people with developmental disabilities and autism: Two self-advocates' perspectives. *Focus on autism and other developmental disabilities, 14*(3), 133–140.

Wolen, S. J., & Wolen, S. (1993). *The resilient self: How survivors of troubled families rise above adversity.* New York: Villard.

CHAPTER 7

THE DISABILITY DISCRIMINATION MODEL IN SOCIAL POLICY PRACTICE

GARY E. MAY

INTRODUCTION

The Disability Discrimination Model is designed to give professional social workers a way to conceptualize disability so that their work can play a role in the transformation of how people with disabilities are treated in our society. The guiding principle of this text is that disability-related impairment is a social construction rather than an immutable, objective reality. Impairment operates as a set of beliefs supported by theories and practices within society so that deviations from normative expectations in physical and biological construction and functionality are defined as limiting and excluding. The Disability Discrimination Model proposes a theoretical model along with a set of practice principles upon which social workers can restructure their practices.

The view advocated in this book, namely, that disability-related impairment is a consequence of the environment, is a view that *demands* that social workers approach policy practice from a broad, ecosystemic, dynamic perspective. The Disability Discrimination Model rejects the unchallenged assumptions that have shaped disability-related policies in the past. It rejects the assumption that disability is accompanied by impairment, that disability-related impairment is an objective consequence of disability, that people with disabilities need to be protected from others. In disability policy and disability policy practice for social workers, the medically-oriented perspective has resulted in selecting from an array of policy options, the premises of which have not been questioned, and the poor consequences of which are commonly seen as evidence of the enormity of the challenges of disability, not as an indictment of the policy-making process.

The need for social work's active engagement in this process of critically examining policies targeted at addressing the "problem" of disabilities is enormous.

According to the National Organization on Disability, persons with disabilities and their families rank appreciably lower than the general U.S. population on important quality-of-life indicators (NOD, 2001). The Human Genome Project and the high-profile work of Peter Singer (2001, 2002), raise the specter of genetic cleansing and eugenics. Many breathlessly await the arrival of the day when genetically driven disabilities can be eliminated, ostensibly to preclude needless suffering by the potential person with the disability and his or her family. Social work should have a role in this discussion, in keeping with our tradition of advocacy and empowerment for the disenfranchised and overlooked.

Such involvement is best predicated on a comprehensive understanding of the issues. For example, the much anticipated ability to predict birth anomalies and to obviate their development, doesn't address what, to most, is the surprising reality that 85 percent of persons with disabilities have adventitious disabilities (U.S. Census Bureau). They were acquired sometime after birth through accident, illness, injury, or other environmental causes. Indeed, the development of policy in the area of disability rests on incomplete information and limited perspectives concerning disability and disability-related impairment.

This chapter describes the application of the Disability Discrimination Model, using the policy analysis framework proposed by Barusch (2002). Case studies will be used as a vehicle to differentiate between a Disability Discrimination Model perspective and other constructs, notably the medical model, for understanding disability and disability-related impairment. The influence of a social constructionist perspective on understanding social work, its clients and context, and our understanding of disability will also be explored.

CONSTRUCTIONIST PERSPECTIVE ON SOCIAL WORK

Payne (1997) asserted that social work is socially constructed. "Three sets of forces construct social work: those which create and control social work as an occupation: those which create clienthood among people who seek or are sent for social work help: and those which create the social context in which social work is practiced" (p. 13). This creates a dynamic, ever-changing relationship among these three defining components. In social work policy practice in the area of disabilities, this dynamic relationship has historically been defined in the context of the medical model, characterized by a focus on deficiency, defect, restoration, or cure. According to Payne (1997), social work theory develops in "response to demands made by clients on agencies and workers affecting the interpretation or acceptance of theoretical ideas" (p. 24). Increasingly, in recent years, this interpretation and acceptance has been evolving to include a more instrumental role for the person with a disability, as discussed in Chapters 1–3. Furthermore, the increasing awareness of the role that social construction of disability plays in popular culture, has come to the forefront (Norden, 2000; Van Houten & Bellemakers, 2002). This evolution necessitates accommodation by the profession if social workers are to continue to contribute to the improvement of life for persons with disabilities.

DISABILITY POLICY

Scotch (2000) observed that public policies are based on generalizations about public perceptions about issues and appropriate governmental responses. In the area of disability policy in the United States, "the certification of disability constitutes a social process of labeling and, frequently, stigmatization, which colors social expectation in ways that constrain people who have impairments" (p. 7). Disability policy's persistent theme is its incorporation of cultural constructs of worthiness and morality. These themes are apparent in the cases that follow.

Social work has a long tradition of policy practice and advocacy. Unfortunately, such advocacy has been less evident in the area of disabilities (Thompson, 2001). The need for change is evident (N.O.D. Harris Poll). Social work, with its commitment to "improving the general welfare," is the likely profession to lead the charge to challenge assumptions about disability-related impairment, to construct new paradigms, and to evaluate the Disability Discrimination Model as an explanation for disability-related impairment. Policy practice is one important avenue for this challenge to follow.

POLICY PRACTICE IN SOCIAL WORK

Jansson (1999) argued in support of the integral role that policy practice plays in the life of social work. Specifically, he identified three important reasons why social workers should be engaged in policy practice:

1. To promote the values that lie at the heart of social work and that are codified in the profession's code of ethics, such as social justice, fairness, self-determination, and confidentiality.
2. To promote the well-being of clients, consumers, and citizens by shaping the human services system so that it conforms to the latest findings of social science and medical research.
3. To create effective oppositions to groups and citizens that run counter to the Code of Ethics and to the well-being of clients, consumers, and citizens—and to put pressure on decision makers to approve and retain policies that advance citizens' well-being (p. 3).

Given the pervasive presence of disability in American culture and the experiences of persons with disabilities in encounters with the "helping network" (Hayashi, Chapter 3), policy practice in the area of disability issues should occupy a considerable part of the profession's attention and the attention of individual social workers. In spite of the dimensions of disability, the Council on Social Work Education's standards are essentially silent on the issue (1999 CSWE Accreditation Standards).

The author's experience suggests that Master's-level social work students generally have little interest in policy practice, opting instead to engage in direct clinical practice. Barusch (2002) suggested that this focus deflects social work from its historic and traditional mission and orientation. She advanced an argument for the pursuit of social justice in public policy by the profession and its practitioners.

In recent years, with the passage of the Section 504 of the Rehabilitation Act, the Americans with Disabilities Act, and other civil-rights legislation, there has been renewed attention focused on viewing disability issues and policy related to them from a civil rights perspective. For example, in the area of employment, Bruyère (2000), pointed out the need for ongoing vigilance, as the disparity between employment of persons with disabilities and their nondisabled counterparts persists. Among the forces to be resisted are those predicated on negative, limiting stereotypes about persons with disabilities. Bruyère asserted that the future will hold additional challenges for those interested in policy improvements that will improve opportunities for persons with disabilities.

BARUSCH'S FRAMEWORK FOR POLICY ANALYSIS

Barusch's (2002) framework for policy analysis focused attention on the question of fairness and the distributive elements of public policy. It is but one of several policy analysis models that might be used. Specifically, Barusch posed five essential questions that must be answered in policy analysis:

Question 1: What are the costs and/or benefits under consideration?
Question 2: Who bears the cost, who receives the benefits, and what is the relationship between these two entities?
Question 3: Is anyone who is affected by this policy being labeled "other" and does everyone affected by this policy have an equal voice?
Question 4: What are the rules, both formal and informal, that govern who receives and who pays?
Question 5: Is this policy fair? (p.5).

The following case, from the author's experience, serves as a useful vehicle for considering possible answers to Barusch's policy analysis queries and to demonstrate the important implications for alternative answers to her suggested policy analysis questions.

In the spring of 1998, the chair of the strategic planning committee of Epi-Hab of Evansville, Inc. contacted me. The chair solicited my suggestions as to how Epi-Hab might attract more persons with disabilities to work in its segregated workshop.

My approach was to challenge the assumptions that supported Epi-Hab and to point out to the board member that the preferred methods for assisting people with disabilities were predicated on community inclusion, not separation. I was invited to visit the facility and to present my views to the strategic planning committee and, ultimately to the full Board of Directors.

A brief history of the facility, my analysis and recommendations, and the board decision to close their facility and fund a Center for Disability Studies at the University of Southern Indiana follows.

CASE STUDY 1

Epi-Hab

BACKGROUND

Epi-Hab of Evansville, Inc. was founded in 1964 ". . . for the purpose of providing job-training employment to persons with epilepsy and other disabilities but (who) are otherwise employable" (Epi-Hab brochure, 1998). It was patterned after a similar organization in California. This not-for-profit organization served business and industry in the Evansville area by providing contractual services/products not performed by the client businesses.

The Board of Directors was facing the challenge of a declining workforce, a competitive disadvantage relative to other segregated employment settings for people with disabilities (the sheltered workshops at Evansville Association for Retarded Citizens, Goodwill Industries, and the Evansville Association for the Blind). Epi-Hab did not receive Vocational Rehabilitation or other state/federal funds on behalf of its employees. Workers were paid prevailing minimum wage, received a benefit package, and bonuses.

Factors which seemed to contribute to the labor shortage included:

1. the need for prospective employees to identify themselves as persons with disabilities (the emergence of the disability rights movement, and disability pride notwithstanding, disability is still a low status and avoided identity) (Baynton, 1997).
2. the need for relatively high skill levels when compared with traditional sheltered workshops ("These employees at Epi-Hab demonstrated everyday that persons with epilepsy are capable of working in an industrial environment and of producing quality work" (Epi-Hab Brochure, 1998).
3. the efficacy of current medications which control the symptoms of epilepsy.
4. the fact that epilepsy is among the category of disabilities for which relatively low unemployment for people with disabilities is experienced (Trupin, Sebesta, Yelin, & LaPlante, 1997).
5. the region was experiencing a strong economy with growth in the forms of new industry and expansions of existing industries (Indiana Business Review, 2000).
6. the trend in public policy and practice and in consumer-driven initiatives for people with disabilities has been toward community inclusion in all spheres of living (Shapiro, 1994).
7. structural barriers to employment (loss of SSI, Medicaid, Food Stamps, etc.).

continued

ALTERNATIVES

The goals of Epi-Hab have been and will continue to be that of providing the person with epilepsy or other disability an opportunity to be self-supporting, independent, and productive in life (Epi-Hab Brochure, 1998).

The Board faced the critical challenge of determining: (1) whether the current segregated industrial operation is the best way to achieve this goal, (2) what other alternatives existed to achieve the organization's goals, and (3) whether the organization had a future.

Trends in employment of persons with disabilities have been *away from* segregated employment. The State of Indiana, a long-time supporter of separate "employment," is clearly moving away from this alternative (State Plan for Services to Persons with Disabilities, 1995). The growing civil rights movement regarding people with disabilities also challenges the notion of separation and "special" treatment. Empowerment and self-determination are principles that underpin this movement toward full community inclusion. There may continue to be a competitive disadvantage—on the basis of cost—until the state fully withdraws funding for sheltered employment services/outcomes. At least one area sheltered workshop (Southern Indiana Resource Solutions) is committed to making the transition from a sheltered workshop to totally community-based services/outcomes. At least one other (Evansville Association for Retarded Citizens) seems to be moving in this direction.

Alternative strategies to achieve the organizational goal include using organizational assets to advocate for nonsubsidized competitive employment for people with disabilities in area businesses and industry. Most vocational outcomes for clients served by the state/federal Vocational Rehabilitation program are in competitive private-sector positions. The Americans with Disabilities Act prohibits discrimination in employment and other activities against people with disabilities. State and local ordinances follow this initiative. Trupin, et al. (1997) found that people with disabilities are adversely affected by general labor market trends that adversely affect other disadvantaged populations—women, members of other minority groups, young workers, and older workers. There have been no attempts to ameliorate these adverse consequences for other (nondisabled) populations by providing separate, segregated employment for them. There is a need for vigorous, sustained, broad advocacy that educates employers and policymakers as well as the general public.

It seemed that the brightest prospects for the future of Epi-Hab were to be found in charting a new course in the Evansville area that recognized the changes in the policy and practice arena regarding conceptualizations of disability and impairment and which is responsive to the changes in the marketplace and in society in general.

BOARD DECISIONS

Having solicited the assistance of a pro bono consultant (the author), who provided them with the above analysis, the governing board of Epi-Hab considered the analysis. In the summer of 1998, they voted to close the sheltered workshop, having concluded, in part, that the organization had accomplished its original mission. In consideration of its employees, the board agreed to a severance package for each of them that included a cash payment, the amount of which was determined by the employee's length of employment. The board also agreed to provide one year's paid health insurance for each employee. Arrangements were made for local state-employment service workers to assist the employees with the transition to competitively compensated, integrated employment.

The planned closure was announced at a press conference on August 17, 1998. Within weeks of the announcement, a private, for-profit competitor approached Epi-Hab. The competitor proposed the purchase of the facility, equipment, accounts, contracts, and the hiring of

continued

all the current workers, which numbered thirty-three. The Epi-Hab board voted to accept the offer.

Upon the finalization of the purchase, the new owner hired all thirty-three employees of the former Epi-Hab. Each received a pay raise and was employed in an integrated workforce, some in the same building and in the same job they had with Epi-Hab. As recently as October 1999, all the former Epi-Hab workers who wished to remain in the employ of the purchasing company were still on the payroll. The plant manager reported that there were no noteworthy problems when the former Epi-Hab workers were added to the company's existing workforce, and that he and the corporation's executives were very satisfied with the assimilation of the former Epi-Hab assets (personal communication, October 1999). In recognition of the desirability and success of this merger, the combined company, GI Ten-Tech, received a "Profit From Our Abilities Award" from the Indiana Governor's Planning Council for People with Disabilities in 1999.

ASSET LIQUIDATION

As the plans for the sale proceeded, the board was confronted with the question of liquidating and disposing of the agency's assets. During the consultation phase, it had been suggested that the board establish a community-based employment education/advocacy foundation, with current board members providing the leadership. Their decision was to not do this, as they wished to "make a clean break." They solicited a proposal from the consultant. It was estimated that the proceeds available for distribution would total approximately $2 million.

A proposal was submitted from the University of Southern Indiana to use the money to establish the USI/Epi-Hab Center for Disability Studies. The proposal suggested depositing the money with the Vanderburgh County Foundation, in order to qualify for a matching distribution from the Lilly Foundation.

The board voted to give the University of Southern Indiana $1.2 million (through the Vanderburgh County Community Foundation Alliance). Another $1.2 million was given—also through the Foundation—to the Evansville Rehabilitation Center to re-establish a free epilepsy clinic, which had been closed several years previously because of lack of funding. The Lilly Foundation match totaled $300,000, bringing the total invested for each entity to $1.35 million. Pursuant to state law, the board agreed to establish an escrow account, from which unanticipated claims against the agency would be paid. After three years, these funds, approximately $300,000, would be divided equally between the university and the Rehabilitation Center.

The following analysis follows Barusch's (2002) five questions outlined earlier.

ANALYSIS

What are the costs and/or benefits under consideration?

In the case above, the board initially considered the benefits to include "employment" opportunities for persons with disabilities. The costs included resources required to investigate options to get more employees with disabilities to work in their facility. Other costs that were considered included the costs related to morphing the company into a different method of operation. (For example, the board was revisiting an earlier opportunity to become a direct vendor for a building supplies company. In this case, they would devote resources exclusively to the production and packaging of a patio support foundation that would be retailed by the building supply company.) Ultimately, the board decided that the benefit to employees was where they would invest.

The board had cause to reframe their cost benefit analysis with the help of outside consultation. Questions were raised about the true benefits to the workers. There was little opportunity for upward mobility for the employees. To a very major extent, the board saw their provision of opportunities for employment as charity, as they were aware of the history of their employees having difficulty in finding and holding competitive, nonsubsidized jobs. Additionally, the board was encouraged to broaden their view of costs to include the social cost of the message they were sending to their peers in the business sector. The message affirmed the stereotypic, limiting depiction of people with disabilities as defective, requiring special employment opportunities apart from those commonly available in the private sector.

Who bears the cost, who receives the benefits, and what is the relationship between the two?

In the Epi-Hab case, as is historically often the case, people with disabilities bore the cost of the beneficence of the board by submitting to the charitable option of minimum-wage employment in a segregated setting with little opportunity for advancement. The mostly able-bodied management of the facility was paid handsomely and had opportunities for upward mobility through their extensive contacts with others in business and industry in the region.

Among the beneficiaries of the status quo were board members, many of whom were employed by Epi-Hab client companies. Through their influence in acquiring contracts with Epi-Hab for quality services at low prices, their stature in their companies rose. They also benefited from the appreciation of their fellow board members, as they brought more business into the facility, thereby enabling the facility to serve more people with disabilities. Finally, the board benefited from positive community perceptions about their work in the charity business that was Epi-Hab.

So, the image that Epi-Hab presented to the community was that of workers who, *because of their disabilities,* were disqualified from competitive, nonsubsidized, integrated employment in nominal work settings; who required special support services that necessitated a segregated employment setting; whose lives could be improved by businesses bringing work into the workshop for them to perform; whose well-being was managed by a beneficent board; and whose presence served as tangible proof of the positive effects of the tolerant attitude that the community felt toward them.

Is anyone who is affected by this policy being labeled "other," and does everyone affected by this policy have an equal voice?

Clearly, the workers at Epi-Hab were labeled as "others." They were distinguished from the qualified able-bodied workforce by their disabilities. The disabilities were not seen as benign expressions of difference, but as disqualifiers for regular employment because of assumptions made, and accepted without challenge, about accompanying impairment. Marketing by the facility played on the acceptance of this disqualification by presenting opportunities for client companies to bring work into the workshop as a charitable, Christian act.

The obvious, but unarticulated paradigm was one where Epi-Hab, in agency for its workers, depicted them to potential client companies as pitiable, deserving sufferers, but had expectations of them as employees that rivaled those found in the client companies themselves. In effect, the "others" were depicted stereotypically and negatively to get business, but were treated as capable, potential human capital by Epi-Hab management. In any case, the assignment to "otherness" was obvious in the operation of Epi-Hab.

What are the rules, both formal and informal, that govern who receives and who pays?

At Epi-Hab, the expressed rules about who benefits clearly identified the employees with disabilities. In expressed policies, there was no reference to parties who bore the cost. Client companies paid for the services from Epi-Hab, but they received benefits that frequently exceeded their cost. The community was led to believe that the employment arrangement at Epi-Hab was an expression of acceptance and beneficence toward poor, but deserving people with disabilities who couldn't find work elsewhere.

The informal rules governing costs and benefits were a bit different. There was subtle and direct pressure on employees to remain at Epi-Hab (P. Shankland, personal communication, 2001). The existence of Epi-Hab and its population, almost exclusively, of workers with disabilities reinforced the belief held by many of the employees that they were indeed disqualified for regular employment. "If (s)he can't get a job elsewhere, why should I believe that I could?" Similarly, the board seemed to believe that their employees couldn't "make it on the outside." Limited board contact with employees while they were at work generally reinforced this belief, as accommodations required by employees were the focus of observations. In effect, the board operated for years without questioning the necessity of what they were doing. The outside consultant was able to help them see this and adopt an alternative course of action.

Is this policy fair?

This became an essential question for the board as they contemplated Epi-Hab's future. The conclusion that it was not became inevitable as the board considered alternative views of their work and its impact. The chair of the Strategic Planning Committee, in his report and recommendations to the board to close the sheltered workshop, said, "We are exploiting our workers, not helping them. We have done what we needed to do, the times have changed. It's time for us to move on and to allow our workers to prosper" (Shovers, 1998).

Ultimately, the Board came to see the presence of Epi-Hab, and its explicit and implicit communication regarding disability and work, in the context of progress and shifting priorities regarding employment and disability. Continuation of the facility, in its historic form, would serve as an ongoing counter message to the one espoused by disability advocates, state government, and the expressed wishes of persons with disabilities. The board arrived at the inescapable conclusion that continuing would be patently unfair, both for their workers with disabilities and the broader community.

In this case, a social worker, serving as a pro bono consultant for the board of directors, was able to provide information and perspectives that permitted the board to make what seems to be a socially just policy decision.

The second case represents the antithesis of this scenario. It is replete with unchallenged negative stereotypes and limiting assumptions about the ability of people with disabilities, indeed their desire, to live in the nominal community.

CASE STUDY 2

Jacob's Village

BACKGROUND
Documents filed with the Area Plan Commission by the Beacon Group proposed a thirty-five-parcel planned unit development (PUD) on 132.5 acres of land zoned for agricultural use. Backers proposed an essentially self-contained village, where primarily persons with disabilities would live, work, recreate, and undergo "training," ostensibly preparatory to their assuming roles in the nominal community.

The proposal necessitated rezoning from agricultural to planned unit development (PUD), including residential, light industrial, recreational, parking, and conference-center components. The project's construction schedule projected initial conference center site preparation to begin by June 1, 2000. Construction of the, ". . . first housing alternative locations and small industry and commerce buildings was expected to commence in early to mid-2001." A phase-in approach is described: as one phase is completed, planning and fund-raising for the

continued

next phase would be undertaken; as each phase is complete, villagers will begin to use it. All construction was projected to be completed by December 31, 2024.

People with developmental disabilities were the only identified "villagers" in the documents filed with the Area Plan Commission. "Jacob's Village will be a safe harbor for people with special needs, no matter what age. Parents will have the comfort of knowing their 'special needs' children have a safe home for as long as they live."

Documents described "expected outcomes & accomplishments" of the Village: "A training center will equip 'villagers' for a variety of employment opportunities. They may work at an 'on-site' facility—cottage industry, sheltered workshop, farming, gardening, etc.—or, they may choose to work at a facility in Evansville. Recreation opportunities will include such programs as camping, fishing, and sports. An activity center will offer recreational and socialization opportunities while a chapel will provide spiritual support" (Vanderburgh County Area Plan Commission).

ANALYSIS

What are the costs and/or benefits under consideration?

Proponents of the village identified the benefits to include parental peace of mind, villagers' protection from deferential treatment from the community, opportunities for economic productivity, and protection for the community. Christian beneficence was also an important component cited by the proponents, who proclaimed themselves "Christian businessmen" in their introduction of their idea to the community.

The Christian beneficence appeal resulted in the mobilization of high-profile community business and other leaders in support of the proposed village. The daily newspaper editorialized in support of the proposed village and testimonials from selected families who supported it were publicized.

Proponents were dismissive of critics who questioned the true benefit that would accrue to the residents of the village. Opponents' advocacy for community inclusion, with appropriate supports, was dismissed as an unrealistic pipedream that wasn't practical. Similarly, the state's movement toward community-based supports and services was dismissed as a "fad" and not a viable long-term solution.

In short, the motivation and assessment of benefits of the village were strongly skewed in favor of the nondisabled proponents and backers. The expression of their Christian beneficence was predicated on a pejorative, limiting, and stereotypic understanding and depiction of persons with disabilities. They were not persuaded by their critics' arguments that the "reality" of disability-related impairment that their proposed village sought to address was a consequence of a set of unexamined and unchallenged assumptions that they had made about persons with disabilities and disability-related impairment.

Who bears the cost, who receives the benefits, and what is the relationship between the two?

In the proposed village, the opponents asserted that the nondisabled organizers and supporters of the village were the true beneficiaries. For example, the prime mover for the village project is a restaurateur whose plan for the village includes the production of foodstuffs that his restaurants would use. Additionally, the owner of the property to be rezoned will benefit from the sale of the property to the village.

The villagers themselves would realize few benefits. There would be little opportunity to accumulate wealth. The distance of the proposed village from the community and the prohibition against villagers driving cars on the property, would effectively sequester the villagers, making them totally dependent upon village caretakers and staff.

Is anyone who is affected by this policy being labeled "other" and does everyone affected by this policy have an equal voice?

Clearly, the proposed village created and perpetuated "otherness." The proponents frequently spoke of villagers in the third person passive voice. Potential villagers were commonly depicted as "damaged," or as "mistakes" whose parents would decide what they needed and where they needed to get it. As is frequently the case with charity-based appeals, the objects of the charitable giving are distinguished from the donors in important ways, with the clear implication that the objects of charity possess undesirable characteristics. Charitable giving and sequestering persons with disabilities in a village assuaged the anxiety of nondisabled donors, who are in fact only separated from the "undesirable characteristics" of persons with disabilities by an accident, illness, injury, or other uncontrollable circumstance.

What are the rules, both formal and informal, that govern who receives and who pays?

The rules that govern who pays and who benefits from the proposed village were predicated on assumptions about entitlement, potential for benefit, and the community's wishes regarding full-fledged community membership. The village leadership has appropriated an extensive tome of rules, policies, procedures, and rights and responsibilities under the guise of client empowerment. In reality, the rules serve to maintain the unchallenged currency of the values, philosophies, and beliefs upon which the village concept is constructed.

The existence of rules offered "proof" that assistance is needed, which resulted in second-class citizenship for persons with disabilities. The operative rules simply perpetuate a circular, victimizing paradigm of disability.

Is this policy fair?

Opponents of the proposed village asserted that it was patently unfair to accept limiting stereotypes about people with disabilities and to construct a segregated village on the basis of these stereotypes. Proponents of the village countered that there was nothing inherently unfair about the proposed village because residents would have a choice about whether or not to live there. Because the facility would not be eligible for public underwriting, the costs would be borne either by residents or through a corporate resident sponsorship scheme that proponents developed.

Larger questions about the diversion of resources from community inclusion and community support were never addressed by proponents. The entire state delegation supported the village. The likelihood that they would not be favorably disposed to consider and fund community-based supports and services was not addressed.

SUMMARY

The Vanderburgh County Area Plan Commission passed the rezoning request unanimously. Construction, ostensibly using 100 percent in private funds, is underway at this writing. Although fundraising and the construction timetable seem to be behind projections, the proponents insist that the village will become a viable resource for persons with disabilities in the foreseeable future.

CONCLUSION

Policy decisions that affect the lives of people with disabilities are being made every day. Social workers, who are foremost among the helping professions, have an obligation to advocate for and help empower persons with disabilities. Advocacy and empowerment necessarily include challenging the status quo.

The large numbers of persons with disabilities in the United States, their poor showing on quality-of-life indicators (N.O.D./Harris), increasing self-advocacy, and inclusive community life predict that disability-related policy issues will be prominent in policy deliberations for the foreseeable future. Social work must take an active, informed role in these deliberations. We must initiate and frame challenges to the conventional assumptions about disability and impairment. We must recognize our obligation to improve the general welfare and improve the opportunities for all citizens—including citizens and others with disabilities.

REFERENCES

Barusch, A. S. (2002). *Foundations of social policy: Social justice, public programs, and the social work profession.* Itasca, IL: F. E. Peacock Publishers.

Baynton, D. C. (1997, Spring). Disability: A useful category of historical analysis. *Disability Studies Quarterly, 17*(2).

Bruyère, S. M. (2000, Summer). Civil Rights and Employment Issues of Disability Policy. *Journal of Disability Policy Studies, 11*(1).

Chambers, M. (1993). Group home backers want law change (28 January 1998). Indianapolis: Evansville Courier and Press.

Council on Social Work Education (1999). Educational policy and accreditation standards. Alexandria, VA: [AU: PUBLISHER?]

Division on Disability, Aging and Rehabilitation Services (1995). *Five year plan for community integration.* Indianapolis, IN: State of Indiana.

Epi-Hab (1998). *Epi-Hab* [Brochure]. Evansville, IN: Author.

Evansville Courier and Press (1998). Group home backers want law change.

[Author] (2000). 2001 Outlook. *Indiana Business Review, 75*(4).

Jansson, B. S. (1999). *Becoming an effective policy advocate: From policy practice to social justice.* New York: Brooks/Cole.

Kasnitz, D., Bonney, S., Aftandlean, R., & Pfeiffer, D. (2000, Spring). Programs and courses in disability studies at universities and colleges in Canada, Australia, the United States, the United Kingdom, and Norway. *Disability Studies Quarterly, 20*(2).

National Organization on Disability (2000). N.O.D./Harris Survey of Americans with disabilities. Washington, DC.

Norden, M. F. (2000). Bitterness, rage, and redemption: Hollywood constructs the disabled Vietnam veteran" (pp. 96–114). In D. A. Gerber (Ed.), In *Disabled veterans in history.* Ann Arbor, MI: University of Michigan Press.

Pappas, V. (2000). *Tell it like it is! Survey results: Indiana's state disability plan 2000–2003.* Indianapolis, IN: Indiana Governor's Planning Council for People with Disabilities.

Payne, M. (1997). *Modern Social Work Theory* (2nd ed.). Chicago: Lyceum Books.

Scotch, R. K. (2000, Summer). Disability policy: An eclectic overview. *Journal of Disability Policy Studies, 11*(1), 6–11.

Shapiro, J. P. (1994). *No pity: People with disabilities forging a new civil rights movement.* New York: Times Books.

Shovers, A. (1998, July). Oral presentation to Epi-Hab Board of Directors. Evansville, IL.

Singer, P. (2002). *Unsanctifying human life: Essays on ethics.* Oxford: Blackwell Publishers.

Singer, P. (2001). *Writings on an Ethical Life.* Hopewell, NJ: Ecco Press.

Stoddard, S., Jans, L., Ripple, J., & Kraus, L. S. (1998). *Chartbook on work and disability in the United States, 1998* [*InfoUse* Report]. Washington, DC: U.S. Department of Education National Institute on Disability and Rehabilitation Research.

Thompson, N. (2001). *Anti-discrimination practice* (3rd ed.). New York: Palgrave.

Trupin, L., Sebesta, D. S., Yelin, E., & LaPlante, M. P. (1997). *Trends in labor force participation among persons with disabilities, 1983–1994.* San Francisco: Disability Statistics Rehabilitation Research and Training Center, Institute for Health and Aging, University of California.

U. S. Department of Commerce, Census Bureau (1997). Current population reports; Americans with disabilities: 1994–1995. Washington, DC.

Vanderburgh County, Indiana (2000). Area Plan Commission.

Van Houten, D. & Bellemakers, C. (2002, March). Equal citizenship for all, Disability policies in the Netherlands: Empowerment of marginals. *Disability and Society, 17*(2), 171–185.

CHAPTER 8

THE EVOLUTION OF A NEW PARADIGM FOR DISABILITY RESEARCH

HARLAN HAHN AND MARTHA B. RASKE

INTRODUCTION

A guiding principle of the Disability Discrimination Model, introduced by May in Chapter 5, is that disability-related impairment is a social construction, not an objective reality. Such a perspective disputes current theories upon which many current practice models are based. If disability is produced by the interaction of public perception, self-identity, environmental barriers, atypical appearances, and functional deviations, then what set of concepts must be defined and measured to mark the existence of disability or note changes that take place over time? If disability can be cause for celebration as well as grief, then how should the full range of reactions and feelings about disability be measured? If the concept of impairment is to replace disability as the benchmark for pathology, then how will it be defined? Once defined, how will it be tested? Research is the essential building block to develop and test the Disability Discrimination Model.

This chapter will focus attention on the role of research in developing and testing the discrimination model, as well as other emerging disability perspectives. First, the chapter describes emerging trends in disability research and lays out a conceptual and theoretical framework for the discipline of disability studies. Second, the authors offer methodological alternatives to current research practices and introduce a model for changing the research agenda.

EMERGING THEMES IN DISABILITY STUDIES

During the final decades of the twentieth century, the discussion of disability research reflected some interesting changes. New controversies emerged, the field gained renewed interest and respectability, and new groups were attracted to the study of disability. Many of these individuals were themselves persons with disabilities who brought a fresh and badly needed perspective to the analysis of fundamental issues (Bucaro & Kapfstein, 1999; Gilson, Bricout, & Baskind, 1998; Hahn, 1997; Pfeiffer, 2000; Rioux & Bach, 1994; Ward & Meyer, 1999).

The developments also provoked a critical reassessment of the linkages between researchers, political activists, and the public. In many respects, the disability rights movement was a fruitful source of innovative ideas for some members of the academic community, and activists soon adopted numerous concepts spawned by researchers. On the other hand, much research on disability was relatively unaffected by these trends, and most of the general public as well as the mass media seemed to remain oblivious to these changes. The studies conducted in universities were based on the assumption that they would eventually shape common understandings about disability as well as other subjects, but most of the information used as a basis for decisions by legislators, judges, policymakers, and professionals appeared to bear the imprint of traditional approaches to the analysis of these issues (Hahn, 1982; Mackelprang & Salsgiver, 1996; Merrick, 1994; Morris, 1991).

The last quarter of the twentieth century was a particularly significant period in disability research because it marked a time when a new conceptual framework was at least introduced into the discourse. The basic elements of this new model were relatively simple. First, the environment was granted a status equivalent to the individual in assessing the components of disability (Hahn, 1982, 1985a, 1985b). An initial attempt was made to wean rehabilitation from a clinical orientation that had confined the search for explanatory measures to the physiological dimensions of the human body. Second, emphasis was placed on the stigmatizing effects of visible or labeled characteristics that produce social discrimination and segregation or avoidance. Both factors marked the gradual shift from a "functional limitations" perspective of disability, which focuses on the repair of personal defects or deficiencies, to a "minority group" model, which identifies discrimination as the principal problem confronting people with disabilities (Hahn, 1997). Hence, disability could be regarded as a difference, essentially similar to variations in other human attributes that have elicited prejudice and oppression for years.

These views established the foundations for important civil rights laws such as Section 504 of the Rehabilitation Act of 1973 and the Americans with Disabilities Act of 1990. Yet the implementation of such measures has been severely hampered by the pervasive acceptance among the general public and policymakers, and especially judges, of a functional orientation that tends to ascribe the unequal status of the disabled minority to the effects of bodily impairments instead of social discrimination. These developments seemed to have relatively little impact on the conduct of health professionals, rehabilitation counselors, and other administrators of programs for persons with disabilities. Only a few fields, such as rehabilitation science and engineering, sought to accommodate environmental influences within a basic model for research (Brandt & Pope, 1997). In general, plans concerning rehabilitation and disability at the close of the century appeared to be relatively unaffected by ideas related to stigma and the environment. Despite the emphasis placed on scientific investigations, for example, few attempts were made to devise empirical measures of either of these concepts. The failure to pursue these goals meant that innovative approaches often could not be effectively applied to the examination of problems facing the disabled portion of the population. Most practices in the field of disability and rehabilitation bore little trace of these influences. Most of the research funded during this period was still based on the traditional model of disability. Particularly striking was the lack of a younger group of researchers to replace the pioneers who had begun to talk about the effects of stigma and the environment. The significance of this void is underscored by the fact that, unlike most disadvantaged groups, disability is not a characteristic that ordinarily is transmitted from one generation to the next. Another and related obstacle has been the absence of an academic discipline or curriculum founded on research encompassing the "minority group" model. Although initial explorations of these issues had generated brave plans for a comprehensive field of disability studies to consolidate fragmented curricula in the health professions, rehabilitation counseling, science and engineering, and special education, such innovations were seldom implemented in higher education in secondary and elementary schools.

The explanation for the relative lack of change in disability and rehabilitation research must be traced to the power of entrenched interests. These influences are particularly evident in academic disciplines, professional groups, the media, and the nondisabled public. Ideas may sometimes be victorious in the conflict between opposing forces, but, far more often, the greatest strength is displayed by viewpoints that have been institutionalized. Thus, established educational programs are more likely to possess the support of a loyal group of adherents than a newly invented curriculum, regardless of the merit of the insights that they may contain. In fact, administrators of traditional departments are apt to be especially vigilant about the threat of new plans that might infringe upon their terrain. Moreover, graduates of these programs are frequently stalwart defenders of the value of the training they received. They commonly form professional associations that exert a determinative impact on the administration of many areas of public policy. In some areas of specialization, these groups may have virtually uncontested access to the decision makers who control such policies. As a result, opportunities to challenge hegemonic influences in research and government programs have been relatively limited.

These patterns seem to be especially prevalent in disability and rehabilitation policy. Unlike other disadvantaged groups, people with disabilities have never been entirely successfully in refuting the claim that their subordinate position in society has resulted from biological inferiority, or an inability to function at a level commensurate with the physical or mental capabilities of nondisabled counterparts. The nondisabled have often responded to this perceived disparity in functional skills with sympathetic or charitable feelings. The media and the public frequently interpret the accomplishments of women and men with disabilities as unusual occurrences, rather than evidence of the gains that would become increasingly possible through continuous measures to modify the environment and to end discrimination. Instead of reporting efforts to gain equal rights in education, transportation, housing, and public accommodations as legitimate news, the media have tended to confine their coverage of disability issues to the presentation of feature stories about the achievements of some disabled individuals. The unspoken implication of course, is that persons with disabilities ordinarily are inferior and unequal.

The consequences of these stereotypes about disability have had a particularly devastating impact on the resolution of issues that are often presented to physicians and lawyers. Because many disabilities are, by definition, permanent, they cannot be substantially ameliorated by medical intervention. As a result, physicians are often left in the position of monitoring chronic conditions. Or they may be compelled to act as gatekeepers by supplying evidence about disabilities that qualify for public benefits by extrapolating from a medical model that was not designed to permit predictions about functional capacities from diagnostic classifications (Stone, 1985). For lawyers and judges, on the other hand, the twin requirements of Section 504 and ADA that a plaintiff must be both "handicapped" or disabled and "qualified" has often resulted in decisions that persons are "qualified" if they are not "handicapped" and that they are not "qualified" if they are "handicapped." More than 90 percent of all cases of employment discrimination under ADA end in victories for employers (Hahn, 1999a). As a result some analysts have begun to contemplate alternative policies that do not depend on medical certification as a means of gaining needed benefits or upon litigation as a method of securing equal rights.

Another indication of the need for innovations in disability research and policy is revealed by the current state of standard measures of rehabilitation outcomes. Many techniques attempt to assess subjective quality of life (Brown, Renwick, & Nagler, 1996). To some disabled individuals, this instrument may have a certain appeal from an egalitarian perspective because it suggests that disabled people ought to enjoy at least a quality of life comparable to their nondisabled peers. And yet "quality of life" has a sinister and even draconian connotation as a criterion that has been used by bioethicists as a standard to determine which disabled infants and adults should be allowed to survive and what "life is unworthy of life" (Glass, 1997). The negative effects of these methods have been especially evident in efforts to develop a collective assessment of the public health of an entire population. DALYs (Disability Adjusted Life Years), reflect two of the most popular of these techniques, as well as another measure called "healthy life without a disability" (Hahn, 1999b). In both projects, disability is viewed as an intrinsically negative trait, and healthy life with a disability is perceived as inherently impossible. This judgment places persons with disabilities under the aegis of a functional concept of "quality of life." The possibility of healthy life with a disability is virtually precluded. Most ominously, there is a significant threat that these measures will be joined with remnants of the eugenics movement as well as new dangers, such as offshoots of the genome project to produce circumstances that could rationalize a sort of genocide against people with disabilities. Not all statistics pose such a risk; a version of the ICIDH that includes adequate assessments of the environment and participation, for example, could produce a census of the proportion of intersections with curb cuts in different communities. Obviously, this information, documenting a widespread lack of compliance with antidiscrimination laws, might be of significant educational value in promoting the interests of disabled citizens. By contrast, the DALYs and related measures are based on the simple and often erroneous assumption that a decrease in functional capabilities will automatically result in a reduced quality of life.

The struggle to advance a new paradigm for any field of research is hampered by many entrenched interests, including dominant concepts and practices of academic disciplines. The supposition that the element of disability should be subtracted from the factors that contribute to a healthy life, for instance, seems to reflect the unstated notion that the joint aims of medicine and the health professions are encompassed by the objectives to prolong life and to restore functional abilities to the maximum extent possible. Implicit in these goals is a vague image of an infinitely perfectible, or at least a "normal," living organism with unspecified functional capacities that lends credence to the common statement that everyone has at least some kind of disability. The inability to achieve anatomical perfection and to "fix" or repair most permanent disabilities also seems to raise serious questions about the viability of the latter objective. Yet most of these professionals would not be content with the exclusive pursuit of attempts to prolong life. Despite the lack of conceptual clarity in the premises and aspirations of such disciplines, the likelihood that health professionals will abandon their efforts to remedy functional impairments is exceedingly low. If medicine were ever to fulfill the goal of eradicating disability, a vital element of diversity would be removed from society. Because biases in the dominant conceptual model may pose a threat to the very existence of people with disabilities, the struggle to combat this danger must be conducted not only in the realm of academic discourse but also in the arena of political conflict.

The entrenched interests molding academic disciplines also are reflected in the major organizations that have influenced policies and programs concerning disability. Significantly, as the segment of the population that is most centrally concerned about this subject, persons with disabilities probably have had less impact on decisions affecting their status than predominantly nondisabled groups. The American Association of Persons with Disabilities notwithstanding, there is no powerful national organization of citizens with disabilities, and even the disability rights movement has failed to spawn an enduring institutional structure. Some researchers with disabilities from various fields have played a major role in the Society for Disability Studies, but it has not gained the prestige or the prominence of organizations representing separate academic disciplines. Groups of nondisabled professionals like the National Rehabilitation Association, the Council of State Administrators of Vocational Rehabilitation Programs, and associations representing rehabilitation medicine and engineering have had the greatest effect on disability issues. Moreover, the attitudes and perspectives of members of these organizations frequently seem to have been shaped more by their education or professional training than by the knowledge or preferences of their clients. Perhaps to a greater extent than any other portion of the population, the opinions and assessments of people with disabilities have been ignored or neglected in the design and implementation of policies that focus primarily upon them. Thus they have been consigned to the margins of a political process that might otherwise be expected to produce a major change in the dominant paradigm for research on disability.

The barriers to a radical transformation of prevalent approaches to the study of issues and problems related to disability are indeed formidable, and ideas generated in the crucible of academic discussions might seem to be puny weapons in the arsenal required to wage such a struggle. Nevertheless, in the absence of the power needed to achieve change through other means, researchers may have few alternative resources. Perhaps the best available strategy, therefore, is represented by the proposal to reformulate major concepts that are integral to the analysis of this subject. This plan is not advanced in the belief that substantial progress can be achieved soon. It is simply predicated on the hope that this sort of reconceptualization could create a new agenda that may encourage adherents of the traditional paradigm to alter the direction of future research in ways that might have the cumulative effect of promoting increasingly extensive changes.

During the final decades of the twentieth century, the dominant notion of disabilities or impairments, which focused on functional deficits or deficiencies, was increasingly challenged by an alternative orientation that emphasized differences that could be a source of prejudice and discrimination. Whereas the former model considers impairment in an almost entirely negative way as a factor that detracts from optimal human performance, the latter perspective simply regards disability as a trait that may be perceived by other people in a negative manner. Hence disability is not intrinsically bad. This shift enabled many individuals with disabilities to release a psychological burden of guilt or shame, and it even permitted a few to redefine disability as a source of dignity and pride. But most of them soon learned that prejudice on the basis of disability was a pervasive phenomenon and that they had to contend constantly with an oppressive environment permeated by unfavorable attitudes (Oliver, 1996). Thus, even though the advent of a sociopolitical understanding produced a major change in the personal identity of many individuals who grasped its message, the ubiquitous nature of the stigma attached to disabilities appeared to preclude the assessment of these kinds of differences from a neutral or objective perspective. As a result, the approach of many researchers may still be tainted by the preconception that disability is only an undesirable characteristic.

There is, however, another path to the study of this subject that might enable researchers and policymakers to escape some of the connotations of prior conceptualizations. Instead of regarding disability exclusively as a functional limitation or as a difference that may evoke discrimination, it can also be viewed simply as an experience. For those who are still influenced by the traditional notions of functional limitations or loss, the experience of disability may still be cast in a negative light. On the other hand, for individuals who have lived beyond the trauma of a disabling event and for researchers who have studied the subject in detail, careful scrutiny or introspection is apt to yield a more balanced understanding of the entire range of elements that are common features of life with a disability. For most people, disability is not simply an inconvenience or limitation. It is part of a full range of life experiences. The creation of a "level playing field," therefore, cannot be achieved simply by applying unmodified principles of impartiality or objectivity. The remedy must be based on an accurate and complete evaluation of the comparative merits of disabled and nondisabled individuals.

In addition, however, the unremitting efforts by numerous people with disabilities to devise alternative means of coping with environmental obstacles has produced a vast body of information and knowledge that could become the foundation for a new research paradigm. In countless circumstances, they have had to create innovative methods of combating both the stereotypes and the structural barriers that they encounter constantly. Individuals with mobility limitations, for example, frequently have been compelled to find ways of circumventing common impediments such as stairs or steps that might otherwise prevent them from moving from place to place. The approaches that they have developed for dealing with such difficulties often may be ad hoc or situational, but they could be codified and explicated by relating similar impairments and common environmental features in everyday life. The aim of this research agenda would be to uncover distinctive features of the experience of people with disabilities that can become a basis for the development of theory and practice (see Saleebey, 1997).

The focus on experience is not inconsistent with a sociopolitical definition and a "minority group model" of disability. An important initial project for researchers interested in any portion of society is the work, usually conducted by anthropologists, of recording common features of the life of the group. This sort of ethnographic study may be an especially crucial element in the development of a conceptual framework for the examination of possible solutions to the social problems faced by this minority. The findings could reveal techniques that have permitted people with disabilities to successfully surmount pervasive impediments and negative aspects of disability. In addition, although the issue has received relatively little attention from the news media or academic journals, one of the most significant topics for people with disabilities is the question of whether or not they possess an identifiable culture. The investigation of all facets of living with disability might also open many new pathways to the exploration of this topic.

The accumulated experiences of people with disabilities, especially in coping with environmental barriers, comprise a valuable resource that may be appropriately conveyed to subsequent generations. Because this information seldom can be transmitted within families, knowledge derived from the analysis of this subject could become a crucial element for professional practitioners who might otherwise be consigned to the limited role of monitoring or describing permanent disabilities and chronic health conditions. The application of data obtained from persons with disabilities to the development of practical as well as theoretical implications of an analytical perspective represents a self-reflexive research strategy that may promote increased cooperation and respect between the professional community and this minority group.

Additional investigations might be launched to explore the suggestion that the continual experience of seeking a means of overcoming environmental barriers may instill a habit of thought that could be transferred to other situations and problems. Although interpretations of the meaning and significance of disability may vary widely, some observers have indicated that after a disabling event most people tend to form a different perspective, or an altered understanding of their circumstances, that may be a source of original insights or creativity (Hahn, 1997). Ironically, everyday occurrences that reinforce the capability to devise innovative solutions to the challenges posed by inaccessible and even inhospitable surroundings may be regarded as factors that offset an exclusively negative view of disability by molding skills and perspectives that are not as readily available to others.

Perhaps the most important potential result of the analysis of disability as an experience, however, might be an increasingly balanced understanding that could promote the empowerment of persons with disabilities. In many respects, the major impediments to the advancement of citizens with disabilities cannot be ascribed solely to the bodily impairments of individuals in the group or to the influence of discriminatory attitudes and structural barriers in the environment. Another formidable problem has been the failure to mobilize massive political influence commensurate with their size and possible strength in the U.S. population. Some significant advances have been achieved by the disability rights movements, but a candid assessment of opposing forces would also require an acknowledgment that a large portion of people with disabilities have remained politically dormant. Much of this passivity undoubtedly can be attributed to the absence of a firm basis for identifying with disability that would promote increased participation. Many citizens with disabilities have been reluctant to join this struggle because of the legacy of stigma and shame that still surrounds this trait. The prevalent interpretation of disability as an exclusively negative attribute has had extensive political as well as scientific repercussions. Moreover, the conceptual framework for the study of disability certainly must be included among the influences that have contributed to this result. In comparison with other sources of social and economic power that have direct and immediate consequences, the reorientation of research to center on the experience of disability rather than the impact of different or functional limitations might appear to be a relatively weak proposal. Yet the overwhelming negative image of disability that permeates society may be a crucial factor that has hampered the emergence of a political force that could vigorously challenge traditional interests. Part of the explanation for the lack of cultural support for a more positive or at least a somewhat balanced interpretation, however, can be traced to the nature of research about the subject that evolved over a relatively long period of time. Altering the dominant paradigm for the investigation of the problems related to disability is not likely to prompt the defeat of entrenched interests or inspire a prompt change in traditional attitudes and practices about the subject. But the understandings of disability supported by the general public, the media, organized lobbies, and health professions bear the indelible imprint of the paradigm that has shaped research for many years. The present state of political conflict as well as dominant interpretations of disability are the product of gradual incremental processes, and attempts to change either of these matters may occur through similar means.

As much of the Western world experiences a sense of entering another century and even another millennium, probably the principal risk facing researchers interested in the evolution of a new paradigm for the study of disability is the danger of indulging prematurely in a spirit of self-congratulation. The formulation of a sociopolitical definition and a "minority group" model of disability that directed attention at the effects of stigma and the environment represented slight progress. But the influence of entrenched interests as well as the traditional allocation of resources and funding for research or other purposes remained basically undisturbed. Although the creation of these concepts provided a foundation for antidiscrimination laws such as the Americans with Disabilities Act, the subsequent enforcement or implementation of these measures has created serious doubts about the effectiveness of litigation as a means of securing the civil rights of people with disabilities. Moreover, despite the intense strivings of the disability rights movement and groups such as the Society for Disability Studies, people with disabilities have not been able to rival the position of well-financed interest groups that play a powerful role in the political process or of the nondisabled professionals who often administer programs that are allegedly designed to serve their needs.

Although there does not appear to be any prospect of achieving a sudden or complete reversal of the principal model for the study of disability, reforming the emphasis slightly may prompt incremental changes by dislodging some traditional notions about the subject. The proposed emphasis on experience instead of difference or functional impairments may promote an increasingly balanced perspective that could yield modest gains in theoretical understandings, professional practice, and the social and political influence of people with disabilities. Perhaps the major danger entailed in this plan, however, is the possibility that it might encourage the self-indulgent celebration of minor progress at the expense of preparing researchers for the major conflicts that can be anticipated in the future.

USING THE DISABILITY DISCRIMINATION MODEL TO BUILD A RESEARCH METHODOLOGY

> It commonly happens that the choice of a problem is determined by the method instead of a method being determined by the problem. This means that thought is subjected to an invisible tyranny. (Daly, 1973, pp. 11–12)

In spite of an increasing research focus on the needs and experiences of persons with disabilities (Brooks, 1991; Cook, Cook, Tran, & Tu, 1997), traditional views that support the discrimination of persons with disabilities remain intact. This means that research methods that support the majority view of disabilities perpetuate existing views. Critics note the limitations that existing research places on building complete knowledge about the nature of disability and impairment (Brown & Ringma, 1989; Felske, 1994; Ramcharan & Gordon, 1994). Hypothesis testing limits the selection of variables to a few of interest to a particular investigator.

Experimental designs structure events and remove opportunities to make observations in natural environments. Standardized measurement instruments reduce the rich variety of responses to a predetermined list devised by scientists. Applied statistical tests reduce findings to a set of numbers, often neglecting unique or novel reactions to life or treatment events. To release the restrictive nature of traditional research methodologies, a paradigm shift is needed to infuse new methodologies that ask broader research questions and include the experiences, both positive and negative, of persons with disabilities.

Whether we like it or not, social work practitioners, supervisors, and administrators are engaged in the research process. Disability service providers, for example, collect and report data about how many and how often clients receive services. Agency funding sources require outcome studies to show whether or not programs or therapies have achieved the promised or expected results. Clients and family members are routinely asked to rate services and report levels of satisfaction. Physicians, psychologists, and social workers, among others, have their practice patterns tracked by managed-care companies. Public and private grants require applicants to demonstrate the efficacy of treatment and educational interventions on predetermined criteria. We collect data before we ask questions. We ask questions without thinking if there are alternative questions to ask. If research has failed to reveal fresh insights it is because restrictions that rely on traditional views of disability perpetuate the problem. Social work practitioners, supervisors, and administrators unwittingly participate in the tyranny that keeps us from questioning practices and services that may oppress the clients we seek to empower. A new way of thinking about disability is needed to help reframe the "problem" of disability. Perhaps the best available strategy, therefore, is represented by the proposal to reformulate major concepts and methods that are integral to the analysis of this subject.

Because the aim is to transform how social workers think about disability, theories are needed to guide us through the change process (Brzuzy, 1997; Gleason, 1994; Pfeiffer, 2000). A theory is an organized way to think about a problem. Theories typically include a set of concepts, hypotheses, and principles that convey the specific aspects of an issue that the theorists mean to bring to our attention. We are fortunate to be living at a time when transformative ways of thinking abound and are widely accepted by social work. Four perspectives form the basis for the strategies needed to reshape disability research: feminist theories, postmodernism, social constructionism, and the Disability Discrimination Model.

Feminist Theories

Feminist theories grew out of a need to understand how gender had marginalized women (Cummerton, 1986; Fraser & Gordon, 1994; Harding, 1987). In the absence of knowledge derived from women, feminists urged women to theorize from their own experiences. The feminist critique revealed three flaws in traditional research: (1) Women were not included in studies; (2) commonly accepted methods and theories did not fit women's experiences; and (3) differences between men and women, and diversity of women and their experiences, were not analyzed.

To reframe feminist analysis to fit disabilities we can simply replace "women" with "people with disabilities" and see the result: (1) People with disabilities are not included in studies; (2) commonly accepted methods and theories do not fit the experiences of people with disabilities; and (3) differences between people with disabilities and people without disabilities, and diversity of people with disabilities and their experiences have not been analyzed.

Postmodernism

Postmodernism, which is more of a movement than a theory, drew our attention to how language describes and shapes our thinking (James & Thomas, 1996), that language of any particular theory distorts and restricts our view of reality. Scientific theories name concepts and assign meaning (Allison, 1999). The selection process is based on accepted "truths" in the context of culture and from a historical perspective. Truths are influenced by those who control language and are spoken by those given a public voice. Social workers are trained to see disability and impairment in predetermined categories. Diagnostic criteria are, perhaps, the most obvious example of categorization of disablement, and the concept of normalcy is another. False dichotomies create artificial distinctions such as pathological and normal, or, disabled and nondisabled. The bias of language extends even further so that a named abnormality identifies not only the impairment but the person diagnosed as having the impairment. For example, a person with a specific cluster of symptoms becomes a schizophrenic. If we view people as their disease or disability, we fail to observe or collect information about their strengths or novel ways they interact in the world. Meaning is derived from what is reported and observed in each context (Ringma & Brown, 1991; Simpson, 1995). The language of diagnosis, prepackaged treatment plans, and standardized outcome measurement instruments may keep us from listening and looking for persons whose voices have previously not been included in knowledge building (Burack-Weiss, 1991; Fisk, Rowe, Brooks, & Gildersleeve, 2000; Gilson, Bricout, & Baskind, 1998; Thapar & Bhardwaj, 1999).

Social Constructionism

Social constructionism essentially states that the social forces at work at any point in history construct and shape all knowledge. In social work, these forces embrace empiricism and the scientific method. We have excellent reasons. Our clients deserve the best interventions evaluated using the most rigorous research methods. As we embrace science we join other adherents of the medical model and advance our own professional status. Science is one way to build knowledge; it is not the only way. To remedy this imbalance knowledge must be derived from multiple perspectives. In addition to studies about deficits and functional limitations we need studies that reveal the environmental and cultural constraints imposed on people with disabilities.

Disability Discrimination Model

As described in previous chapters, the Disability Discrimination Model views impairment associated with disability as a social construction rather than an immutable consequence of disability. Disability operates as a set of beliefs supported by theories and practices within society so that differences in physical and biological make-up are redefined as limiting and excluding. This perspective stands in stark contrast to the medical model, the reigning standard for understanding and treating problems associated with all forms of disability. The medical model views disability as a pathological condition that must be eliminated or reduced. The goal is restoration to "normal," with normal defined as the absence of disability. Thus, people with disabilities are placed outside the "norms" of society, and the meaning attached to normality constitutes the basis of exclusion and discrimination. The Disability Discrimination Model rejects the classification of people with disabilities on the basis of functional limitations or medical diagnoses. Instead, it sees impairment associated with disability as the result of discrimination, poverty, and marginalizing special services, such as special education and group homes. People with disabilities must claim authorship for defining what they need. People with disabilities must make a space for themselves in society and in research by asserting and demanding their rights. In fact, change is well underway.

Unfortunately, these efforts had relatively little impact on the conduct of social work and programs for persons with disabilities (Mackelprang & Salsgiver, 1996). Few disciplines have addressed the need to incorporate environmental influences into their research models (Brandt and Pope, 1997). Initial explorations in the field of disability studies have laid the groundwork, however, the impact is not yet evident in social work practice or agency policies (Moxley, 1992).

Thus, a new research perspective can be built on the lessons emerging from disability studies and on the concepts and principles of transformational theories. Feminist theories show ways to eliminate disablement bias throughout the research process. Post-modernism calls us to look for local meanings and contexts and to scrutinize the language we have created that reinforces impairment. Social constructionism shows us how our assumptions about disability shape what we allow ourselves to see and study. The Disability Discrimination Model brings people with disabilities center stage to take charge of defining, organizing, and challenging the terms and conditions of disabilities research. Thus we have ways to organize our thinking about disability and methods to create social change. We have ways to examine the role and impact the service system plays in creating the very impairment we allege to treat. These theories must now be translated into strategies for change. Four strategies can help shape a new vision of research for and about disabilities: 1) Redefine the rules for each phase of the research process, 2) Create space for people with disabilities to become principal research investigators, 3) Infuse all studies with multiple methods and competing questions, and 4) Develop and disseminate a critique to help all disability researchers detect bias and discrimination patterns in research studies.

STRATEGIES FOR A NEW SOCIAL WORK RESEARCH PARADIGM

Redefine the Rules for Each Phase of the Research Process

One way to ensure that research is transformed is to imbed new rules into each phase of the research process. The phases of the research process typically begin with problem formulation, followed by selection of research design and measurement instruments, identification of study participants, data collection, data analysis, detailed examination of the study findings and implications, and dissemination of results.

Problem formulation   Investigators routinely review prior research, identifying problems already examined and concepts previously operationalized. It is hard to break new ground when the rule is to first examine what is already known. It is hard to ask novel questions when one must be shaped by questions posed by earlier investigators. It is at this phase of the research process that new ways of thinking can have the most significant impact.

There is, however, another path that might enable disability researchers to escape some of the connotations of prior conceptualizations. Instead of regarding disability exclusively as a functional limitation or as a difference that may evoke discrimination, it can also be viewed simply as an experience. For those who are still influenced by the traditional notions of functional limitations or loss, the experience of disability may still be cast in a negative light. On the other hand, for individuals who have lived beyond the trauma of a disabling event and for researchers who have studied the subject in detail, careful scrutiny or introspection is apt to yield a more balanced understanding of the entire range of elements that are common features of life with a disability. As stated earlier in the chapter, in an environment designed and constructed almost exclusively for the nondisabled population, people with disabilities have a different life experience that must be documented and understood.

Thus, investigators are justified in learning how persons with disabilities overcome environmental barriers. Although interpretations of the meaning and significance of disability may vary widely, such studies will give social work fresh insights about how people cope with impairment and environmental barriers, how they gain strength or inspiration from disabilities, and how social work agencies and services are experienced and interpreted. This research approach is supported by the strengths perspective, an approach widely accepted by social work and applied to practice with such groups as persons with serious mental illness and the elderly (Saleebey, 1997).

Likewise, the Disability Discrimination Model opens other avenues for research problems, namely the nature of impairment related to disability and the nature of discrimination. Because impairment is separated from disability, it must now be considered as a separate research problem. New definitions for disability and impairment are needed to guide investigators to consider these separate concepts. Emancipatory disability research (Barnes, 2003) links the research agenda with the problems of oppression and discrimination, making both the central topics for the study of disabilities.

Selection of research design   This is perhaps the most limiting aspect of the research process, as design decisions describe the evidence-gathering strategies and the setting in which a study will take place. In recent years, qualitative research has gained prominence among social workers. Qualitative research methodologies are important tools for focusing attention on the lives and diverse experiences of persons with disabilities (O'Day, 2002). For example, case study interviews with graduates of special education and rehabilitation programs and their families would expose more about agency practices than standard client satisfaction surveys. Logs and tape recordings made by clients about their daily life experiences in the community and in agencies may reveal oppressive practices that remain hidden from agency staff. New insights may be exposed using ethnographic studies of residential facilities where the researcher becomes a participant-observer and temporary resident of the facility. Quantitative methods are powerful tools for revealing the extensive nature of discrimination and oppressive practices.

Measurement instruments   Refocusing disability studies on new concepts and theories necessitate the development and testing of new instruments, a time-consuming but necessary task. Qualitative studies are likely to reveal new concepts that can be operationalized for further testing and inclusion as standardized measures. For example, there may be a broad range of attitudes among nondisabled persons that warrant further study. Once these attitudes are documented and conceptualized, researchers can devise standardized instruments that can measure the nature and extent of oppression and discrimination related to disability.

Research participants   Study participants should include more than those typically selected for study, such as patients and clients undergoing treatment and rehabilitation. What is needed are more studies that focus on people with disabilities when they are not in treatment. Additional research participants are family members and friends. If new research is to address environmental issues, then, study subjects must include those elements in the environment that may foster discrimination. Important research subjects include practitioners, professional societies, academic disciplines, and the media, as well as sidewalks, buildings, and schools. It is as important to observe how the general public relates to persons with disabilities as it is to note how persons with disabilities interact with the general public.

Data collection and analysis methods   Traditionally, research has relied on standardized tests that limit the types of events and information that lie within the scope of the study. Yet important events may be taking place in categories that fall outside the boundaries of traditional study variables. For example, the efforts by people with disabilities to devise alternative means of coping with environmental obstacles could yield a vast body of knowledge that could become the foundation for a new research paradigm. The aim of this research agenda would be to uncover distinctive features of the experience of people with disabilities that can become a basis for the development of theory and practice.

Study findings and dissemination of results   The results or findings section of a research study includes a summary of the data collected by the researcher. Here we find out what the study participants did or said in response to the research questions. If new methodologies expose new insights about disability, it will be important to disseminate study results to a wide audience in written reports to funding sources, presentations at professional conferences, and publication in professional journals. Typically, dissemination of results does not include audiences beyond the researcher's professional peers. To reach a wider audience research reports must be modified so that differing audiences will be able to understand and make use of research findings. Although Internet and Web-based communications are not yet universally accessible, this forum to disseminate research information has the additional feature of facilitating feedback from audiences who read or hear the study findings online. Such a dialogue between researcher and multiple audiences can add more voices to the research base.

Create Opportunities for People with Disabilities to Become Principal Research Investigators

The goal of this strategy is for people with disabilities to be involved in all phases of the research process, and to become the authors of how their experiences are conceptualized and studied. Persons with disabilities must:

- be included on teams that review grants and research proposals for acceptance and funding.
- participate in the beginning stages of formulating research problems. This means meetings and discussions must take place between researchers and their participants before issues of study question and method are decided.
- be included in making methodological decisions, including selection of measurement instruments, study participants, study design, and how data will be collected and analyzed. They should be co-investigators and should be provided with training or mentoring if it is needed.

- be included in preparing research reports. Their reflections and concerns about the study findings should be included in the reports, including the meanings they attach to the findings, as well as observations about study strengths and limitations.
- be involved in the dissemination of study findings. They should be included as copresenters and coauthors, take part in accommodating reports for the needs of various audiences, and make presentations to funding sources and agency boards.

There are numerous barriers related to this strategy. First, experts in disability research have already occupied all the spaces at the table, and they use a coded language to conduct business. Even when advisory groups recruit consumer members, professional service providers often control the dialogue by using the acronyms and professional language of their privileged communication. Second, tokenism is an accepted method of bringing new stakeholders into power. This places the burden on new players to invent their roles and create their source of power. Third, it takes time to include those formerly excluded from setting the research agenda. Yet, there are numerous people with disabilities who have the skills and insights needed to participate in all the research phases outlined above.

Infuse All Studies with Multiple Methods and Competing Questions

The investigation of all facets of living with disability might also open many new pathways to the exploration of this topic, such as learning about the cultures of disabilities or the cultures of impairments. Among the important questions and issues are:

- Ask persons with disabilities to define the concepts and variables (e.g., What do you have in your life that makes you feel supported?).
- Encourage studies that combine quantitative and qualitative methods.
- Use communication methods other than verbal (Ramcharan & Gordon, 1994).
- Study everyday life. Understand it without comparison to the life of others (Gleason, 1994), an anthropological view. Sociology would consider the ethnographic method of direct observation of others to understand what occurs and what meaning it has. Seek the meaning from the lived experience.
- Add disability as a demographic characteristic in all studies. Do not simply exclude persons with disabilities from studies or ignore the presence of a disability.
- Study points of empowerment in daily life via issues of access and living standards.
- Examine structures of inclusion and exclusion in human relationships and activities.
- What are the consequences of oppression? (Linton, 1998).
- Focus on what *can* be known, not what *is* known.

- How are people disabled by social structures?
- Study how those labeled nondisabled perceive those labeled with a disability.
- Focus on the margin, where disability meets nondisability.
- Test whether practices designed to "empower" actually do so from the subject's point of view.

Develop and Disseminate a Research Critique to Help All Disability Investigators Detect Bias and Discrimination Patterns

Scholarly research has a strict set of standards. Academic researchers know that unless the rules of science are honored, acceptance and publication may not follow. Because jobs, funding, and promotion may depend on adherence to strict protocols, it will not be easy to persuade researchers to break the rules. However, within research circles, critics such as Pfeiffer (2000), Goodley and Moore (2000), and Linton (1998) have already created a climate for change. They are raising consciousness from within. A critique from the outside, from the voices not represented among research decision makers, will strengthen and expand the challenge. We need to develop and institutionalize a consciousness-raising critique for all disability researchers. Such a critique might include the following:

- Does the study examine how the environment may be limiting or pathological?
- Is there evidence that people with disabilities played an active researcher role in any phase of the study? If so, which phases? How many people and with what type of disabilities?
- Are the findings communicated so that people with a broad range of understanding about research can clearly understand the nature of the study and the study findings?
- Does the study describe or analyze how power structures play a role in interactions of subjects to organizations?
- Does the study exclude people with certain characteristics or conditions?
- Does the study address strengths associated with disability?
- Does the study examine how disability enhances life?
- Does the study evaluate social participation and quality of life?

CONCLUSION

In recent years we have come to rely on traditional and prescribed research to justify and evaluate programs and services for people with disabilities. However, strict adherence to traditional empiricism has forced us to exclude important sources of knowledge, specifically the locally lived experiences of people with disabilities as well as positive attributes associated with disability.

We need to create a shift in consciousness so that people with disabilities and their previously silenced points of view can occupy the central space at the research table. A collaborative model would make room for new minds and voices and add new dimensions to our thinking that would challenge entrenched views of disability and play a role in removing the policy and environmental barriers that apparently remain hidden to many who do not experience disability.

Another important result of a holistic analysis of disability, however, might be an increasingly balanced understanding that could promote the view that disability is not an exclusively negative attribute. Perhaps such a holistic understanding of disability would help mobilize the massive political influence people with disabilities could have, based on their size and possible strength in the U.S. population.

New research could make a candid assessment of forces that oppose or resist the empowerment of persons with disabilities and investigate why a large portion of people with disabilities have remained politically dormant. The overwhelming negative image of disability that permeates society may be a crucial factor that has hampered the emergence of a political force that could vigorously challenge traditional interests. Altering the dominant paradigm for the investigation of the problems related to disability may not prompt the defeat of entrenched interests or inspire an immediate change in traditional attitudes and practices about the subject. However, the understandings of disability accepted and supported by the general public, the media, organized lobbies, and health professions cannot be changed if no alternative is offered.

Research reforms in social work will bring incremental changes by dislodging traditional notions about the nature of disability and impairment. The strategies proposed in this chapter are designed to promote an increasingly balanced perspective that could yield modest gains in theoretical understandings and professional practice, and improve the social and political influence of people with disabilities.

REFERENCES

Allison, C. E. (1999). Disability as diversity: A sociolinguistic construct for the new millennium. *Reflections, 5*(4), 47–51.

Barnes, C. (2003). What a difference a decade makes: Reflections on doing "emancipatory" disability research. *Disability & Society, 18*(1), 3–17.

Brandt, E. N., Jr., & Pope A. M. (Eds.) (1997). *Enabling America: Assessing the role of rehabilitation research and engineering.* Washington, DC: National Academic Press.

Brooks, N. A. (1991). Self-empowerment among adults with severe physical disability: A case study. *Journal of Sociology & Social Welfare, 18*(1), 105–120.

Brown, I., Renwick, R., & Nagler, M. (1996). The centrality of quality of life in health promotion and rehabilitation. In I. Brown, R. Renwick, & M. Nagler (Eds.), *Quality of life in health promotion and rehabilitation: Conceptual approaches, issues, and applications.* Thousand Oaks, CA: Sage Publications.

Brown, C., & Ringma, C. (1989). The myth of consumer participation in disability services: Some issues for social workers. *Australian Social Work, 42*(4), 35–40.

Brzuzy, S. (1997). Deconstructing disability: The impact on definition. *Journal of Poverty, 1*(1), 81–91.

Bucaro, T., & Kapfstein, R. (1999). Coming out: Claiming disability in and out of the classroom. *Reflections, 5*(4), 71–81.

Burack-Weiss, A. (1991). In their own words: Elders' reactions to vision loss. *Journal of Gerontological Social Work, 17*(3/4), 15–23.

Cook, P., Cook, M., Tran, L., & Tu, W. (1997). Children enabling change: A multicultural, participatory, community-based rehabilitation research project involving Chinese children with disabilities and their families. *Child & Youth Care Forum, 26*(3), 205–219.

Cummerton, J. M. (1986). A feminist perspective on research: What does it help us see? In N. Van Den Bergh & L. B. Cooper (Eds.), *Feminist visions for social work.* Silver Spring, MD: National Association of Social Workers.

Daly, M. (1973). *Beyond God the father.* Boston: Beacon Press.

Felske, A. W. (1994). Knowing about knowing: Margin notes on disability research. In M. H. Rioux & M. Bach (Eds.), *Disability is not measles* (pp. 181–194). North York, Ontario: L'Institut Roeher Institute.

Fisk, D., Rowe, M., Brooks, R., & Gildersleeve, D. (2000). Integrating consumer staff members into a homeless outreach project: Critical issues and strategies. *Psychiatric Rehabilitation Journal, 23*(3), 244–253.

Fraser, N., & Gordon, L. (1994). A genealogy of dependency: Tracing a keyword of the U. S. welfare state. *Signs: Journal of Women in Culture and Society, 19*(2), 309–336.

Gilson, S. F., Bricout, J. C., & Baskind, F. R. (1998). Listening to the voices of individuals with disabilities. *Families in Society, 79*(2), 188–196.

Glass, James M. (1997). *Life unworthy of life: Racial Phobia and mass murder in Hitler's Germany.* New York: Basic Books.

Gleason, J. J. (1994). Theoretical framework for what persons with severe and profound multiple disabilities do in context. In M. H. Rioux & M. Bach (Eds.), *Disability is not measles* (pp. 213–232)). North York, Ontario: L'Institut Roeher Institute.

Goodley, D., & Moore, M. (2000). Doing disability research: Activist lives and the academy. *Disability & Society, 15*(6), 861–882.

Hahn, H. (1982). Disability and rehabilitation policy: Is paternalistic neglect really benign? *Public Administration Review, 43*, 385–389.

Hahn, H. (1985a). Disability policy and the problem of discrimination. *American Behavioral Scientist, 28*, 293–318.

Hahn, H. (1985b). Toward a politics of disability: Definitions, disciplines, and policies. *Social Science Journal, 22*, 87–105.

Hahn, H. (1997). An agenda for citizens with disabilities: Pursuing identity and empowerment. *Journal of Vocational Rehabilitation, 9*, 31–37.

Hahn, H. (1999a). *Healthy life with a disability: Conceptual and measurement issues.* Unpublished paper. Santa Monica, CA: Disability Forum.

Hahn, H. (1999b). Accommodations and the ADA: Unreasonable bias or biased reasoning? Unpublished paper presented at the Boalt Hall School of Law, University of California, Berkeley.

Harding, S. (Ed.). (1987). *Feminism & methodology.* Bloomington, IN: Indiana University Press.

James, P., & Thomas, M. (1996). Deconstructing a disabling environment in social work education. *Social Work Education, 15*(1), 34–45.

Linton, S. (1998). *Claiming disability.* New York. New York University Press.

Mackelprang, R. W., & Salsgiver, R. O. (1996). People with disabilities and social work: Historical and contemporary issues. *Social Work, 41*(1), 7–14.

Merrick, L. (1994). The disability triage: Denial, marginalization, and legislation. *Journal of Religion in Disability & Rehabilitation, 1*(1), 39–43.

Morris, J. (1991). *Pride against prejudice.* Philadelphia: New Society Publishers.

Moxley, D. (1992). Disability policy and social work practice. *Health and Social Work, 17*(2), 99–103.

O'Day, B. (2002). Research on the lives of persons with disabilities: The emerging importance of qualitative research methodologies. *Journal of Disability Policy Studies, 13*(1), 9–15.

Oliver, M. (1996). *Understanding disability: From theory to practice.* New York: St. Martin's Press.

Pfeiffer, D. (2000). The disability paradigm. *Journal of Disability Policy Studies, 11*(2), 98–99.

Ramcharan, P., & Gordon, G. (1994). Setting one agenda for empowering persons with a disadvantage within the research process. In M. H. Rioux & M. Bach (Eds.), *Disability is not measles* (pp. 195–212). North York, Ontario: L'Institut Roeher Institute.

Ringma, C., & Brown, C. (1991). Hermeneutics and the social sciences: An evaluation of the function of hermeneutics in a consumer disability study. *Journal of Sociology & Social Welfare, 18*(3), 57–73.

Rioux, M. H., & Bach, M. (Eds.). (1994). *Disability is not measles.* North York, Ontario: L'Institute Roeher Institute.

Saleebey, D. (Ed.). (1997). *The strengths perspective in social work practice* (2nd ed.). New York: Longman.

Simpson, M. K. (1995). The sociology of "competence" in learning disability services. *Social Work & Social Science Review, 6*(2), 85–97.

Stone, D. (1985). *The disabled state.* Philadelphia: Temple University Press.

Thapar, N., & Bhardwaj, S. M. (1999). Overcoming the tyranny of space: Experiences of multiple sclerosis patients. *Reflections, 5*(4), 64–70.

Ward, M. J., & Meyer, R. N. (1999). Self-determination for people with developmental disabilities and autism: Two self-advocates' perspectives. *Focus on Autism and Other Developmental Disabilities, 14*(3), 133–140.

THE CHALLENGE
FOR SOCIAL WORK

GARY E. MAY

INTRODUCTION

This work has presented and discussed the application of a new model, or perspective of disability, which we hope will facilitate a more helpful and informed
orientation for social workers in their work with and for persons with disabilities.
I believe that many social workers have arrived at such a perspective on their own
as a reflection of their commitment to the values of our profession and their com
mitment to those they serve.

As described in Chapter 5, there is incongruity between the position of disability scholars and our profession. Social work, as a profession, does not yet seem
to have recognized the importance of challenging itself to reexamine its stance—
or lack thereof—on disability issues or the importance of making a strong, clear
statement about our commitment to this issue.

Gilson and DePoy (2002) argued that viewing disability from a constructionist perspective has more utility for social workers than the more traditional,
deficit-oriented diagnostic perspective. The implications for viewing disability from
a social construction perspective are reflected in disability-related content in key
elements of professional social work education (p. 158, table 1). The essential differences are the aperture through which disability is defined and the environment
in which change is sought. In the diagnostic (medical) model, disability-related
impairment is held to exist as an objective condition residing in the person with a
disability. The constructionist perspective asserts that disability-related impairment is a consequence of the arbitrary assumptions made about disability.

The latter perspective underpins the Disability Discrimination Model. This
shifts intervention to the person with a disability AND his/her environment
and establishes shared "ownership" of disability-related impairment. Consequently, interventions to remediate disability-related impairment must be shared
and require accommodations in the individual with the disability and his/her

environment. This stands in sharp contrast to the nominal position taken by the academy relative to the education of social workers regarding disability (Gilson & DePoy 2002).

The Council on Social Work Education's 1992 Curriculum Policy Statement and the 1994 Handbook of Accreditation Standards and Procedures are ambiguous regarding disability definition and content requirements (Gilson & DePoy 2002). Most commonly, disability is defined diagnostically and persons with disability are aggregated in the "populations at risk category". Thus, pedagogy, limited though it is, is confined to diversity content courses, already chock full of mandates and advocacy for including numerous discreet populations thought to be "at risk" as a consequence of their membership in identified out groups. A sad consequence of this reality is that disability content is irregularly included and education is frequently superficial. Some instructors report that there isn't enough time to "cover" the plethora of specifically identified populations in such diversity courses. The consequences include some sad confessions by diversity instructors, as elaborated in Chapter 5.

Payne (1997) identifies three views of social work: reflexive-therapeutic; socialist-collectivist; and individualist-reformist. The reflexive-therapeutic view sees social work as a reactive therapeutic response aimed at achieving "the best possible well being for individuals, groups, and communities in society by promoting and facilitating growth and self-fulfillment" (p. 4). The socialist-collectivist view sees social work as seeking "cooperation and mutual support in society so that the most oppressed and disadvantaged people can gain power over their own lives" (p. 4). Finally, the individualist-reformist perspective sees social work as individually therapeutic as well as improving the service delivery systems, "it meets the individuals' needs and improves services of which it is a part, so that social work and the services can operate more effectively" (p. 4).

Gilson and DePoy (2002) advocated for a combination of the diagnostic and constructionist viewpoints in disability content in social work education. "The knowledge, theory, and skills that would emerge from this complex, multifaceted, and contemporary treatment of disability would reflect social work's professional commitment to social justice and locate discussions of disability within the larger discourse on diversity" (p. 163). This would seem to place it within the socialist-collectivist view of social work in Payne's (1997) typology.

Payne (1997) advances the premise that social work itself is socially constructed. This construction includes creating a social worker. Thus, social workers are defined by occupational expectations in encounters with clients. Social and political forces and perceptions about need shape the response to needs. The organization of services and agencies within the broader culture reflect legislative and popular sanction for social workers and their services. These definitions, based on occupational expectations, perceptions about needs and responses and the existence of services and agencies in the context of the broader culture, expose areas of actual or potential conflict. In the area of disability, such conflicts, actual or potential, may center on the role of social workers in the lives of individual persons with disabilities.

Should the worker strive for rather passive "acceptance" of the disability-related impairment by the owner of the disability? To what extent do the worker's definition and understanding of disability influence what roles they enact? What is the obligation regarding client education and broadening horizons regarding self advocacy, empowerment, or self actualization? What is the role for social work when social and political forces de-value or narrowly reframe needs and responses to needs? How does social work rise to the challenge when the consumers of our services are defined as undeserving and unworthy? Finally, what should social work's position be when the definition of the "problem" of disability is narrowly crafted and leads to a one-dimensional response?

These questions suggest that social work is but a component in a network of related professions and occupations that have roles in improving the opportunities for persons with disabilities. Our understanding of theories that explain and predict human behavior needs to be seen as reflective of the assumptions and beliefs that we accept. Gilson and DePoy (2002) seemed to suggest that, as it pertains to disability, many of the assumptions and beliefs we accept do not serve the broad, long term interest of persons with disabilities. Acceptance of the medical model, especially when not critically examined, and assuming a diagnostic framework for understanding and intervening in disability, is limited and limiting.

Hiranandani (2002) has suggested that social work would be well served by a more critical perspective regarding disability. Relevant questions from this critical perspective include, "How are deficits of the body and mind interpreted and dealt with in different societies? How is an individual's identity as a person affected by the cultural connotations of disability? How do processes of cultural transitions shape local understanding of disability?" (p. 10). Definitions of disability constructed around measurements of functional limitations fail to address these cultural and contextual issues.

So, constructing and defining clients with disabilities as composites of impairments caused by their disabilities predicts a narrow, reflexive-therapeutic approach (Payne, 1997) by the social worker. This linear depiction minimizes and suppresses the full range of possible social work responses. Conversely, defining impairments as caused by the broader socio-cultural construction of disability unleashes the inclusive, dynamic social system orientation that characterizes social work.

Social work is failing persons with disabilities and social workers who expect leadership and guidance for working with and working for people with disabilities. Chapter 3 pulls the covers off the helpless role of social workers in institutional settings. The powerful narratives Hayashi includes serve as cries for help from a population that our profession has ignored—in much the same manner that the broader society has ignored them.

Our profession, through its professional organizations and associations, should take a leadership role in provoking a dialogue about disabilities in this country. Such a dialogue will necessarily include those about whom the dialogue is engaged—persons with disabilities—and their families, and those of us who have professional responsibilities to this population. Such a dialogue should include forthright consideration of policy alternatives, empowerment, self-determination, resource allocation, and training implications. This is all very familiar territory for our profession.

Social work, more than any other profession, has the heritage, the understanding of the values, and the capability to transform the way persons with disabilities are viewed and treated. To continue to ignore this opportunity and the obligation that accompanies it is unacceptable.

REFERENCES

Gilson, S. F., & DePoy, E. (2002). Theoretical approaches to disability content in social work education. *Journal of Social Work Education,*(1).

Hayashi, R. (2003). The environent of disability today. In G. E. May & M. B. Raske (Eds.), *Disability discrimination: A model for social workers' conceptualization of disability.* Boston: Allyn & Bacon.

Hiranandani, V. S., (2003). Rethinking disability in social work: Interdisciplinary perspectives. In G. E. May & M. B. Raske (Eds.), *Disability discrimination: A model for social workers' conceptualization of disability.* Boston: Allyn & Bacon.

Payne, M. (1997). *Modern Social Work Theory,* (2nd ed.) Chicago: Lyceum Books.